*Resistance and Reformation in Nineteenth-Century*
*African-American Literature*

# Resistance and Reformation in Nineteenth-Century African-American Literature

Brown, Wilson, Jacobs, Delany, Douglass, and Harper

JOHN ERNEST

University Press of Mississippi    *Jackson*

Copyright © 1995 by the University Press of Mississippi
All rights reserved
Manufactured in the United States of America

98  97  96  95    4  3  2  1

The paper in this book meets the guidelines for permanence and durability of the
Committee on Production Guidelines for Book Longevity of the Council on
Library Resources.

Library of Congress Cataloging-in-Publication Data

Ernest, John.
    Resistance and reformation in nineteenth-century African-American
literature : Brown, Wilson, Jacobs, Delany, Douglass, and Harper /
John Ernest.
        p.  cm.
    Includes bibliographical references and index.
    ISBN 0-87805-816-8 (cloth : alk. paper). — ISBN 0-87805-817-6
(pbk. : alk. paper)
    1. American literature—Afro-American authors—History and
criticism.  2. American literature—19th century—History and
criticism.  3. Literature and society—United States—History—19th
century.  4. Afro-Americans—Social conditions—19th century.
5. Social problems in literature.  6. Afro-Americans in literature.
7. Race in literature.  I. Title.
PS153.N5E76  1995
810.9'896073—dc20                                    95-17113
                                                      CIP

British Library Cataloging-in-Publication data available

For
*R. M. Ernest,*
". . . something of a mystery . . . ,"
and for my parents,
*Phyllis and Norman Ernest*

# Contents

# Preface

> It will always be a mystery, history.
> —Ishmael Reed, *Flight to Canada*

In the fall of 1994, in an Introduction to African-American Literature course, my students and I were engaged in the last day of what had proven to be an energetic and detailed discussion of William Wells Brown's *Clotel; or, the President's Daughter*. Usually, when I have taught this novel in the past, I have had to argue for the value of this text—but not this time. My students had entered zealously into the novel's rich complexity, its subtle strategies; and in the last minutes of our discussion, they wondered about a detail that we were in danger of overlooking. Chapter 27, entitled "The Mystery," tells the story of former slave George Green's chance reunion with his long-lost lover Mary in a graveyard in France. Mary faints when she sees George, who does not recognize her behind her veil. She is taken back to her home, and she might have lost him forever were it not for the fact that George inadvertently leaves behind the book he is reading, identified in *Clotel* only as Roscoe's *Leo X*. In the book is George's name, as well as a card of the Hotel de Leon, where George was staying at the time—and thus he is found, and the couple is reunited. My students were by this time accustomed to providential encounters in the literature we were reading, but they wondered at Brown's selection of Roscoe's *Leo X* as the providential device. I had to confess that I knew nothing about Roscoe and this book, for I had forgotten completely William Edward Farrison's suggestion that Roscoe provided Brown with a valuable theory of history, by which "the value of history consisted primarily not in what it was but in what it did—in the extent to which it influenced the course of human affairs" (445). Still, we all agreed that *Clotel* rewards attention to detail, and that Brown almost certainly had a reason for choosing this book. I suggested that this would be a good subject for a paper.

One student, Tiffany Johnson, took the suggestion seriously, and began her search for William Roscoe's *The Life and Pontificate of Leo the Tenth*, published in London in 1827. She did not find the book in our library, and was insufficiently schooled in the mysteries of interlibrary loan (and the timing it requires) to acquire a copy in time for the paper. But she did discover another of Roscoe's books, *The Life of Lorenzo de Medici*, and she followed through with research on Roscoe and then on Leo X himself. In her paper, entitled simply "An Important Book," Ms. Johnson notes various levels of significance in Brown's use of this book. First, it is significant that Brown uses the book as a providential device, the means by which two people torn apart by slavery are reunited. Second, it is significant that the book is by a prominent British abolitionist, representative of the power of individual and combined political action. Third, Ms. Johnson argues, it is significant that the book is about Leo X, thus drawing our attention to the Protestant Reformation. In a frankly speculative but intriguing reading, Ms. Johnson argues that Brown uses this book to draw parallels between the religious reformation of the past and the one necessary in the present. And underlying these various levels of significant findings is a simple revelation: "Ultimately," Ms. Johnson announces, "my findings led me to believe that Brown saw literature as the best way to promote change."

I couldn't agree more—and in the following chapters I simply perform my own version of the investigative task that Ms. Johnson took upon herself for her paper. I have tried to avoid bringing to this task assumptions about what literature should be and how it should work, looking instead for ways to understand what *this* literature is and how it *does* work. I have tried to account for the power of this literature, and I have tried to convey the deep pleasure that awaits those who read beyond first impressions and learn to ask questions about the design of and details in each work. Like Ms. Johnson, I keep returning to simple revelations. Each book began for me as a mystery, a book of unaccountable power and sometimes surprising complexity; and each book led me, as it led Ms. Johnson, to other histories, to various texts to be discovered and read. Most of us educated in the United States are ill-equipped to read nineteenth-century African-American literature in its historical and cultural context, for we do not know enough about history and culture to do so. We bring to the task a distorted and partial understanding of the past. In my research for this book, I have tried to construct a context for understanding these autobiographies, novels, and narratives by learning to follow each text's implicit guidance: reading my way into the context, asking questions about details that lead to other details, and asking myself what would happen if one were to assume that each text is a literary achievement instead of merely an important historical document. In short, I examine the "cultural work," as Jane Tompkins has termed it, of six important nineteenth-century African-American writers, each of whom acted upon a deep faith in the power of literature to promote change. Taking the world as they find it, as they must take it, these authors try to change the world by changing how it is envisioned, revealing problems where before there were none, multiplicity where before there was unity, and possibilities where before there were problems. This is not simple work, however simple and morally comforting it may seem when blandly summarized, for the problem was not merely to promote a moral program or solve clear problems, but rather to influence those who believed themselves to be part of the solution to reconsider their world, their roles in it, and even their ability to understand the problems they hoped to address.

I've tried to be attentive to Brown's reminder that books can influence history, and that seemingly chance encounters can draw one into an understanding of larger designs. During the same semester in which Tiffany Johnson undertook her own literary investigations, studying the significance of a discovery of a book that led to a significant reunion in Brown's *Clotel*, I read a review of a novel published in 1994 that brought Brown's subtitle to renewed prominence, Barbara Chase-Riboud's *The President's Daughter*, and I obtained a copy of the novel for our class. The review had said nothing of Brown's own story of the President's daughter, and so I was ready to complain about the novel, but I found (and I should not have been surprised to find) that Chase-Riboud is carefully attentive to the lives and works of nineteenth-century black authors and activists (though she exercises considerable poetic license throughout the novel, changing and mixing lives and facts freely with fiction along the way). At one point in this *The President's Daughter*, Harriet Hemmings, daughter of Thomas Jefferson, meets with Sarah Hale, editor of *Godey's Lady's Book*, at Brown's Hotel, where Hale hands Hemmings a copy of " 'the newest antislavery romance from London,' " William Wells Brown's *Clotel; or, the*

*President's Daughter*. Hale is thinking of serializing an American edition of the story, though she finally passes it by to publish "a new American romance about slavery written by a free black doctor, Martin Delany, who had graduated from Harvard in 1852" (326–28). Harriet reads this fictional version of her own biography—and particularly the scene in which the President's daughter jumps into the Potomac and dies—with understandable interest, and enjoys the idea that her story might now be used as antislavery propaganda.

When Brown first presented his story of a chance encounter in the graveyard, he presented it not as fiction but as history; and now this creative act has entered into a new realm of historical fiction as his story is read by its subject. Chase-Riboud presents here a complex mix of fiction and history that is characteristic of African-American literature generally: history developing into legend inspiring fiction that influences history, leading back to a fictive representation of history in which the protagonist enjoys a novel that addresses her "actual" life. Creators of fiction who become subjects of subsequent fiction, Brown and Delany, like the other writers I study, are still very much present in our cultural landscape. They've left their books behind at the graveyard, there to be discovered by those recovering from the shock of recognition.

# Acknowledgments

All of the authors I study in the chapters that follow argue that under-standing is not a solitary activity, and while writing this book I have been reminded time and again of my own dependence on a large community of scholars and friends. Whatever scholarly virtues I can claim for this book are grounded ultimately in the instruction I received from David Levin and Alan Howard at the University of Virginia. I have not yet learned all their lessons well, but I continue to be inspired by their example and guided by their standards of scholarly method and intellec-tual integrity. I continue to be inspired and challenged also by friendships that began in Virginia and that now connect me to broader regions. Steve Arch, John Grammer, Tom Prendergast, and Susan Schultz all have read portions of this manuscript; they've listened to me talk my way through changing conceptions of the project and different versions of individual chapters; and they've tolerated my obsessions beyond the call even of the duty of friendship. I am indebted also to Deborah Garfield, who encour-aged me to develop my ideas on Harriet Jacobs, and who with Rafia Zafar helped me to discover and realize my argument.

I owe a great debt to the members of the English department at Florida International University, who encouraged me to pursue my developing interests and provided me with a congenial and supportive environment in which to do so. Exchanging works in progress with Meri-Jane Rochelson helped me to develop my methods and clarify my concerns, and I was fortunate to begin my career by meeting Sheila Post-Lauria, a wealth of knowledge and a source of energy, whose work has been an inspiration. And I owe a special debt to Adele Newson, who encouraged me to consider a book-length study after reading an early draft of an essay on Harriet Wilson; I have been guided throughout the process of writing this book by her example of untiring devotion to black literature. Above all, I am grateful to Mary Free, to whom I owe so much, and who proved to be the right mentor at the right time (despite her fondness for British literature) when I was completing the essay on Frances E. W. Harper that eventually led me to write this book.

The book was only half finished when I moved north from Miami, and I could not have finished it—either on time or as well—without the encouragement, guidance, and support of my colleagues at the University of New Hampshire. My thinking about African-American literature and culture has developed considerably during conversations with Les Fisher and David Watters, both of whom helped me define my role in the department's ongoing commitment to African-American studies. Lisa MacFarlane, who provided me with an apt phrase for my consideration of the education of Frederick Douglass, encouraged me to develop my ideas in a different context; the essay I wrote under her guidance helped me to clarify my thinking for this book. Briggs Bailey generously agreed to read a very long draft of my chapter on Douglass. That she read it so carefully is simply characteristic; that she read it so quickly is heroic. Sarah Sherman and Melody Graulich, both of whom offered good advice when I reached the final stages of this manuscript, have provided me with forums in which to present my ideas and to learn from others. And Doug Lanier has listened to constant stories of frustration and mystification, and has helped me find my way and hold to my course. This is but a partial list of the members of a vital department who have influenced this manuscript, directly and otherwise.

This book began in the classroom, and many of my students have played a significant role in its development. I am especially grateful to Malvina Engelberg, whose questions about *Iola Leroy* helped me to refine my thinking about Harper's novel. Malvina was one of a trio of students at Florida International University (the other two were Elizabeth Accola and Phylis Grosholz) who were an important influence in my early career as a teacher. I am grateful also to Tony Thomas and Kitty Oliver, graduate students at FIU and writers I admire, who helped me shape my ideas.

My lessons continued when I began teaching at the University of New Hampshire. Tiffany Johnson and Joan Duhamel, undergraduate students at the University of New Hampshire, taught me much by asking simple questions and developing profound responses, and graduate student Joe Poulin indulged my taste for surprising finds and rare books by introducing me to a book he had discovered in a used book store. And I am grateful beyond measure to the members of my graduate seminar on the subject of this book in the spring semester of 1994: Michelle Bellion,

Molly Doyle, Dot Kasik, Alysson Parker, Bruce Peppard, Kristen Peters, Joe Poulin, David Stockwell, and Lance Suehla.

I must thank also those friends I've been fortunate enough to meet along the way who have taken an interest in my work. Andy Scheiber, in particular, has been a part of my professional life since shortly after I left graduate school; a good reader, a good friend, Andy has played a significant role in the creation of this book. And one of the many benefits of my move to New Hampshire is my acquaintance with Dan Reagan, whose reading of an early draft of the introduction was immeasurably helpful. Thanks also to Kathy Fishburn for her early and substantial encouragement and guidance. Finally, though he might not recognize his influence, Gordon Hutner helped me considerably as I wrote the conference papers and essays that led me to write this book.

The chapters on Harriet E. Wilson, Harriet Jacobs, and Frances E. W. Harper all began as papers prepared from 1991 to 1993 for the "Other Voices: American Women Writers of Color National Conference" sponsored by Salisbury State University. Clearly, I am indebted to the codirectors of that conference, Connie L. Richards and Thomas L. Erskine, for providing me with a yearly opportunity to test my ideas before a challenging but supportive audience. I've presented versions of various chapters also at Michigan State University; the 11th Annual Women's History Month Conference at Florida International University; the American Studies Association Annual Meeting; the MLA convention; and the Conference on the "New Economic Criticism" held at Case Western Reserve University. Shorter versions of some chapters have appeared elsewhere: on Wilson, in *PMLA* 109 (1994); on Harper, in *American Literature* 64 (1992); and on Jacobs, in Deborah Garfield and Rafia Zafar, eds., "Harriet Jacobs and *Incidents in the Life of a Slave Girl*: New Critical Essays," forthcoming from Cambridge University Press.

I am particularly grateful to the University Press of Mississippi and to its energetic editor-in-chief Seetha A-Srinivasan, whose early and continuing faith in this project has been a guiding light, and whose insightful and judicious suggestions have made this a better book than the one I would have written without her.

This long list of debts is still an incomplete one, and it barely manages to indicate my gratitude to those who are so much a part of my life—and I cannot hope to find words to express my thanks to my life's center, Rebecca, who has helped me write my ideas by helping me learn to live them.

*Resistance and Reformation in Nineteenth-Century African-American Literature*

# Introduction

In the penultimate paragraph of Frances E. W. Harper's serialized novel *Minnie's Sacrifice* (1869)—the tragic conclusion of which clearly is meant to be uplifting—Harper addresses the significance of her attempt to shape the available cultural materials into a new plotting of the imagination, a new cultural script: "While some of the authors of the present day have been weaving their stories about white men marrying beautiful quadroon girls, who, in so doing were lost to us socially, I conceived of one of that same class to whom I gave a higher, holier destiny; a life of lofty self-sacrifice and beautiful self-consecration, finished at the post of duty, and rounded off with the fiery crown of martyrdom, a circlet which ever changes into a diadem of glory" (91). Harper here and elsewhere looks to weave together the materials of the time into a different story, one in which the protagonist speaks for the glory of choosing death of the individual over death of the community, thus symbolizing the sacrifice necessary to building, maintaining, and strengthening the black community. This is a story that gestures towards another realm, a "holier destiny," the closure that comes to a narrative that begins with duty and ends in martyrdom, and that binds together self-sacrifice and self-consecration. Harper's claim for *Minnie's Sacrifice* lies not only in the story she has told but also in the imaginative possibilities she has opened. What matters is that her story differs from others that are being told, stories that are damaging to the community at large. She has imagined a narrative that connects earth with heaven, human struggle with divine reward—but what matters is not only the tale but the telling, the "weaving" together of profane and sacred.

Lives are shaped, Harper knew, by stories both told and untold, by stories that attract and stories that repel—and one must learn how to narrate what must be told along with what can be hoped. In her novel *Trial and Triumph*, published serially in 1888 and 1889, Harper tells of Mrs. Lasette, whose daughter cannot imagine her mother's fondness for the troublesome Annette, a girl who is otherwise "very unpopular" (*"Minnie's Sacrifice," "Sowing and Reaping," "Trial and Triumph"* [cited hereinafter as *MST*], 256). Mrs. Lasette explains that her daughter would not be so unkind if she knew Annette's story, but she hesitates to tell her daughter that story. When pressed, Mrs. Lasette begins by telling her daughter, "My child, I want this story to be more than food for your curiosity; I want it to be a lesson and a warning to you" (*MST* 257). At the end of that novel, Harper's narrator echoes Mrs. Lasette's conception of the nature and purpose of storytelling, and of the responsibilities of the reader: "And now, in conclusion, permit me to say under the guise of fiction, I have essayed to weave a story which I hope will subserve a deeper purpose than the amusement of the hour, that it will quicken and invigorate human hearts and not fail to impart a lesson of usefulness and value" (*MST* 285). The hope is familiar, as is the lesson on which this hope is placed; and the need to serve a deeper purpose and the desire to "quicken and invigorate human hearts" are also familiar. The question Harper faced in telling this story concerns the extent to which Harper's readers would respond to her message; the extent to which Harper's hopes could be supported by the world as it then was; the extent to which she could hope to change that world by quickening individual hearts; and the grounds for her hope. She would need of her readers more than idle curiosity; she would need to offer more than abstract moral lessons on usefulness and value. Like Janie in Zora Neale Hurston's *Their Eyes Were Watching God*, Harper recognized that " ' 'tain't no use in me telling you somethin' unless Ah give you de understandin' to go 'long wid it' " (Hurston 7). For Harper, as for the other authors I study in the following chapters, the reader's understanding would be most fully attentive and wholly human if the author could renegotiate the relationship between the human and sacred realms, between human systems of order and the all-encompassing divine order.

Stories matter because they can create community, and because they can regather the materials of the world into a newly imagined moral order. Underlying all of the texts I study in the chapters that follow is a belief summarized well by the great black clergyman-abolitionist J. W. C. Pennington in his 1859 essay "The Self-Redeeming Power of the Colored Races of the World." "Human progress," Pennington argues, "next to human redemption, must, indeed, enter into the economy of every enlightened state and Christian church. In the economy of God's moral government, no provision is made for waste human materials; and it is not easy to see how the state or church can afford to waste those precious materials which God has committed to their care" (*Anglo-African Magazine* 314). As Harper laments the postbellum waste of human materials, those lost to the black community, so Pennington here laments the broader waste of human materials left out of the national economy. Pennington points to a fundamental discrepancy between United States social order and that of God's moral government, and he argues that the recognition of that discrepancy is the motive force needed to ignite the "self-redeeming power of the colored races of the world."

Each of the works I examine in this study looks to expose that discrepancy, and to imagine a possible reorganization of human governance according to the terms of what Pennington calls "the economy of God's moral government." As it is impossible to understand the terms and significance of Pennington's vision of human governance without accounting for the nature and depth of his belief that there is a Christian framework for all human life, so understanding the cultural work of William Wells Brown, Harriet E. Wilson, Harriet A. Jacobs, Martin R. Delany, Frederick Douglass, and Frances E. W. Harper requires that one take seriously the dynamics of religious belief. I have tried to be attentive to the ways in which each author weaves her or his belief into the vision of the text, and to each author's faith in what might be called (building on Pennington's vision) belief's economizing potential, its power to serve as the motive force for reconfiguring human society, inspiring individuals and communities to begin the large task of reconstructing the house of order in accordance with God's plan.

Understanding the visions of divine order that serve as the foundations of the texts I here study, let me emphasize, requires one to accept that these authors had and took seriously religious beliefs. This is not to say that the critic must accept belief uncritically, or that the critic must believe or pretend to believe as the author did. But the responsive and responsible reader of these texts must take seriously the prominent presence of belief in the economy of the individual writing consciousness. Foster has noted that many in cultural studies "walk past six storefront churches and two cathedrals while looking for a bar or rap group where we can get in touch with the 'real' folk" (Introduction to *MST* xxxv), and I agree that this approach will not lead to an understanding of these texts. Nor can we settle for an intellectually comforting master discourse that places bar and cathedral, sermon and gansta rap in a complex but still monolithic neighborhood. The complications and contradictions suggested by the diversity of beliefs within the various neighborhoods of literary culture, even operating within the same minds and hearts of individual neighborhoods, might be many—and we will do better by studying individual examples of and responses to that rich diversity than by enclosing it within strict ideological or scholarly boundaries. The question of how to support their own claims for the truth of these beliefs is, in fact, at the center of their works and, as will be clear, at or at least close to the center of my study.

In *Resistance and Reformation in Nineteenth-Century African-American Literature* I examine the ways in which six important authors work to influence their readers' understanding of history and progress. Each of these authors relies upon an individual version of what Paul Ricoeur has called "a Christian interpretation of the mystery of history," and each might well appreciate Ricoeur's conception, in his essay "Christianity and the Meaning of History," of the "false problem" of "the clash between Christian eschatology and the concept of progress" (81). Asserting that "the subject of the natural and uninterrupted progress of mankind is the aftermath of a secularization and . . . rationalist corruption of Christian eschatology," Ricoeur argues that "nothing is more misleading than to oppose progress and hope or progress and mystery" (81). The writers I study operate on the faith that God's ways are mysterious, and that human history, properly understood, is contained within that essential mystery. We best understand ourselves, these authors suggest, when we recognize the limitations of human understanding, and therefore conduct ourselves with appropriate caution and self-questioning. We should keep in mind

Foster's reminder that Frances Harper, for one, had a very specific conception of the cultural work of literature, arguing throughout her work that "Christianity is a system claiming God for its author, and the welfare of man for its object," and that "compared to the truths of Christianity" philosophy, science, and literature are "idle tales" ("Christianity" 96, 98). Harper's task, in effect, was to write a narrative capable of demonstrating the significant correspondence between the stories we construct for ourselves—in the actions, decisions, and perspectives that plot our lives and character—and the larger narrative which, according to her beliefs, we cannot read but by which we are contained. Similarly, all of the authors I study here looked for the authority of a transcendent author to support their own narratives of progress, hope, responsibility, and community; all try to rescript their worlds by referring to a more significant stage of events. Of course, many in the nineteenth-century United States would agree with this; the writers I study here were by no means alone in this need to sanctify their visions of human progress. The question was how to do so, and how to claim this authority for one's efforts.

In this regard, it is useful to compare the efforts of many nineteenth-century African-American writers to construct the relation between divine governance and human events with that of George Bancroft, nineteenth-century U.S. historian and politician, whose influence on the national mythology has been so pervasive that he has been called the father of American history. Bancroft was perhaps the most determined and certainly the most prominent promoter not only of American providential destiny but also of American history as a science in support of that destiny—for though most readers have no trouble reading the Jacksonian democrat's biases in Bancroft's *History of the United States*, Bancroft himself considered his monumental study to be objective. Consider this one of many of Bancroft's reminders that he believed his *History* (published in ten original separate volumes over a forty-year period beginning in 1834) to be a scientific study of the relation between human and providential history:

> By comparison of document with document; by an analysis of facts, and the reference of each of them to the laws of the human mind which it illustrates; by separating the idea which inspires combined action from the forms it assumes; by comparing events with the great movement of history,—historic truth may establish itself as a science; and the principles that govern human affairs, extending like a path of light from

century to century, become the highest demonstration of the superintending providence of God. (3:398)

At issue here is how one determines "historic truth" and how one identifies evidence of "the superintending providence of God"—which, Bancroft argued, was a matter not of ideological positioning but of careful scholarly method. For Bancroft, the democratic scholar is he or she who can use the materials of facts and documents to construct a "path of light." That is, behind Bancroft's obvious and persistent emphasis on method throughout the *History of the United States* lies a mystification of scholarship; the scholar lives in a privileged realm and is a key player, even facilitator, in the great movement of history.

Sharing his belief in divine Providence, many of Bancroft's African-American contemporaries questioned his transference of that belief to historical method, for they were subject to different documents and bound by different facts than those which propelled Bancroft's *History*. Indeed, Bancroft's name appears with some frequency in essays and speeches by his African-American contemporaries. For example, the black abolitionist William J. Watkins, responding to Bancroft's 1854 oration "The Necessity, the Reality, and the Promise of the Progress of the Human Race," argued that "Our theory is well enough; but our practice is as far removed from it as the east is from the west." Noting Bancroft's assertion that "our country is bound to allure the world to Liberty by the beauty of its example," Watkins wondered, "Where has Mr. Bancroft been living that with all his wisdom and erudition he has not found out that the great object of this Government, *as developed in its policy*, is the extension, the consolidation, and the perpetuity of a system of robbery, of plunder, and oppression, aptly characterized the vilest that ever saw the sun" (257). Working their way *from* the realm of secular history *to* an understanding of moral history, the nineteenth-century African-American writers I examine here invert not the ideological but rather the historiographical relationship between divine and human history. Like Bancroft, though on significantly different terms, these writers necessarily directed themselves towards the "separating [of] the idea which inspires combined action from the forms it assumes." Bancroft compares the "forms" to look for essential continuities; all that does not fit into the discernible pattern of "the great movement of history" may be dismissed as evidence of transient human error, the imperfect historical manifestations of a gradually unfolding Providence. In their responses to such visions of history, African-American writers look to discontinuities, for contradictions within and among the forms, finding there evidence of a growing disjunction between the human (mis)management of affairs and God's "superintending providence." Accordingly, the hope for a renewed awareness of the motive "idea" that informs human history requires not the reapplication of old "forms" but rather the dependence on new.

These "new forms" were individuals themselves—products not of Bancroft's ideal culture but of the actual working assumptions, laws, and policies of the United States—who insisted on testing the nation by its cultural productions, by the individuals it produced. In the texts I study in the chapters that follow, "historical truth" is linked to the mutually contradicting cultural signifiers embodied in the slave and the culturally enslaved "free" black. The authors' response to this situation was not to write works capable of transcending cultural limitations but rather to rearrange the existing cultural forms into new narratives of social order and progress—a pragmatic and revealing use of available cultural materials that exposes the facade of the existing cultural system while claiming authority over the philosophical grounds of that culture. In their strategic manipulations of available discursive and literary conventions, these writers present themselves as the most willfully determined products of the culture and argue that they therefore are the only ones who can successfully negotiate the culture's contradictions, transgress its boundaries, and return its discursive conventions to stable meaning. In their interrogation of the process of production that defines their lives—and in their exposure of the traces of the material production of slavery in U.S. philosophical and moral idealism—these writers do not look to undermine the ideals themselves. Rather, they seize upon the hermeneutical potential of those ideals to transform misreadings into new readings, readings that justify new conceptions of authorship and social agency.

In effect, they follow Ricoeur's theoretical narrative of "a Christian interpretation of the mystery of history," which leads one through "three stages in the flux of history, three ways of understanding and recovering meaning, and three levels of interpretation: the abstract level of progress, the existential level of ambiguity, and the mysterious level of hope" (81, 82). For Ricoeur, what is commonly called *progress* is simply the ongoing "*accumulation of acquirements*," the development of human tools of production and understanding. By *acquirements,* that is, Ricoeur means "tools in the broadest sense of the term: material or cultural tools, tools of knowledge, and even tools of consciousness and of the spirit" (81). Progress is the ongoing manifestation of human development over time, as humankind refines the tools it needs for higher aspirations and responsibilities, for such tools are not the end of human endeavor. Of course, human beings can easily overvalue such acquirements, mistaking the tools for the essential work the tools should serve. Certainly, this was the version of progress used by many white writers as evidence of racial supremacy and justification of racial domination, as they contrasted Anglo-Saxon acquirements to those of other cultures and often used the tools to define notions of racial difference. It was a powerful argument, and Brown, Delany, Douglass, and Harper especially worked hard to respond to this evidence by offering counterevidence of black acquirements. They knew, though, the limitations of such arguments; Delany, for example, devotes a number of chapters of *The Condition, Elevation, Emigration, and Destiny of the Colored People of the United States* to a listing of the achievements of black men and women, only to note finally that such achievements will come to nothing in the struggle for the rights of citizenship.

And so these writers question the function and value of the tools of U.S. civilization, and develop frameworks by which the culture's tools might be reevaluated—and in this way, they anticipate Ricoeur's conception of the "level of ambiguity" in the larger project of the Christian interpretation of history. The "level of ambiguity," Ricoeur argues, begins with the recognition of "the inadequacy of knowing about the equipment (even in the broadest sense) of a civilization in order to understand it." It is at this level of historical interpretation, Ricoeur suggests, that one can recognize that the significance of a culture's "equipment does not lie within the equipment itself; it depends upon the fundamental attitudes taken by the men of a given civilization in respect to their own technical possibilities" (87). "[T]he tool," Ricoeur observes, "is not even useful unless it is valued" (87)—and, being a tool, it cannot be adequately valued unless its function is itself recognized and valued. Certainly, the writers I study here would agree; in fact, they argue in a variety of ways that white U.S. culture does not value its physical and conceptual tools, as is evidenced by its insistence on either misusing them (for example, its reliance on corrupted American political and religious ideals) or ignoring them completely (for example, the cultural dismissal of the intellectual talents and perspectives of black Americans). Ricoeur's conception of the "level of ambiguity" depends upon the recognition that "the destiny of a civilization always remains uncertain." Civilizations and history alike are not monolithic, Ricoeur reminds us, and in fact both have "many ways of being *multiple*," a multiplicity that both increases and complicates any complacent sense of a civilization's destiny (89). Accordingly, "The consciousness of an era," Ricoeur explains, should be viewed as "the confused and massive synthesis of this entanglement" of different and contradictory histories and "schemata" of civilization (89, 88). Aware of the importance of confronting and negotiating this confusion, the writers I study here based their cultural authority on the fact that they were the most fully realized embodiments of such entanglement—the complex subjects of an as-yet-undeveloped explanatory system that their oppressors were not equipped to invent. As such, black Americans became emblems of the nation's uncertain destiny, the collective site of guilt in the national theology.

And so they can present themselves as the ones best suited for the hermeneutical task of the last stage of Ricoeur's "Christian interpretation of the mystery of history," the "level of hope." This level, Ricoeur explains, can be "summarized in two words"—"meaning and mystery"—that "in some way nullify each other but are nevertheless the contrasted language of hope" (93). And one might say that Ricoeur's conception of these terms is the same conception that we discover at the heart of each of the works I here study: "Meaning: there is a unity of meaning; it is the fundamental source of the courage to live in history. Mystery: but this meaning is hidden; no one can *say* it, rely upon it, or draw an assurance from it which would be a counter-assurance against the dangers of history. One must risk it on signs" (93). In nineteenth-century U.S. culture, a good deal of cultural power was generated in the interpretive space between meaning and mystery. That is, many in the nineteenth century claimed cultural power by claiming the ability to determine the relation between human events and providential destiny. Bancroft is just one reminder of the extent to which the national mythology was devoted to what Ricoeur calls the "Christian meaning of history"—"the hope that secular history is also a part of that meaning which sacred history sets forth, that in the end there is only *one* history, that all history is ultimately sacred" (94). Such claims were used both to justify slavery and to argue for its abolition; the interpretation of U.S. history within the framework of an imagined Providence was the common and contested rock upon which John Brown and John C. Calhoun both stood.

In my studies of Brown, Wilson, Delany, Jacobs, Douglass, and Harper, I examine individual attempts to claim authority over this interpretive space, attempts based on each author's belief in a unity of meaning and each author's conception of the essential mystery of that meaning. Each of these writers was aware of the extent to which this faith in a meaning that remains hidden would resonate for a nation largely devoted—in its political mythology and its discourse—to just this conception of history. In other words, I present a study of authors who know that they must "risk it on signs": the signs of their connection to the mystery of history, the signs that they construct in their texts to speak to others of that possible connection, and the signs of other writers to which they respond and which they appropriate in their efforts to read and write their way into new configurations of secular meaning and identity.

We see one version of this struggle over the signs within the context of an encompassing sacred history in Anna Julia Cooper's conception of the necessity of racial conflict. "Each race," Cooper argues, "has its badge, its exponent, its message, branded in its forehead by the great Master's hand which is its own peculiar keynote, and its contribution to the harmony of nations" (152). When races are left alone—"out of contact, that is, with other races and their opposing ideas and conflicting tendencies"—human life is reduced to a single keynote, to "unity without variety, a predominance of one tone at the expense of moderation and harmony, and finally a sameness, a monotonous dullness which means stagnation,—death" (152). Cooper thus reenvisions racial struggle as a rich and entangled confusion of human life and history that requires the active presence of all different groupings of individuals, all different notes in a symphony that no single group is equipped to write.

Similarly, in his address of 30 May 1881 entitled "Did John Brown Fail?" Douglass notes that "To the broad vision of a true philosophy, nothing in this world stands alone. Everything is a necessary part of everything else"; "The universe . . . is continually proving itself a stupendous whole, a system of law and order, eternal and perfect" (10–11). And upon this vision of an encompassing economy Douglass bases his hopes for justice—hopes that Douglass is thus enabled to extend beyond abstract philosophical notions of brighter days coming to a narrative that places John Brown's revolutionary struggle within a vision of sacred history:

Every seed bears fruit after its kind, and nothing is reaped which was not sowed. The distance between seed time and harvest, in the moral world, may not be quite so well defined or as clearly intelligible as in the physical, but there is a seed time, and there is a harvest time, and though ages may intervene, and neither he who ploughed nor he who sowed may reap in person, yet the harvest nevertheless will surely come; and as in the physical world there are century plants, so it may be in the moral world, and their fruitage is as certain in the one as in the other. The bloody harvest of Harper's Ferry was ripened by the heat and moisture of merciless bondage of more than two hundred years. That startling cry of alarm on the banks of the Potomac was but the answering back of the avenging angel to the midnight invasions of Christian slavetraders on the sleeping hamlets of Africa. The history of the African slavetrade furnishes many illustrations far more cruel and bloody. (11)

Douglass here reads one past (that of John Brown at Harper's Ferry) to read the future in terms of sacred history, a reading designed to move his readers to reread the ominous text of other aspects of the past (for example, the history of the African slave trade). This vision of an eventual harvest reorganizes human history and redirects individual behavior, calling upon those implicated in the secular narratives of the past to consider their position in the larger sacred narrative with its ominous closure.

In their attempts to not only tell stories but also to give their readers the means to understand those stories, these authors necessarily confront the stories that exist and try to undermine the conventions of understanding that we bring to such stories. Consider, for example, the story Douglass tells in the opening pages of the "Third Part" of his revised *Life and Times of Frederick Douglass* (1892). Douglass complains of the American people that "When an unknown man is spoken of in their presence, the first question that arises in the average American mind concerning him and which must be answered is, Of what color is he? and he rises or falls in estimation by the answer given." And, as he continues, the most famous black American of his day demonstrates that behind this question awaits a series of increasingly specific questions, all amounting to an insistence on racial identification:

I have often been bluntly and sometimes very rudely asked, of what color my mother was, and of what color was my father? In what proportion does the blood of the various races mingle in my veins, especially how much white blood and how much black blood entered into my composition? Whether I was not part Indian as well as African and Caucasian? Whether I considered myself more African than Caucasian, or the reverse? Whether I derived my intelligence from my father, or from my mother, from my white, or from my black blood? Whether persons of mixed blood are as strong and healthy as persons of either of the races whose blood they inherit? Whether persons of mixed blood do permanently remain of the mixed complexion or finally take on the complexion of one or the other of the two or more races of which they may be composed? Whether they live as long and raise as large families as other people? Whether they inherit only evil from both parents and good from neither? Whether evil dispositions are more transmissible than good? Why did I marry a person of my father's complexion instead of marrying one of my mother's complexion? How is the race problem to be solved in this country? Will the Negro go back to Africa or remain here? (939–40)

Together, these questions indicate a cultural habit of thought and a determination to mark clear racial boundaries even where the boundaries resist all delineation. When Douglass lists the many questions he is asked, he presents a fundamental and persistent fact of his life; and he does not have the liberty to define himself wholly in other terms, for the questions will always be a part of his public self. But he can *arrange* the questions into a series that begins with questions about his parents' color(s); proceeds to questions about the influence of white and black blood in his makeup; and then to questions about the specific implications of that blood; leading to questions about his marriage that are in fact questions about the appropriate response to these conditions of identity; which then leads to a broader application of the same question, now concerning the appropriate response to the "race problem . . . in this country"; and concluding with the question that indicates the inquisitor's implicit answer to the race problem and that indicates also the underlying assumptions that drive all of the questions: "Will the Negro go back to Africa or remain here?" Douglass's response to these questions is to arrange them into a narrative that reveals a certain cultural plot, a plot that joins various aspects of U.S. racialized culture and points to the narrative's escapist fantasies of a closure that insists on separatism. But as the questions themselves make clear, this closure simply does not follow from this narrative, for the narrative reveals in each of its questions the fact that whatever racial lines one might want to imagine have long ago been crossed. What we have is a narrative of white racial insistence that undermines its own foundations and that draws one to an ethical interpretation of the urge to mark clear lines, the need to ask the questions in the first place. Using only the questions he has been asked, Douglass constructs a narrative that suggests a larger question that he turns back on his inquisitors.

And so, too, Brown, Wilson, Jacobs, Delany, and Harper—like Douglass—work to reshape the cultural narratives in which they find themselves placed into new narratives that challenge the foundational assumptions that govern collective and individual identity, public roles and private lives. The stories they construct challenge the existing interpretive modes for determining the relation between human and sacred history. Each of these authors begins by recognizing and then continues on the hope fostered by the recognition that, as white abolitionist Joseph C. Hathaway puts in his 1847 Preface to Brown's first *Narrative*, "among a reading people like our own, their books will at least give character to their laws," an influence that kindles "the fires of freedom, which will one day break forth in a living flame to consume oppression" (23). Beyond what Hathaway might have in mind, Brown along with the other writers I study clearly looks to the flame not only of a newly impassioned readership but also of significantly new readers, black and white alike, trained to read their worlds differently. Hathaway also notes that Brown's "little book is a voice from the prison-house" (23), a reminder that these writers had to write within prison-houses of discourse from which there was no escape. As I suggest in my chapter on Douglass, writing one's way out of one racially inscribed identity does not mean that one has reached a free discursive space in which one can assert complete control over one's own story, and thereby over one's identity. There are other rooms and fields still contained within the walls. But if one cannot escape, one can still teach one's readers to recognize just how all-encompassing the prison is, and just how many are contained within its walls.

Working within these walls, *Resistance and Reformation in Nineteenth-Century African-American Literature* presents six case studies in literary activism, six attempts to construct understandings of Christian mystery capable of opening new vistas of human history, six writers who challenge their readers' reliance on the undervalued and misapplied tools of a culture devoted to dangerously deceptive notions of human order and progress. Throughout, I have considered these texts as individual modes for reenvisioning the world, and I've operated on the faith that individual texts reward individualized attention.

In the chapter on William Wells Brown's *Clotel* I examine this fictive narrative's rich combination of cultural documents, legends, discourse, and plots. Brown's *Clotel*, which in many ways resembles Ishmael Reed's *Flight to Canada*, might best be described as Reed's Raven Quickskill describes his poem in the opening sentences of his narrative: "Little did I know when I wrote the poem 'Flight to Canada' that there were so many secrets locked inside its world. It was more of a reading than a writing" (7). The reading Brown presents in *Clotel* is no less complex and no less rewarding than Raven's (and Reed's) all-encompassing and disorienting novel. Presenting evidence throughout *Clotel* that U.S. culture is dangerously incoherent, devoted to contradictory and otherwise inconsistent arguments and ideals, Brown points to a possible coherence available to those who learn to read the implied narrative of Providence through the interstices of the chaotic human text.

Like Brown's *Clotel*, Harriet E. Wilson's *Our Nig* resists neat generic categorization, and I read this blend of autobiography and fiction to consider the ways in which Wilson shapes the raw material of her experience to create not only a product for sale (the narrative itself) but also to redefine the terms of cultural interaction and exchange. That is, in her appeal for patronage, Wilson looked not for charity but rather for an economic exchange by which the cultural value of her critique of the mid-nineteenth-century northern states could be acknowledged. The narrative defines this exchange as an entrance into a moral economy, a system of social relations based not on an ideal of cooperation but on the recognition that conflict and distrust among and within culturally defined social groups are inevitable. In this way, *Our Nig* responds to proslavery forces that found ready arguments in the injustices of capitalism and calls attention to the ethical motivations behind economic relations. Placing human transactions within the context of what Martin Delany termed "God's Economy," Wilson tells a fictionalized story of her life to transform the terms of an identity not wholly under her control, and demands the aid of those whose lives have been shaped by the world that created her protagonist Frado.

Harriet Jacobs similarly looks to reconfigure the terms of identity, transforming herself from an object of pity into a representative subject, the embodiment of the very contradictions that define the lives of her white readers, and therefore the only reliable guide through the uncertain cultural terrain of veiled practices and deceptive discourse. As I argue, Jacobs faces, and returns to her readers, an epistemic challenge, arguing that new ways of knowing and new modes of understanding will be necessary if a world of mutually exclusive allegiances (the system of slavery and God's moral government) is to be restored to order. Arguing that her readers' understanding of their own world is hidden by the ideological screens they use to maintain the fiction of cultural coherence and moral stability, Jacobs's pseudonymous narrator, Linda Brent, enters into the realm behind the screens and reconstructs the fragmented cultural text that will make clear her readers' moral predicament and their attendant responsibilities.

Next I examine Martin R. Delany's attempt to revolutionize the minds of his readers, deconstructing the self-sustaining logic of the system of slavery and constructing a vision of moral government that justifies militant black agency. Delany identifies a "White Gap," the realm between national principles and actual practices, and he guides his readers through that gap on a kind of Underground Railroad journey that extends beyond the provisional destination of Canada to Africa, Cuba, and ultimately back to the heart of slavery in U.S. racialist thought. Ultimately, Delany creates a fictive community of unified black revolutionaries in order to change a more incoherent and fragmented reality, and his narrative tells the story of an increasingly apparent vision of moral order that both follows from and guides moral action.

Delany's more famous and generally more moderate colleague Frederick Douglass understood keenly the need to construct a model for black moral agency, and I examine his attempt to construct and maintain a vision of his life as a representative man. My study of Douglass's sequential versions of his life reveals the extent to which he tried to respond to the increasingly complex cultural politics of public identity, involving the multiple ways in which black identity was defined and delimited. Ultimately, I argue, Douglass's attempt to maintain a unified representative identity breaks down into multiplicity, a series of discrete responses to the various forces that defined his life and reputation—and instead of representative selfhood Douglass eventually presents his life as a sentimental role performed on the public stage, working to bring an individual performance to a script whose authorship was beyond his control. Douglass, that is, becomes representative in his inability to reconcile human history and Providence, as the weight of events and cultural constructions of identity obscure his vision of a clear moral narrative.

*Resistance and Reformation* concludes with a consideration of Frances E. W. Harper's *Iola Leroy*, which in many ways combines the concerns and strategies of the other texts I examine. Like Brown, Harper constructs her narrative from a variety of historical sources; like Wilson, Harper recognizes the relations among various systems of order and looks to reconstruct a coherent vision of individual, communal, commercial, and moral economies; like Jacobs, Harper challenges her readers' ability to understand their own worlds and argues that understanding must be a combined effort, extending from a genuine cultural reciprocity; like Delany, Harper deconstructs prevailing racial attitudes and constructs a vision of a moral order that requires black agency; and, like Douglass, Harper recognizes the multiple threats to the black community—threats from within as well as from without—and tries to construct a narrative capable of providing a unified vision for responding to a complexly incoherent world, trying to account for everything without losing the simplicity and coherence needed to provide practical and moral instruction. Noting that the dominant culture's "acquirements" can offer only a limited knowledge—a world of mysteries that cannot be solved—Harper operates on her faith in a more essential mystery and presents a story devoted to moral uplift that is also a story of the hidden histories that inform the lives of her readers.

Since my fundamental contention is that these writers use available materials to construct new houses of culture, it is appropriate to conclude this introduction as I conclude the book, with what might be called Frances Harper's architectural vision of the post-Reconstruction United States. In the centerpiece of *Trial and Triumph*, Annette argues in her commencement speech that because "[s]ome races had been 'architects of destruction,'" the black American "mission" is accordingly "grandly constructive" (*MST* 241). A subplot of this novel involves the building of churches, and when Mr. Thomas—educator, minister, and carpenter— talks with Reverend Lomax about a people who are in some respects "sheep without a shepherd," he offers a vision of the black church capable of countering the multifarious forces of a restrictive world. "I hope the time will come," he says, "when every minister in building a church which he consecrates to the worship of God will build alongside of it or under the same roof, parish buildings or rooms to be dedicated to the special wants of our people in their peculiar condition" (*MST* 247). Thomas's vision of this church is too lengthy to reprint here, but it is a vision of the church as "the great centre of moral, spiritual and intellectual life for the young," and of a building in which "earnest men and women" could "come together and consult and counsel with each other on the best means to open for ourselves, doors which are still closed against us" (*MST* 247–48). It is important to note that the mission of that church is defined by the "peculiar condition" of U.S. culture; the church's conception of its mission is necessarily responsive, and its goal must be to acknowledge conditions as they are in the process of envisioning and realizing conditions as they could be. And the materials needed to build that church are themselves of the world—the same materials used to construct the institutions to which the church must respond. One can, of course, use those materials differently, and in reenvisioning the architectural requirements of the church, one both responds to necessity and creates possibilities by reenvisioning the activities that the church can contain. But my point is not to celebrate what should be for my readers a familiar vision of the black church as a cultural, social, political, and moral center. My point is that Mr. Thomas's vision for the church is also Harper's vision for her literature, and that each of the writers I study in the following chapters offers similarly architectural innovations on familiar designs and looks to build new structures from existing materials. To understand the houses of culture they have built, we need to set aside the familiar blueprints and enter into each structure, and into the world that the structure both contains and resists.

I

# The Profession of Authorship and the Cultural Text

## William Wells Brown's *Clotel*

Deception, discursive complexity, multiple contexts, and documentary confusions await those who enter the world of William Wells Brown's *Clotel; or, The President's Daughter: A Narrative of Slave Life in the United States* (1853). In describing this world, critics have been so frustrated by the presence of so many sources and plots in one text that they have had trouble seeing the one in the many—a unified artistic achievement greater than the sum of its parts. Vernon Loggins complained in 1931 that "[t]he great weakness of *Clotel* is that enough material for a dozen novels is crowded into its two hundred and forty-five pages" (166); by 1970, Arthur Davis had reduced the number of potential novels in *Clotel* to five, asserting that Brown "tried to cram too many things into one work: antislavery lectures and verse; enough situations to supply at least five novels; newspaper accounts, some pertinent, others flagrant digressions; minstrel jokes and sketches; and every slavery anecdote he considered even remotely pertinent" (xv). Putting the best light on this wealth of material, J. Noel Heermance noted in 1969 that "What we finally have in *Clotel* . . . is not so much an artistic novel as a loosely structured skeleton of a plot on which the author can hang true and vivid anecdotes, stories, advertisements and Virginia legislature speeches." *Clotel*, Heermance concludes, is "not a work of sculptured unity resting on American soil," but rather "a nineteenth century 'deus ex machina' mobile, propitiously hanging from the sky" (164–65).

Virtually all the critics who have viewed this conglomeration of suspended unity have either reached the conclusion or begun with the assumption that *Clotel* does not hold together when set on hard critical ground. Of course, one might say the same of Melville's *The Confidence-Man*, another work with enough material for a dozen novels that presents difficulties to those in search of novelistic structure, consistency, and unity. But whereas one might proceed through *The Confidence-Man* with the assumption that it will make sense, different assumptions usually are brought to *Clotel*. As recently as 1989, even so great an advocate of African-American literature as Blyden Jackson found it necessary to approach Brown's *Clotel* only indirectly, asserting virtually as a matter of fact that the work "cannot pretend to be great fiction, novelistic or otherwise. Everyone agrees on that. But it must be conceded to be a historical fiction" (326). This kind of evaluation is characteristic of approaches to nineteenth-century African-American literature in that it begins by submitting to the authority of traditional, hierarchical critical standards. But my point is not that advocates of African-American literature should provide the critical apparatus *Clotel* needs to "pretend to be great fiction"; rather, my point is that we should take this text as an entrance into a world in which the work's apparent lack of unity and overabundance of materials are entirely appropriate.

Our best critical guide might be Brown himself, as represented in a story told in his earlier work *Three Years in Europe* (1852) and quoted in the memoir that opens *Clotel*. Finding himself "without any means of support during the winter," Brown looks for work at a barber shop, and when he is turned down, he opens his own shop across the street. A resourceful businessman, he places over the door of his shop a sign that reads "Fashionable Hair-dresser from New York, Emperor of the West," a sign that is, he notes, "the most extensive part of the concern." Extensive, indeed, for Brown's success in drawing business is a matter of fulfilling the identity invented by his sign: "Of course I had to tell all who came in, that my neighbor on the opposite side did not keep clean towels, that his razors were dull, and, above all, he never had been to New York to see the fashions. Neither had I" (*Clotel* 39–40). In this enterprising act of economic self-creation, Brown plays with the psychology of fashion and places himself within the world of self-conscious cultural marginalism. He appeals to the unseen New York and to fashion-as-concept, and his investment in the fictive empire city of taste is returned by his customers' investment in his professional identity. He would later play this game yet more seriously in New York City itself, when he set up his office to practice medicine.[1]

One needn't invoke Henry Louis Gates's conception of "signifyin(g)" to understand the nature and significance of this "trick of mediation" (*Signifying* 56), this sign that provides its agent with the identity necessary to invest the sign with authority and meaning. Indeed, as he tells the story, Brown locates himself simply as one confidence man among others, one of many in what Karen Halttunen has called "the anonymous 'world of strangers' that was the antebellum city" (xvi). As William L. Andrews has noted, "Brown was . . . a trickster, a very accomplished one in fact" (*To Tell a Free Story* 144).[2] One could say of Brown what Gary Lindberg has observed about many Americans of the nineteenth century: that in a world of "ceaseless movement" and change, the usual badges of identity were insufficient, and so strangers "had to confront each other as mere claimants, who can at best try to persuade each other who they in fact [were]" (5).[3] Brown's enterprise is the usual form of advertising and marketplace competition—one that pays because he is in fact a competent barber (though perhaps no more so than his untraveled competitor).

But insofar as Brown lived in a world that restricted black agency, his ability to create confidence in himself and to create the image of an identity that would authorize a profitable public role was both significant and necessary.[4] One might apply to Brown's career as a whole what Andrews says of the "performing selves" that Brown presents in his *Narrative of William W. Brown, A Fugitive Slave*. Andrews notes the distinction between Brown's different names—William W. Brown, the subject of the narrative, and Sandford, the name Brown was forced to assume when under enslavement, selves related to and representative of but not identical with William Wells Brown; and Andrews suggests that the narrative voice seems directed by Simon Suggs's motto, "It is good to be shifty in a new country," and thereby indicates Brown's belief that "it is good . . . to shift out of constricting poses, to be self-seeking in both a positive and negative sense, not self-satisfied." "By the same token," Andrews argues, "the reader must shift with Sandford to be liberated from the unsatisfying narrative perspective of William W. Brown" (*To Tell a Free Story* 151). Following those shifts, one finds oneself in an uncertain relationship to the usual interpretive moorings upon which one relies for understanding, and drawn to Brown as a practiced and suitably sly guide in this deceptive world. Accordingly, what Lindberg has said of the confidence man, the "covert hero" of the nineteenth-century world of strangers, also applies to Brown—that he is "a manipulator or contriver who creates an inner effect, an impression, an experience of confidence, that surpasses the grounds for it. In short, a confidence man *makes belief*" (3, 7). Making belief was for Brown both an economic and an ideological imperative—the means by which he could earn his bread, and the means by which he could struggle against a culture of such deliberately restrictive means. In effect, Brown had to write his way into authorship to authorize his career as a writer and public figure. As there is a difference between being a capable barber and getting customers to frequent your shop, so there is a greater difference yet between opposing the culture of racism and getting that culture to finance its own opposition. As Andrews has demonstrated, black writers, restricted by their dependence on a white readership, "instead of either conforming to the rules of the literary game or refusing to play . . . set about changing the rules by which the game was played even as they played along with it" (*To Tell a Free Story* 6). Recognizing both the ideological and financial value of the game, Brown similarly had to "make belief" in himself so that he could manage the confidence man's task of taking from a transaction something more than or something different from what the sponsor had bargained for.

I will argue that Brown works to guide familiar antislavery arguments towards unfamiliar results. His basic claims seem simple enough: as he puts it in the Preface to the 1853 edition of *Clotel*, "[t]he great aim of the true friends of the slave should be to lay bare the institution" and thereby "cause the wise, the prudent, and the pious to withdraw their support from it, and leave it to its own fate" (*Clotel* 16). But Brown knew that to accomplish this, to expose the institution, he had to redefine *wise, prudent,* and *pious*; that is, he had to expose the institution as it exists in each individual. Doing so meant working to establish and then reconstitute a correspondence between the public and private, the communal and the individual realms—or, more to the point, between culture and individual character. Brown does this by drawing from the materials of the culture and then serving as cultural editor, rearranging those materials in a revealing demonstration of cultural contradictoriness and tension. At the same time, he establishes his role as cultural product and author, editing himself into being in a grand act of self-governance, rearranging the materials of his life and of his world into a new economy of perspective.

## The Cultural Editor

In Nella Larsen's novel *Quicksand* (1928), protagonist Helga Crane works for a while as "a traveling-companion for a lecturing female on her way to a convention," the "Negro Women's League of Clubs" (35, 38). While "correcting and condensing the speeches," Helga notices how little in them is actually new:

> These speeches proved to be merely patchworks of others' speeches and opinions. Helga had heard other lecturers say the same things in Devon and again in Naxos. Ideas, phrases, and even whole sentences and paragraphs were lifted bodily from previous orations and published works of Wendell Phillips, Frederick Douglass, Booker T. Washington, and other doctors of the race's ills. For variety Mrs. Hayes-Rore had seasoned hers with a peppery dash of Du Bois and a few vinegary statements of her own. (38)

One discovers similar patchworks in the various books published by William Wells Brown, though most of Brown's readers have never seen the sources themselves. Readers of William Edward Farrison's biography of Brown will be aware of the presence of other texts in those published by Brown, and readers of Farrison's edition of *Clotel* can benefit from footnotes directing the reader to most of the sources Brown used. Most readers today, too, are aware that Brown drew one of the main plot lines in *Clotel* directly from Lydia Maria Child's story "The Quadroons." Still, one is likely to forget the presence of texts one has never read, and even with a map it is often difficult to keep track of Brown's continued and varied use of the same sources throughout his career. Most of Brown's books are patchworks, and many of his later works are such complex patchworks of his earlier works and of his earlier uses of his sources that they seem new while containing very little new writing.

In itself, the use of material lifted bodily from other works was neither an unusual or questioned practice in the nineteenth century. Like Larsen's Mrs. Hayes-Rore, historians would often copy or alter or both, as Richard C. Vitzthum has noted, ideas, phrases, and even whole sentences and paragraphs (8)—indeed, even whole chapters—from other works. In his study of historical writings in the nineteenth-century United States, George H. Callcott has demonstrated the prevalence and legitimacy of this practice, noting that "[t]he early nineteenth-century historian felt no need to argue for originality, and he would not have understood why he should make a fetish of reworking material when what he wanted to say already had been better said by another" (136). "As contemporary critics understood the altering of quotations," Callcott notes, "they also understood and approved what the plagiarizers were doing. Critics were aware of having seen the same words before and frequently compared the later account with its source, remarking on the improvement that had been made over the earlier account but seldom considering it a matter of dishonesty in the use of phraseology" (137). Old passages in new contexts served new ideas, new applications of familiar knowledge, and new arrangements of accepted truths. To observe creative versions of this practice in what is today distinguished as literary writing (as was historical writing in the nineteenth century), one would need to look no further than to Herman Melville. Still, Brown's practice is particularly intriguing, both when he acknowledges his debt to outside material (as he does in general terms at the end of *Clotel*), and when he does not (as, for example, in *The Rising Son* [1873]). At a time when it was important for black writers to secure the authority of authorship ("written by himself"), Brown's practice carried risks.[5] For example, Martin R. Delany, in *The Condition, Elevation, Emigration, and Destiny of the Colored People of the United States* (1852), critiques a work "purporting to be a history of ancient great men of African descent, by one Mr. Lewis, entitled 'Light and Truth.' This book is nothing more than a compilation of selected portions of Rollin's, Goldsmith's, Furguson's, Hume's, and other ancient histories; added to which, is a tissue of historical absurdities and literary blunders, shamefully palpable, for which the author or authors should mantle their faces" (128). "If viewed in the light of a 'Yankee trick,'" Delany continues, "simply by which to make money, it may, peradventure, be a very clever trick," though he reminds the publishers that edification should be the first object of concern and expresses his regret that "there are but too many of our brethren who undertake to dabble in literary matters, in the shape of newspaper and book-making, who are wholly unqualified for the important work" (128–29).[6] In the same footnote in which Delany presents this critique, he praises Brown as one of those "authors of narratives, written by themselves, some of which are masterly efforts, manifesting great force of talents" (128). Delany wrote this before Brown published *Clotel* or any of his historical works, and one can only wonder how Delany would have responded to a source study of those later works. These many years afterward, whether or not we view them as Yankee tricks, we misunderstand Brown's writings when we ignore his borrowings, though one could say that Brown's self-creation as author included his ability to speak with great force of talent through the words of others either to ears too willing to accept or to eyes too complaisant to see.[7]

Brown's career as writer began with his *Narrative*, published in 1847; his career as editor began with his publication of *The Anti-Slavery Harp; a Collection of Songs for Anti-Slavery Meetings. Compiled by William W. Brown*, published in Boston in 1848 and in Newcastle in 1850. In this latter work, Farrison notes, "Brown erred in saying that 'the larger portion of the songs' had not been previously published," for "only 17 of the 48 songs had not been included in either Jairus Lincoln's *Anti-Slavery Melodies* or George W. Clark's *The Liberty Minstrel*." Farrison notes further that Brown found many of the remaining seventeen songs "in anti-slavery newspapers" (*William Wells Brown* 123).[8] Included in this collection was the poem "Jefferson's Daughter," published, according to Farrison, in *Tait's Edinburgh Magazine* in July 1839 (*William Wells Brown* 125). This poem speaks of the legend from which Brown would later draw in his fictive narrative about "the President's Daughter," and marks an early instance of Brown's ability to chart the course of his later career by following the maps provided by the material he encounters along the way.[9]

Some of those maps mark the terrain of selfhood, and finding Brown in the maze of this grand journey of self-creation can be difficult. Certainly, one should begin with his popular *Narrative*, which offers the main one of many versions of his life—autobiographical, biographical, and fictional—that he presented through the years in his works.[10] Included are not only Brown's own four American and five British editions of the *Narrative*, but also the account of Brown's life that opens *Clotel* and *The American Fugitive in Europe* (more commonly called *Sketches of Places and People Abroad* [1855]); William Farmer's "Memoir of William Wells Brown," which appears at the beginning of Brown's *Three Years in Europe*; and Alonzo Moore's "Memoir of the Author" that opens *The Rising Son*.[11] In addition, Brown's daughter Josephine published a biography which, as

Farrison notes, "follows . . . Brown's *Narrative* as far as that goes and draws freely upon the biographical and autobiographical data found in *Three Years in Europe, Clotel,* and *Sketches of Places and People Abroad.* In many instances it follows its sources almost verbatim" (Farrison, *William Wells Brown* 272).[12] And completing this strange cycle of self-representation, Brown's own *Memoir of William Wells Brown* (1859), Farrison notes, "is principally a condensation in the first person of Josephine Brown's *Biography of an American Bondman*" (*William Wells Brown* 313). The various versions correspond generally but sometimes contradict one another in their details, and often present inaccurate information; and one can easily become confused as to whose authority one is accepting in any given account. Beyond this biographical mix is a mix of genres, drawing Brown's life in and out of fiction, autobiography, biography, and history. For example, included among the biographical sketches in *The Black Man; His Antecedents, His Genius, and His Achievements* (1863) is a fictionalized account of Brown's own life, under the title "A Man Without a Name," which then becomes chapter 36 of his history *The Negro in the American Rebellion: His Heroism and His Fidelity* (1867), under the title "A Thrilling Incident of the War." A lengthy episode concerning a steamboat race in the "Memoir of the Author" one encounters at the beginning of *The Black Man* becomes a chapter in more than one version of *Clotel*. As Russ Castronovo has argued, "These diverse autobiographical accounts do not so much constitute a complete life, inviolable in the authority of its own experiences, as they subtly reconstitute history, implying its mutable and selective aspects" (528).

Yet more complex is Brown's use of his sources, of his own earlier writings, and of his own earlier use of sources. To miss this use is to misevaluate the nature and course of Brown's career, for one can never be sure of distinguishing between Brown's own writing and that of his sources. For example, in his overview of Brown's career, Heermance singles out *St. Domingo: Its Revolutions and Its Patriots* (1855) as an example of "Brown's ability to see detachedly and objectively both sides of a man's nature and both sides of a historical struggle. Thus while he is able to celebrate the heroic Christophe in almost Classical cadences, he is also able to give Rigaud, Petion, and Boyer their due as men, even as they represent the enemy in this speech of liberation and revolution" (170). In this work, however, Brown borrows heavily—and often verbatim—from John R. Beard's *Life of Toussaint L'Ouverture*. While much of the writing is not to be found in Beard's book, it is difficult to credit Brown with all examples of balanced historical perspective and stylistic cadences.[13]

These borrowings become more difficult to trace as Brown's career continues. He drew from Beard again, from his own *St. Domingo*, and from other sources in *The Black Man*. For example, he drew half of his sketch of Denmark Vesey from a sketch by Thomas Wentworth Higginson, and he "quoted," Farrison reports, "almost verbatim" the *Memoir and Theatrical Career of Ira Aldridge, the African Roscius*. In *The Negro in the American Rebellion*, Brown borrowed heavily from Livermore's *An Historical Research Respecting the Opinions of the Founders of the Republic on Negroes as Slaves, as Citizens, and as Soldiers* (1862). Indeed, as Farrison reports, "Brown's original writing in chapter 1 consists of only a few introductory and linking paragraphs" (411). Brown borrowed heavily also from his own *The Black Man*, and from sources quoted in that work—but in *The Negro in the American Rebellion* the quotation marks disappear, placing entire series of paragraphs into the new work without the indication of quoting that Brown found necessary in the earlier work. This is the case also in *The Rising Son*, very little of which, by my count, is new writing. Much of it comes from *St. Domingo*, *The Black Man*, and *The Negro in the American Rebellion*, and quotation marks again disappear. At times, Brown revises the judgments he presented in earlier works or selectively omits paragraphs from sections taken from earlier works; at other times, as Farrison notes, Brown "failed to make simple changes in wording which were necessary to bring his statements up to date" (442). Finally, Brown's *My Southern Home* (1880) is largely a work made up of earlier writings. As Farrison notes, Brown "repeated a considerable amount, often verbatim, of what he had said in the several editions of his *Narrative*, the four versions of *Clotel*, *The Escape*, his *Memoir of William Wells Brown*, and also *The Negro in the American Rebellion*" (447).

Even more confusing is the trail one must follow to keep track of the various versions of *Clotel*.[14] The trail begins with *Clotel; or, The President's Daughter: A Narrative of Slave Life in the United States*, published in London in 1853; this was followed by *Miralda; or the Beautiful Quadroon*, serialized in the *Weekly Anglo-African* in 1860–1861; in 1864, Brown returned to this material to publish *Clotelle: A Tale of Southern States*; and in 1867 he published *Clotelle: or, The Colored Heroine; A Tale of the Southern States*. Sometimes considered revisions of the same book, these works are better considered as four books drawn from the same material. In *Miralda*,

Brown changed the names of the principal characters—and, as Farrison summarizes, "changed the setting and order of several of the events in *Clotel* and rearranged its division into chapters, omitting all or parts of some chapters and adding new ones or new parts to old ones." He also "quoted poetry profusely, or made different characters quote it," often inaccurately (*William Wells Brown* 325). In *Clotelle: A Tale of Southern States*, Brown repeated most of the material and form of *Miralda*, omitting most of the poetry, and deleting many passages, along with chapter 36. This version also includes material taken from the "Memoir of the Author" that opens *The Black Man*. In *Clotelle: or, The Colored Heroine*, Brown repeats most of the first hundred or so pages of the previous version, adding four new chapters. None of the books is presented as a revision or new edition of the previous ones or as a new arrangement of existing materials.

It is, then, precisely because it contains an overabundance of materials that I wish to focus on the 1853 *Clotel; or, The President's Daughter: A Narrative of Slave Life in the United States*—that is, on what might be called Brown's initial economy of the materials. Although Farrison identifies in the notes to his edition of *Clotel* the materials Brown uses in each chapter, it is useful to review these borrowings here (beyond the ones Brown himself identifies in the text), for they are seldom and only briefly mentioned in most treatments of this text. Brown takes advertisements for slave sales from Theodore Dwight Weld's *American Slavery as It Is* (1839), itself a compendium of documents, testimonies, and advertisements drawn from the South, and in chapter 16 has Georgiana Peck mouth words originally appearing in that work. In chapters 4, 8, and 23 Brown largely reprints verbatim (with only minor changes, many of names and places) Lydia Maria Child's story "The Quadroons," which she published in *The Liberty Bell* (1842), and then republished (slightly revised) in *Fact and Fiction: A Collection of Stories* (1847). The sermon by Hontz Snyder in chapter 6 is "a combination of passages found in two sermons which had been preached to slaves about 1743 by the Reverend Thomas Bacon" (*Clotel* 250n). In chapter 14, Brown retells the true story of Salome Muller, a native of Alsace, who "lost her suit to regain her freedom" in a New Orleans trial of 1844, though "she appealed to the state's supreme court and won her suit in June, 1845" (Farrison, *William Wells Brown* 222). Brown alters the story considerably, as Farrison notes, "for no apparent reason, unless he was unfamiliar with its details at the time of the writing of his novel" (*Clotel* 251n). Brown's account of Clotel and William's escape is "adapted . . . from the actual experience of William and Ellen Craft," and his account of their "steamboat trip from Vicksburg to Louisville is an adaptation almost verbatim of a report which an unidentified observer had written about the Crafts' steamboat ride from Savannah to Charleston" (*Clotel* 252n). In chapters 23 and 24 he borrows significantly—largely verbatim—from John R. Beard's *The Life of Toussaint L'Ouverture*. Chapter 25 ends with Grace Greenwood's "The Leap from the Long Bridge," with an additional stanza and minor changes in wording, though Greenwood's name is omitted.[15]

Beyond his borrowing from the works and lives of others, Brown also reprints material from his own publications. The sale of Clotel is drawn and enlarged from his "A True Story of Slave Life," which appeared in *The Anti-Slavery Advocate* in 1852. The Rev. John Peck is modeled after a "preacher named Peck from Rochester" who had "set forth essentially the same argument against the doctrine of natural rights" that Brown has Peck present in *Clotel* (*Clotel* 250n). Much of the story of Henry and Althesa Morton in chapter 9 is "an expansion of the story related" in Brown's 1850 *A Description of William Wells Brown's Original Panoramic Views* (Farrison, *William Wells Brown* 222).[16] And in chapter 26 Brown repeats "almost verbatim" his "Narrative of American Slavery" published as letter 22 of *Three Years in Europe* (*Clotel* 254n).

When one approaches *Clotel*, one indeed approaches a compendium of, to use again Davis's list, "antislavery lectures and verse; enough situations to supply at least five novels; newspaper accounts, . . . minstrel jokes and sketches; and every slavery anecdote he considered even remotely pertinent." But I would suggest that to evaluate this compendium according to the traditional standards of novelistic fiction is to misjudge it from the start. As Ann duCille has argued, the strategy that informs *Clotel* is "[o]ften misdiagnosed by critics as sentimental melodrama or badly written realism" (18). In this work that is so often heralded for being the first novel by an African American (one of the few unqualified compliments paid it), it is at least mildly interesting that Brown—an untiring self-promoter who never missed an opportunity to speak for the cause and to secure his own position within it—never thinks to make this claim himself in his 1853 version. The title page refers to the work as "a narrative of slave life in the United States"; Brown ends his Preface with the hope that this work will add to "information already given to the Public through similar publications" (16), missing here a grand opportunity to claim that this is in fact a singular publication.

Like Stowe in *Uncle Tom's Cabin*, Brown concludes *Clotel* by raising and answering the expected question, "Are the various incidents and scenes related founded in truth?" (*Clotel* 245). Of course, Stowe says much the same thing about *Uncle Tom's Cabin*, though again Brown misses an opportunity to ride the popularity of that work, an opportunity certainly not missed by the many who responded to Stowe in works claiming to tell the true story, and that many writers of fiction and nonfiction would not miss in the following years.[17] Answering his question with an unequivocal yes, Brown then offers the following acknowledgment of his sources:

> I have personally participated in many of those scenes. Some of the narratives I have derived from other sources; many from the lips of those who, like myself, have run away from the land of bondage. Having been for nearly nine years employed on Lake Erie, I had many opportunities for helping the escape of fugitives, who, in return for the assistance they received, made me the depositary of their sufferings and wrongs. Of their relations I have made free use. To Mrs. Child, of New York, I am indebted for part of a short story. American Abolitionist journals are another source from whence some of the characters appearing in my narrative are taken. All these combined have made up my story. (245)

One might well read the final sentence here as referring not only to the story Brown tells but also to the continuing story he has lived, joining the first and last sentences here in a full statement of "my story." For Brown's portrayal of slavery and of racial domination in the U.S. follows his experience: not a neat narrative, nor isolated incidents, but a combined effect of various experiences—experiences in print media as well as in events. The effects of a slave culture include the means devised within that culture to understand one's situation, and the stories of others that help one to conceive and articulate one's own.

Like Harriet E. Wilson's *Our Nig*, *Clotel* resists easy and conventional classification, and I don't think our response to this difficulty should be to either insist on *Clotel*'s status as a novel in a story of literary origins and progress or to place it in a special category of black fiction or docufiction. More to the point is duCille's careful consideration of Brown's participation in a "formal strategy" for which there is no adequate critical term:[18] "Brown crafted fact and fiction, image and incident, into what I call an 'unreal estate,' a fictive realm of the fantastic and coincidental, not the farfetched or the fanciful or 'magical realism' but an ideologically charged space, created by drawing together a variety of discursive fields—including 'the real' and 'the romantic,' the simple and the sensational, the allegorical and the historical—usually for decidedly political purposes" (18). A blend of narrative, autobiography, fiction, history, documentary collection, political philosophy, and national legend and myth, *Clotel* most resembles not *Uncle Tom's Cabin* but rather the antislavery journals Brown claims as his source and Weld's *American Slavery as It Is*, itself printed in *The Anti-Slavery Examiner* in 1839. Antislavery journals like *The Anti-Slavery Record* and *The Anglo-African Magazine*, like other periodicals of the time, offered a rich blend of fiction, poetry, reviews, essays, and reprints of speeches and other documents. The first volume of *The Anglo-African Magazine* (1859), for example, included the first published chapters of Martin R. Delany's *Blake; or, The Huts of America*, poems, essays, and a short story by Frances E. W. Harper, a historical essay by Edward W. Blyden, a narrative sketch "Allexandre Dumas," a series of sketches under the title "Afric-American Picture Gallery," "A Statistical View of the Colored Population of the United States from 1790–1850," and the words and music to A. J. R. Connor's "My Cherished Hope, my Fondest Dream," "written, composed and arranged for the piano-forte." To read any single issue of this journal from start to finish is to read a truly multiform work, one that joins poetry, fiction, nonfiction, and social studies under a single political and even discursive roof. Some publications—like Weld's book—included as well documents from the South, many of which were presented without commentary. For example, in 1835, some seventeen years before Frederick Douglass would present his famous speech "What to The Slave is the Fourth of July?," the first volume of *The Anti-Slavery Record* included a piece in which the Reverend Dr. Dalcho of South Carolina offered a foregrounding answer to Douglass's eventual question. Under the heading "Slaves Have Nothing to Do With the Fourth of July" is an excerpt from Dalcho's writings, in which he asserts that "the celebration of the *Fourth of July* belongs *exclusively* to the white population of the United States" (115). The same journal reprints advertisements for slave sales, offering little beyond informative commentary—for example, noting an inconsistency in an advertisement for "young Negroes" in states that claim not to separate families (34).

Certainly, the assumption is that the documents will speak for themselves, but equally important is the arrangement of the documents to make them speak with and against each other. For example, in the inaugural issue of *The Anti-Slavery Record* (January 1835) is a piece (credited to the *Review of Nevin's Biblical Antiquities*) entitled "Contrasts Between the Mosaic Servitude and American Slavery," in which the page is divided into parallel columns (see figure 1). In the left column, Mosaic law is summarized in an overview, which is then followed by "specifications," or summaries of specific laws. In the right column, after an overview of American slave law, corresponding "specifications" are placed parallel to the appropriate Mosaic laws (9–10). The journal *Slavery in America* followed this same format in its piece on "National Consistency" (figure 2), in which "American Declarations" are quoted from the national and state constitutions in the left of the parallel columns and "American Practice" is represented by a series of quotations from advertisements in the right (319). The point of the two columns is obvious but effective, and would serve as one of the most fundamental discursive methods of the abolitionist movement. To mouth the words "Give me liberty, or give me death" while struggling against enslavement, or to distinguish between the "Christianity of this land" and the "Christianity of Christ," as Douglass does in the Appendix to his 1845 *Narrative* (97), is to place before one's audience parallel and contrasting columns that make clear the widening gap between cultural theory and practice. But the point is not that the nation has drifted from its declared ideals, but rather that the nation exists in neither column; and as the columns multiply, the point is that the nation lacks discursive, political, philosophical, and moral unity. The nation exists in the space that separates the columns, the silence left by the warring discourses.

In *Clotel* Brown uses narrative threads to tie together the kind of documentary complexity one encounters in the journals; indeed, *Clotel* might well be considered a narrative journal, one that works to give voice to the world that lies in the spaces between the columns, and to look for bridges between antislavery and proslavery discourses and documents. We have in this work the same sort of documentary richness and ideological consistency that provides any magazine or journal with its textual identity. Just as the identity of a journal is grounded in but transcends the content, tone, or message of any individual article, poem, song, or reprinted advertisement—and just as that identity can both critique and encompass the world of the opposition by reprinting strategically chosen articles or advertisements from other books, journals, and newspapers—so *Clotel* becomes the encompassing document that represents the cultural battles over race and enslavement by encompassing those battles, quoting them, and joining them in an ideological framework and narrative progression that brings the confusion to a determinable point. That is, the claim of authorship in *Clotel* extends beyond any given narrative line or any specific episode; authorship in this work functions as a response to the text that the community is in the act of writing. Brown does not so much represent a world as capture a world in the act of unconscious self-representation. In his role as cultural editor, Brown gathers the documents that reveal the national disunity—not the meaninglessness of the national text but rather its meaningful incoherence—and he constructs or reshapes his various narrative lines to instruct his readers to read beyond the text to a moral realm presented not as the ideals of the left column but rather as the interpretive tools one needs to read one's world.

## The Prisonhouse of Culture

The first pages of *Clotel*'s first chapter introduce the reader to the textual world of U.S. slavery, for there Brown engages in cultural gossip by referring to Henry Clay's talk of amalgamation as the possible end of slavery and John Randolph's claim in the Virginia legislature that " 'the blood of the first American statesman coursed through the veins of the slave of the South' " (59). From the beginning of *Clotel*, the authors of U.S. history speak for themselves in the voices of its most prominent representatives, and in the form of the "fearful increase of half whites" among the enslaved population (59). Here in the interstice of official and unofficial history, the voices of a culturally inexpressible desire remind the reader that the Clotel of the title is defined in relation to "the first American statesman," and that this narrative is as much about those whose blood *courses* "through the veins" of three quarters of the enslaved population as it is about the one quarter who are "the real Negro, or clear black" (59). These voices redefine this text, making it not about the enslaved but about the enslavers, drawing attention to the need to read color as a mark not of race but of morality, for the presence of whiteness

# FIGURE 1

## CONTRAST BETWEEN THE MOSAIC SERVITUDE AND AMERICAN SLAVERY.

### MOSAIC.

The Mosaic law regulating servitude had its foundation in generous compassion for the poor; and every one of its provisions is framed with a view to the relief of such ; tends to encourage a kind and benevolent disposition in the rich and powerful ; and to elevate the character of the poor.

### AMERICAN.

The American slave laws had their origin in avarice ; and are framed with a view to promote the secular interest of the master, and tend to produce and foster meanness of spirit in the slave, and a spirit of cruelty and tyranny in the master, and thus destroy every generous feeling in both.

### SPECIFICATIONS.

1. Two thirds of all the servants in Israel were free at the end of six years; and the fiftieth year gave liberty to all. There was no hereditary servitude.

2. Jewish servitude was voluntary, except where it was the penalty annexed to crime.

3. Servants might contend with their masters about their rights ; and to despise their cause was reckoned a heinous crime. Job xxxi. 13.

4. The law in Israel granted freedom to a servant who had been cruelly or unreasonably punished. Ex. xxi. 26, 27.

5. Servants in Israel were carefully protected in their domestic relations ; so that husbands and wives, parents and children, must not be separated. In case the mother did not get her freedom as soon as her husband, the children remained with her; and the master was bound to receive him to service again, if he chose to live with them.

6. The law of Moses secured to servants the means of religious instruction and consolation.

7. The law of Moses required every one to love the stranger as himself, and forbade any one to vex or oppress him.

8. If a servant escaped from his master and fled to the land of Israel, the law commanded every one to protect him ; and forbade any one to deliver him to his master.

### SPECIFICATIONS.

1. American slavery is perpetual to the last moment of the slave's earthly existence, and hereditary to all his descendants to the latest posterity.

2. American slavery is involuntary, and inflicted for no other crime, than having a skin not colored like ours.

3. Slaves can make no contracts, and can have no legal right to any property. All they have and are, belong to their masters.

4. An American slave may be punished at his master's discretion without the means of redress. And the master can transfer the same despotic power to any other person : so that on the side of their oppressors there is power ; but they have no comforter.

5. American slaves are entirely unprotected in their domestic relations ; so that husbands and wives, parents and children, may be separated at the sovereign will of the master.

6. The operation of the laws in America tends to deprive slaves of religious instruction and consolation ; for their whole power is exerted to keep slaves in a state of the lowest ignorance.

7. The American law views every black stranger an enemy, and considers him a slave until he proves his freedom.

8. If a slave escape from his master, and flee to any part of the United States, the law forbids any one to protect him; but commands that he be given up to his master.

*Review of Nevin's Biblical Antiquities.*

# FIGURE 2

## NATIONAL CONSISTENCY.

*An American Exposition of Acts xvii. 26, " God hath made of one blood all nations of men, for to dwell on all the face of the earth."*

### AMERICAN DECLARATIONS.

" WE HOLD THESE TRUTHS TO BE SELF-EVIDENT, THAT ALL MEN ARE CREATED EQUAL ; THAT THEY ARE ENDOWED BY THE CREATOR WITH CERTAIN UNALIENABLE RIGHTS ; THAT AMONG THESE ARE LIFE, LIBERTY, AND THE PURSUIT OF HAPPINESS."—*Declaration of Independence.*

" All men are by nature equally free and independent, and have certain inherent rights ; of which, when they enter into a state of society, they cannot, by any compact, deprive or divest their posterity ; namely, the enjoyment of life and liberty, with the means of acquiring and possessing property, and pursuing and obtaining happiness and safety."—*Virginia.*

" Through divine goodness, all men have by nature, the rights of worshipping and serving their Creator, according to the dictates of their consciences, of enjoying and defending life and liberty, and acquiring and protecting reputation and property, and, in general, of obtaining objects suitable to their condition, without injury by one to another ; and these rights are essential to their welfare."—*Delaware.*

" All men are born equally free and independent ; all men have certain natural, essential, and inherent rights ; among which are, the enjoying and defending life and liberty, acquiring, possessing, and protecting, property ; and, in a word, of seeking and obtaining happiness."—*New Hampshire.*

" All men are born equally free and independent, and have certain inherent and indefeasible rights, among which are those of enjoying and defending life and liberty, of acquiring, possessing, and protecting property and reputation, and of pursuing their own happiness."—*Pennsylvania.*

### AMERICAN PRACTICE.

1. " Negroes.—A lot of uncommonly likely negroes for sale—fellows and boys. Sold for no fault. Inquire," &c.

2. " Ten dollars reward.—Run away from the subscriber, a boy named January ; rather chunky built ; with thick cheeks or jaws. The small part of his right leg having been broken, or badly hurt, shows differently from the left, which is notable ; and he says done by a horse when he was small. Any person that will bring him to me, or lodge him in some safe gaol, so that I may get him, shall have the above reward from me. William Watson."

3. " Negro men wanted.—Cash will be paid for negro men from 18 to 30 years old. Apply at the store of Graham and Hope."

4. " Negroes wanted.—Cash will be paid for likely negroes of both sexes, from the age of 10 to 20 years. Persons having such to dispose of may apply to Hugh M'Donald."

5. " Brought to Augusta gaol, on the 17th inst. a negro man who calls himself Riley. The owner is requested to come forward, pay expenses, and take him from gaol."

6. " This day, the 6th inst., will be sold, at the north of the Exchange, at 11 o'clock, a wench about 38 years old, a field hand, with her child 10 months old. Also a wench, 45 years old : a good dairy woman, poultry minder, and nurse. Conditions, cash."

7. " Cash ! cash ! cash !—The highest prices will be given for negroes of every description. Apply in Beaufain Street, one door from Coming-street.

8. " Fifty dollars reward. — Run away from the subscriber, his negro woman, Patsey, about 45 years old. She has two scars on the right cheek, made by the whip. The above reward will be given to any person who will deliver her to the subscriber : or 25, if in any goal, so that I can get her. If she was not stolen, it is expected that she has endeavoured to get back to Virginia, where she was raised. She was bought of John Lane, a negro speculator.—Henry Bird."

in the faces of the enslaved offers "the best evidence of the degraded and immoral condition of the relation of master and slave in the United States of America" (59).

But Brown, who makes a point of his temporal position in England as he writes this narrative, begins with this statement not to announce *Clotel* as yet another commentary on the immorality of slavery but rather to present the text as a cultural study. The question is not how this could happen—enslavement, desire, illicit and forced relations—for human nature is capable of evils that are considered unimaginable only by a comforting cultural fiction. Rather, the question is why this *does* happen in a nation with the legal and religious cultural tools to shape and control human nature. The rightness or wrongness of slavery is not the issue; rather, the question is why the cultural system fails to guarantee right behavior and why it also fails to reveal this failure. From his perspective across the Atlantic, Brown reads the cultural system—rather, shows it reading and misreading itself—and draws from his experience within the system to construct the means by which it can read itself in a new light.

In the nine pages of *Clotel*'s first chapter, entitled "The Negro Sale," Brown introduces the reader to a dangerously skewed cultural economy. I use the term *cultural economy* to refer to Brown's attention to the order and operation of various cultural institutions: religion, governance, law, economics, and education. Each institution is introduced as it bears not only on slavery but also on the other institutions, as we see lawyers, statesmen, and clergymen engaged in the defense or perpetuation of slavery. By the logic of nineteenth-century United States "chosen nation" mythology,[19] the putatively *natural* hierarchy of these institutions might be as I have listed them above, in descending order, though the dynamics of this order might be better envisioned as a group of concentric circles. The outermost circle of authority and order, encompassing and securing all the others, would be the divine realm, without which the others will not last. Accordingly, the next encompassing circle is religion, the effort to maintain a communal relationship with God, and to determine the divine will as it reveals itself. Contained by this, and containing all the others, is the national system of governance, an effort to translate God's intended order into a system of human governance that would enable individual and communal progress; the legal code, the practical mode of ensuring justice, is secured by the Constitution and encompasses and secures in turn human transactions, ensuring individual stability and opportunity. Education, the central circle, ensures the ongoing transformation of individuals into citizens, those who have internalized this cultural hierarchy and who embody it in perspective and practice. As laws derive their authority from the Constitution, so each institutional level depends upon its submission to the series of encompassing circles. Thus it was that many antislavery arguments—and especially those that denied the authority of the Constitution—were based on the assumption that governance cannot assume authority over religion. Similarly, economic practice must be legal; and education, the innermost circle, gains its authority from its ability to transmit the cultural code in its ideal order. Education, one might say, is the articulation of the combined and interrelated effects of all the other cultural spheres, by which one negotiates and articulates one's position within this ordered world. And at the center of the wheel is the perfect product of the culture, the Christian republican citizen, secure in his or her identity and confident about his or her role. As with a wheel, the misalignment of any of these circles to the rest will damage the operation of the whole. And if God provides the wheel by which the culture moves forward, at the hub of the wheel is the individual—linked to the God who is both circumference and center—who is both motivated and trained to turn the wheel.

To demonstrate the violation of this order in the United States, Brown focuses on the single institution that participates in and derives its authority and stability from all the others: marriage.[20] Marriage, Brown asserts, is "the first and most important institution of human existence—the foundation of all civilization and culture—the root of church and state" (61). Marriage is, after all, at once a religious, legal, economic, and (always implicitly, often explicitly) political union. As countless domestic handbooks argued, the security of marriage depended upon the security of these various institutions; and the security of the institutions and of the nation itself depended, in turn, upon the security of marriage—a point to which I will return later. As Brown emphasizes, marriage is the practical model for the wheel of culture. "It is," he notes, "the most intimate covenant of heart formed among mankind; and for many persons the only relation in which they feel the true sentiments of humanity" (61). That is, marriage is where abstract concepts become felt concerns. Accordingly, marriage becomes the most intimate of schools, teaching the married partners to develop those virtues that are essential to the broader communal family: "It gives scope for every human virtue, since each of these is developed from the love and confidence which here predominate. It unites all which ennobles and beautifies life,—sympathy, kindness of will and deed, gratitude, devotion, and every delicate, intimate feeling. As the only asylum for true education, it is the first and last sanctuary of human culture" (61–62). And as it is the means by which communal unions are maintained, so marriage is also the means by which those unions are sustained over time, perpetuated in the children who first learn about human society by viewing the union of their parents:

> As husband and wife, through each other become conscious of complete humanity, and every human feeling, and every human virtue; so children, at their first awakening in the fond covenant of love between parents, both of whom are tenderly concerned for the same object, find an image of complete humanity leagued in free love. The spirit of love which prevails between them acts with creative power upon the young mind, and awakens every germ of goodness within it. This invisible and incalculable influence of parental life acts more upon the child than all the efforts of education, whether by means of instruction, precept, or exhortation. (61–62)

In this early argument for what one might today call family values, Brown looks to marriage, the "first and last sanctuary of human culture," as that which transforms cultural ideals into cultural practice, institutions into individual identities, philosophy into lived experience.

The point is less that the violation of marriage is wrong than that it is *revealing*, for such a violation can only be the result of larger violations and misalignments and can lead only to additional cultural decay. As duCille argues, "Brown's primary interest is not in the marital relation in and of itself but in the marriage rite as a fundamental civil and moral right"; and in his portrayal of what both the rite and the right come to in the culture of slavery, "both within and across racial lines," Brown works to "problematize not the marriage relation itself but the 'universal truth' of the traditional marriage story" (22). As Brown asks pointedly, presenting what duCille calls his "discourse on marriage" (22), "If this be a true picture of the vast influence for good of the institution of marriage, what must be the moral degradation of that people to whom marriage is denied?" (62). The wrongness of this violation of marriage is only part of the point, for if one can save the culture by saving the marriage, one can save the marriage only by way of both large and fundamental cultural repairs. Indeed, Brown presents the southern United States as a region with only the pretense of cultural order, a mask that gives license to unchecked human nature, for "amongst the slave population no safeguard is thrown around virtue, and no inducement held out to slave women to be chaste" (63). Those institutions that should provide the order that regulates human nature are devoted instead to justifying disorder, in the form of laws, and in the form of religion, making "ministers of religion, even in the so-called free states, . . . the mere echoes, instead of the correctors, of public sentiment" (62). Even those who look for guidance are not drawn into an institutional light but are instead "plunged into a deeper darkness!" (60). The broken wheel damages itself further as it spins.

The culture Brown presents in *Clotel*, of course, is one in which the outermost encompassing circle is not the divine order but rather the human, the next circle not religion but economics, and the inner hub not the secure republican citizen but degraded and unchecked human nature. The best evidence of this, and the point of the chapter, is the Negro Sale, in which Clotel's price goes up from an initial $500 when she is presented as unformed potential ("She enjoys good health, and has a sweet temper"); to $700 when she is legally certified as ethically sound ("I hold in my hand a paper certifying that she has a good moral character"); to $800 when she is further certified as being capable of education and training ("This paper also states that she is very intelligent"); to $1,200 when her legally certified moral virtue is associated with the cultural institution of religion ("She is a devoted Christian, and perfectly trustworthy"); and finally to $1,500 when she is presented as the product of the ideal cultural system ("The chastity of this girl is pure; she has never been from under her mother's care; she is a virtuous creature") (66–67). The documented embodiment of both the cultural institutions and of the virtues those institutions are designed to produce and secure, Clotel becomes valuable as the ideal "fancy girl" for the "laughing, joking, swearing, smoking, spitting, and talking" crowd of men (67). The breakdown of the cultural economy has transformed value from a carefully produced orchestration of various ideals of human potentiality to simply a gross transaction according to the terms of one cultural institution.

In this way Brown contextualizes his use of Child's "The Quadroons," which begins with chapter 4, transforming it from a moral tale to a story about cultural economy. Although she stands separated from the "fashionable summer residents" of Sand-Hills by "the edicts of society" (62), Child's protagonist Rosalie otherwise seems worlds away from Clotel. Whereas Clotel enters Brown's story by way of a "negro sale," Child's Rosalie is "the daughter of a wealthy merchant, [is] highly cultivated in mind and manners, graceful as an antelope, and beautiful as the evening star" (62). Whereas Child presents Rosalie simply as one who "had early attracted the attention of a handsome and wealthy young Georgian" (62), Brown draws attention to the process of attraction itself, noting that the "great aim" of Clotel's mother Currer was "to bring up Clotel and Althesa to attract attention, and especially at balls and parties" (*Clotel* 64). Clotel, we are told, meets Horatio Green at one such party, a "Negro Ball," one of those "democratic gatherings" where white "gentlemen, shopkeepers, and their clerks, all appear upon terms of perfect equality" to meet "quadroon and mulatto girls" (64).[21] And whereas Rosalie is drawn to Edward by "genuine love[,] that mysterious union of soul and sense, in which the lowliest dew-drop reflects the image of the highest star" ("The Quadroons" 62), not Clotel but Currer is drawn to a union between her daughter and Horatio, looking "forward with pride to the time when she should see her daughter emancipated and free" (65). We do not witness Edward's "proposal" to Rosalie; we do, however, witness the moment when Horatio sits "with the object of his affections by his side," and it is hardly the kind of proposal needed to support Brown's views on marriage. Certainly, the setting is charged with tension and is potentially romantic: "It was a beautiful moonlight night in August, when all who reside in tropical climes are eagerly gasping for a breath of fresh air, that Horatio Green was seated in the small garden behind Currer's cottage, with the object of his affections by his side" (65). The consummation of the scene, however, is more tense than romantic. "And it was here," the narrator notes simply, "that Horatio drew from his pocket the newspaper, wet from the press, and read the advertisement for the sale of the slaves to which we have alluded; Currer and her two daughters being of the number" (65). He leaves Clotel that night with a promise to purchase the object of his affections.

Depending, then, on the text (and thereby the context), we will read differently the slightly different versions of the sentence that one encounters early in both stories: "The tenderness of Clotel's conscience, together with the care her mother had with her and the high value she placed upon virtue, required an outward marriage; though she well knew that a union with her prescribed race was unrecognized by law, and therefore the ceremony would give her no legal hold on Horatio's constancy" (*Clotel* 83–84).[22] Child's and Brown's young women both distinguish between this outward marriage and the inward union, between cultural "semblance" and moral "reality"; both view it—as do the narrators—as "a marriage sanctioned by heaven, although unrecognized on earth" (84). Brown, though, transforms the story into one on the price of virtue in a nation ruled by finance; the story of Clotel is a story not merely of social restrictions and the "tragic mulatto" but of systemic moral transgressions and cultural inversions. What is tragic about this "quadroon" is not her victimization by society but rather her creation and purchase as a product of this society. Horatio is soon tempted by his own "ambition to become a statesman," and therefore by his need to enter into the cultural circle (85). Not only is his relationship with Clotel unacknowledged by the culture, and not only is his own human nature unrestrained and unguided by his culture, but his entrance into politics requires the transgression of the professed moral code: "He had already become accustomed to the dangerous experiment of resisting his own inward convictions; and this new impulse to ambition, combined with the strong temptation of variety in love, met the ardent young man weakened in moral principle, and unfettered by laws of the land" (85). His culture has not only failed to fetter his temptations; it has required him to yield to them.

Indeed, the most fitting emblem of the world Brown portrays is that presented in the brief chapter that follows this installment of Clotel's story, "The Slave Market." In this chapter, Brown takes the reader not to a cabin or hut, nor to a church or government building, but rather to a slave pen, there to find the unofficial national monument in which the actual relations of cultural institutions are represented. When viewed as part of the larger cultural study that is *Clotel*, Brown's reading of the architectural significance of the slave pen is particularly important, drawing attention to the ways in which one social institution influences or is contained within another:

> Not far from Canal-street, in the city of New Orleans, stands a large two story flat building surrounded by a stone wall twelve feet high, the top of which is covered with bits of glass, and so constructed as to prevent even the possibility of any one's passing over it without sustaining great injury. Many of the rooms resemble cells in a prison. In

a small room near the "office" are thumbscrews, cowhides, whips, chains, gags, and yokes. A back yard inclosed by a high wall looks something like the playground attached to one of our large New England schools, and in which are rows of benches and swings. Attached to the back premises is a good-sized kitchen, where two old Negresses are at work, stewing, boiling, and baking, and occasionally wiping the sweat from their furrowed and swarthy brows. (86)

We have here an uneasy combination of prison and New England schoolyard, in the office of which are collected those instruments of torture and restraint that make visible the usually invisible technology of discipline and order. The walls themselves are significant, hiding all from view, and thereby emphasizing the implicitly experienced perspective of the narrator—walls that define order not only by what they keep in but also by what they keep out. Both prison and school, the slave pen is the symbolic center of education in the United States. If the use of the word *swarthy* leads one to question whether this is yet another passage that Brown drew from another source, the presence of the negresses remind us that slavery remains the vital support system of the culture; the only human faces and activity in this portrait, they feed the system that feeds off their enslavement.

Surrounded by these walls that contain and provide spatial unity to both prison and schoolyard, thumbscrews and swings, one has no chance of reading this culture. As the cultural prison shapes the education of "instruction, precept, [and] exhortation" as well as the education of experience, the schoolyard can hope to provide no perspective that extends beyond the defining order of the walls. Brown represents the fruits of this education by having Mr. Peck echo a speech on natural rights that Brown had heard presented by a preacher of the same name from Rochester, at an 1846 Liberty party meeting in New York State (Farrison, *Clotel* 250n). Adam and Eve, Peck argues, might have had what " 'modern philosophy, in its pretended reverence for the name of God, prefers to call natural rights,' " they might have had " 'the right to eat of the fruit of the trees of the garden,' " but even that right was restricted, and " 'their liberty of action' " itself " 'was confined to the garden' " (92–93). However, " 'these were not "inalienable rights," ' " Peck argues, " 'for they forfeited both them and life with the first act of disobedience.' " Accordingly, man no longer had rights, and " 'if he had no rights, he could suffer no wrongs' " (93). And as he draws his conclusions from this line of reasoning, Peck argues for the cultural authority that supports and is supported by the ordering wall: " 'Rights and wrongs are therefore necessarily the creatures of society, such as man would establish himself in his gregarious state. They are, in this state, both artificial and voluntary. Though man has no rights, as thus considered, undoubtedly he has the power, by such arbitrary rules of right and wrong as his necessity enforces' " (93). Peck's conception of rights and of right here is similar to Foucault's conception of truth as "a thing of this world," a thing "produced only by virtue of multiple forms of constraint," and that "induces regular effects of power." "Each society," Foucault argues, "has its regime of truth, its 'general politics' of truth," including "the mechanisms and instances which enable one to distinguish true and false statements" and "the techniques and procedures accorded value in the acquisition of truth." And, most significantly for Brown, Foucault reminds us that the "regime of truth" creates and requires "the status of those who are charged with saying what counts as true" ("Truth and Power" 72–73). Certainly, it is of little comfort to learn that one who enjoys this status—Mr. Peck—claims that "I am one who looks after my people, in a moral, social, and religious point of view" (96). Brown's task, then, is not that of "emancipating truth from every system of power," but rather of "detaching the power of truth from the forms of hegemony, social, economic, and cultural, within which it operates at the present time" (Foucault, "Truth and Power" 75). In *Clotel*, the world of truth is hidden and contained behind the prison walls, the schoolyard is contained within the slave pen, and the individual who stands at the hub of the cultural system finds himself or herself not a subject of culture but its hapless object, as the collective wheel turns the individual hub.

## Reading Culture

What, then, does our world produce? This is the question towards which *Clotel* is directed. As I have argued, much of the narrative—in its documentary fullness and complexity—is designed to raise this question in order to identify the need for a stable interpretive mode, one capable of looking for God's narrative in the confusing chronology of human events. And *Clotel* argues that this interpretive mode begins with the search for disruptions and contradictions, and tests apparent human designs by working back from actual results to veiled causes, looking to the maintenance or disruption of order, and finding significance in strained attempts to make the system *appear* orderly and natural. For example, after Mr. Peck is hit by cholera—and "in less than five hours John Peck was a corpse" (152)—Carlton and Georgiana are surprised to note that "at the parson's death his Negroes showed little or no signs of grief" (153). Taking a walk, they overhear the slaves singing songs that both mock and celebrate Peck's death. When Carlton tries to lead Georgiana away from the scene, Georgiana insists on staying to listen, arguing that "it is from these unguarded expressions of the feelings of the Negroes, that we should learn a lesson" (156). The lesson learned is that the culture of enslavement cannot destroy the idea of liberty, for that idea extends from "the ethereal part of [the slave's] nature, which oppression cannot reach; it is a torch lit up in his soul by the hand of Deity, and never meant to be extinguished by the hand of man" (156).

This, though, is a lesson learned only by observing the contrast between the slave's public behavior and his or her unguarded sentiments, and Brown is well aware that this contrast lends itself to other readings. Carlton represents the dominant interpretation when he observes of Sam's participation in the singing and subsequent obsequiousness, "I could not have believed that that fellow was capable of so much deception" (156). This reading assumes the contrast to be a visible sign of what was by then the white culture's all but standard assumption that blacks were naturally deceptive. Georgiana, though, takes the reading to another level by using the disjunction between behavior and sentiment as a visible sign of a more serious disjunction between human and divine culture. "Our system of slavery," she argues, "is one of deception; and Sam, you see, has only been a good scholar" (156). Adding that Sam is "as honest a fellow as you will find among the slave population here," she looks for conclusions not about race but about culture: "If we would have them more honest, we should give them their liberty, and then the inducement to be dishonest would be gone" (156). By her reading, Sam is the embodiment of a fundamental contradiction between the order of society and the designs of God, and the only answer is to adjust the human system accordingly.

Brown goes to some pains to emphasize that this is a systemic problem and not merely a problem of abstract morality—that, in fact, morality is a function of cultural economy, concerning the management and productions of the cultural system. As Georgiana puts it, "Nothing has been held so cheap as our common humanity, on a national average" (164). Even the problem of liberating the slaves is first expressed in economic terms: "If the slaves were liberated, they must be sent out of the state. This, of course, would incur additional expense" (163). But the economics of liberation go beyond the question of what to do with those who are liberated, and how to finance their journey elsewhere, for an economy that did not hold humanity cheap would recognize the right of the formerly enslaved to live in the South. When Carlton suggests sending them to Liberia, "their native land," Georgiana responds with a familiar American argument, one formerly used in the United States to defend the right of colonization and conquest: " 'What right have we, more than the Negro, to the soil here, or to style ourselves native Americans? Indeed it is as much their home as ours, and I have sometimes thought it was more theirs. The Negro has cleared up the lands, built towns, and enriched the soil with his blood and tears; and in return, he is to be sent to a country of which he knows nothing' " (163). The black community's right to liberty is inherent; the right to *create* by labor and investment, and then live in, one's "native land" is here argued in the most basic economic terms. A system that leads to other views, Brown suggests, is based on an unsound economy.[23]

Thus it is that Brown avoids the possibility of "immediate emancipation" and presents instead Georgiana's and Carlton's attempt to realign the economic system, setting "new rules . . . for the working and general treatment of the slaves on the plantation" (163). Immediately the middle management of the former system recognize the change: "Huckelby, the overseer, saw his reign coming to an end; and Snyder, the Dutch preacher, felt that his services would soon be dispensed with" (163). All the slaves are told that "the whip would no longer be used," that they would be paid wages, and that "the money they earned should be placed to their credit" towards emancipation.[24] The result is quick and widely noticeable:

> The bricklayers had been to work but a short time, before their increased industry was noticed by many. They were no longer apparently the same people. A sedateness, a care, an economy, an industry, took possession of them, to which there seemed to be no bounds but in their physical strength. They were never tired of labouring, and seemed as though they could never effect enough. They became temperate, moral, religious, setting an example of innocent, unoffending lives to the world around them, which was seen and admired by all. (166)

It is not that a systemic change produces a new breed of people; rather, by the theological perspective that informs this text, a systemic change enables the enslaved to align their private and public selves, to identify and fulfill in their behavior their inner nature, to join the physical and the ethereal. No longer *apparently* the same people, they become *possessed* by economy.

One can be discomforted by this lesson if one takes it as evidence that Brown here acquiesces to the logic of enslavement by allowing the enslaved in his narrative to work for their own emancipation. However, one should remember that this passage ends with a reminder that the Carltons' white neighbors are impressed but not fundamentally changed— that, in fact, they largely miss the lesson apparently presented here. Mr. Parker, for example, is moved simply to offer a large sum for the "head workman," Jim. And even when he is told why the slaves are working so hard, he reasons with the embedded logic taught by the school of slavery, "If niggers can work so for the promise of freedom, they ought to be made to work without it" (167). I am suggesting that Brown directs the lesson here not to the workmen (slaves) nor even to the management (slaveholders) but rather to the investors and consumers of the larger system of the U.S. government, those who form the congregation of the implicit state church. Finally, this episode is part of *Clotel*'s ongoing lesson in interpretive method; it is an example of what can be done when one has the luxury of managing others. But the narrative's fundamental message concerns the necessity of self-reading and self-management—and it is a message directed not to the enslaved, nor to slaveholders. Rather, this message directed explicitly to the British public is directed implicitly to those white northern U.S. Christians whose own sympathy for Brown's cause might keep them from applying his lessons to their own lives.[25]

The problem was not only to expose the evils of slavery, for they had been forcefully exposed before; indeed, Brown draws frequently from authors who had presented the case powerfully in the past and integrates their findings and their arguments into *Clotel*. The problem was to reconfigure the terms of the cultural arguments about slavery, terms that implicitly either denied Brown's own authority or limited his voice to that of a witness. Consider, for example, Weld's *American Slavery As It Is*, one of Brown's most important sources. In his introduction to that work, Weld notes the disagreements over the evidence for moral arguments either for or against slavery. "[S]laveholders and their apologists," he notes, "are volunteer witnesses in their own cause, and are flooding the world with testimony that their slaves are kindly treated; that they are well fed, well clothed, well housed, well lodged, moderately worked, and bountifully provided with all things needful for their comfort" (9). Continuing his legal analogy, Weld promises to present "a multitude of impartial witnesses" for the prosecution, "and then to put slaveholders themselves through a course of cross-questioning which shall draw their condemnation out of their own mouths." And as he continues, he amplifies his faith in the sound and indisputable conclusions to be drawn from the case he will present, promising first that "[w]e will prove that the slaves in the United States are treated with barbarous inhumanity"; and then following a listing of examples of such treatment with the assertion, "[a]ll these things, and more, and worse, we shall *prove*"; and then asserting more emphatically, "Reader, we know whereof we affirm, we have weighted it well; *more and worse* WE WILL PROVE" (9).

The emphasis here on proof emphasizes as well the enormity of Brown's own task, for Weld's implicit faith is that once met with evidence of such "barbarous inhumanity," his readers will be moved to pronounce the slaveholders guilty and sentence them to just punishment by rallying behind the antislavery flag. Brown shared this faith, but he knew also its limits, for he would not even be recognized at this bar of justice except as a living document submitted for evidence. Weld promises testimony from those most directly involved in committing or supporting such crimes, and his list of witnesses is revealing even beyond his intentions:

> we will establish all these facts by the testimony of scores and hundreds of eye witnesses, by the testimony of *slaveholders* in all parts of the slave states, by slaveholding members of Congress and of state legislatures, by ambassadors to foreign courts, by judges, by doctors of divinity, and clergymen of all denominations, by merchants, mechanics, lawyers and physicians, by presidents and professors in colleges and *professional* seminaries, by planters, overseers and drivers. (9)

If Weld's own list of witnesses emphasizes the pervasive influence of slavery and provides a portrait of widespread cultural complicity, it also emphasizes the intricate network of the "regime of truth" within which Brown's voice was contained and defined. His task was not just to present authorized *facts* but to reconfigure the cultural constitution itself—to change his readers' ability not just to notice but also to interpret and judge the evidence of experience, to transform the silent jurors of Weld's book (the northern white readers) into either conspirators in or victims of the crimes of slavery, and to present himself not merely as evidence but as judge.

Certainly, *Clotel* offers many examples of the ability of the slave system to harm the lives of those whites most immediately involved in it. For example, Brown presents Horatio Green as a lost soul in the labyrinthine deceptions created and required by the slave system, one whose own human nature is unrestrained and unguided because the cultural system has lost what might be called its productive integrity, its ability to produce the kind of citizens it claims to produce. Eventually, then, we are given a chance to read the moral lesson of Horatio's life, and to thereby measure not only the system's productive integrity but also its moral authority. Green soon finds himself "trying to find relief in that insidious enemy of man, the intoxicating cup. Defeated in politics, forsaken in love by his wife, he seemed to have lost all principle of honour, and was ready to nerve himself up to any deed, no matter how unprincipled" (149), leading him to acquiesce in the sale of Clotel. His wife, who forces her husband to "drink of the cup of humiliation to its very dregs," similarly suffers, and having "felt she had been deceived," she "determined to punish her deceiver"—both her husband and the issue of Horatio's and Clotel's love, Mary (149, 158). But important here is not only the now-visible breakdown of white character but also the newly emphasized racial politics that result from that breakdown, for Mrs. Green, having "hit upon a plan," forces the light-complexioned Mary to work outside "without either bonnet or handkerchief" until the young girl "was but little whiter than any other mulatto children running about the yard" (159). Trying to erase by race the evidence of her husband's love for another and of the thin cultural line dividing the two, Mrs. Green only emphasizes a diseased culture in the act of groping for cosmetic repairs.

Brown works to draw his readers to this thin line, and then to cross it imaginatively through their sympathetic engagement in the story to apply the interpretive lessons learned along the way. As she faces the task of taking over the management of the slaves after her father's death, Georgiana translates Christian ethics into an interpretative method by which one can "try the character of slavery, and our duty in regard to it" (95):

> Long ere this we should have tested, in behalf of our bleeding and crushed American brothers of every hue and complexion, every new

constitution, custom, or practice, by which inhumanity was supposed to be upheld, the injustice and cruelty they contained, emblazoned before the great tribunal of mankind for condemnation; and the good and available power they possessed, for the relief, deliverance and elevation of oppressed men, permitted to shine forth from under the cloud, for the punishment of the human race. (165)

This is application of moral philosophy to the system of slavery, but it is not yet proof of the evils of that system. Although Brown suggests that the new management of the slaves provides proof of the benefits of changing the system, he indicates little application to the white population aside from an appeal to the effect on profits when one has one's workers invest in their own liberty.

For application *and* proof, the sentimental and interpretive strategies of *Clotel* come to a point when Brown draws his readers into an imaginative effort to "try slavery." Responding to the argument that some masters are kind to their slaves and therefore deserve gratitude, Georgiana argues, " 'Everybody knows that slavery in its best and mildest form is wrong. Whoever denies this, his lips libel his heart. Try him! Clank the chains in his ears, and tell him they are for him; give him an hour to prepare his wife and children for a life of slavery; bid him make haste, and get ready their necks for the yoke, and their wrists for the coffle chains; then look at his pale lips and trembling knees, and you have nature's testimony against slavery' " (153). This argument, which Brown presents through Georgiana, actually comes from the first page of Weld's introduction to *American Slavery As It Is*. Weld then follows this statement with a similar appeal to imagine losing one's rights to one's labor: "Suppose I should seize you, rob you of your liberty, drive you into the field, and make you work without pay as long as you live, would that be justice and kindness, or monstrous injustice and cruelty?" (7). The argument itself was not new, even by Weld's time. For example, Samuel Whelpley in his *A Compend of History from the Earliest Times* (1823) includes an entry on Africa in which he refers to the argument that slavery provides Africans with a chance to "learn and embrace Christianity"; noting this line of argument, Whelpley then warns his readers,

The man who justifies slavery upon this principle, let him put himself in the place of one of those ruthless children of misfortune. Let him imagine himself seized, perhaps in the night, and torn from all his friends, and all his heart held dear; bound and forced into a vessel loaded with wretches like himself; his tears answered with scorn; his cries for pity, with the bloody whip. If he does not perish with contagion, hunger or cruelty on the voyage, he is landed at length, and consigned to a master, who drives him into his fields to labor. (148)[26]

By Brown's time, both the facts of slavery and the arguments suggested by the facts were well established; the ongoing task was to fulfill the promise of this application of the condition of the enslaved by looking beyond imagined empathy to a shock of recognition—that is, not by asking his readers to imagine that they are in the world of slavery but by arguing that the world of slavery is in his readers. Whereas Weld begins with this argument in his introduction to the documents that will prove the existence of the horrors of slavery, Brown builds to it after preparing his readers to read it as it stands: not as a prelude to unimaginable horrors but as a mirror in which one can find *imaginable* horrors.

Indeed, Brown leads his readers to a hall of mirrors, a series of inverted reflections of cultural attitudes and habits that together show how arbitrary are the customs that rule U.S. society. As Frederick Douglass comments ironically on U.S. politics in his treatment of the competition within the slave community for *election* to the Great House farm (*Narrative* 23), so Brown comments on racial divisions in his emphasis throughout *Clotel* on prejudice against color within the black community. As the narrator explains, "The nearer the Negro or mulatto approaches to the white, the more he seems to feel his superiority over those of a darker hue. This is, no doubt, the result of the prejudice that exists on the part of the whites towards both mulattoes and blacks" (130). This mirror-image prejudice keeps the dark-skinned Sam, for example, from seeing his image in the mirror while trying to be a mirror of his white master. He dresses in ruffled shirts, butters his hair, greases his face—and, "although Sam was one of the blackest men living, he nevertheless contended that his mother was a mulatto, and no one was more prejudiced against the blacks than he" (133). In this discomforting reflection of white prejudice, Sam plays whiteface to the dominant culture's blackface in a great minstrel romp that demonstrates ultimately complex alliances, desires, and ambivalence behind the carefully staged show.[27]

Brown's point is not only to provide "unmistakeable evidence that caste is owing to ignorance" (133), but also to remind his readers that, as Houston Baker puts it, "Culture is not transcendental and ethereal; while some of its manifestations—some of its arts and artifacts—may often be defined in spiritual terms, culture itself is a more inclusive concept that accurately denotes 'a whole way of life' " (*Long Black Song* 1). Demonstrating to his readers through his often comical treatment of racial prejudice that, in Baker's words, "one necessarily lives a culture" (1), Brown leads his readers to see themselves in the funhouse mirrors of the culture they live, the complex images that constitute the culture within as well as around, the world at home as well as that in the South. Leading into the comical episode where a black man, told that he would have to ride in the luggage van of the train, insists on paying not the fare for a passenger but rather the price for his body as freight, the narrator asserts, "The prejudice that exists in the Free States against coloured persons, on account of their colour, is attributable solely to the influence of slavery, and is but another form of slavery itself" (176). Not only does one live a culture, Brown here suggests, but one is lived by a culture; identifying one's own stance becomes a matter of standing in the place of another.

And deep run the roots of the culture within, roots that, Brown emphasizes, have always had to push through the interstices of profession and practice. At the beginning of chapter 21, Brown constructs a set of historical "parallel lines," extending back to 1620 and the arrival of ships at Plymouth Rock and at the James River in Virginia. Using the ships to typify a clear moral distinction between the North and South (one that he argues against throughout *Clotel*), Brown argues that "these ships are the representation of good and evil in the New World, even to our day" (188). Although he asks dramatically, "When shall one of those parallel lines come to an end" (188), ultimately Brown argues that the two lines are mirror images of each other, too closely joined to be separated. Standing on either of the two lines, one can at best see one's image or one's negative; but always one sees the twin that insures one's identity. To break the parallel, one must adopt the perspective of those who live between the two lines, in the contradictions created by the artificially constructed distinctions of good and evil. As Castronovo argues, instead of challenging "the past which America remembers" Brown challenges "the ways in which it remembers that past" (530).

Operating not along the transcendental cultural line of good or evil but rather in the secular space between, *Clotel* relocates the authorized voice of American political ideals, of American philosophical identity. The white man identified in chapter titles as "the man of honor" and "a true democrat," Henry Morton, can only argue against American practice in his devotion to American ideals. On the other hand, the character in this novel who most fully embodies American political ideals—the one who most convincingly participates in the cultural ritual of invoking the revolutionary zeal of the fathers—is not white but black: George Green, who, like Clotel, "could boast that his father was an American statesman" (224). Morton argues that "the slaves of America . . . lie under the most absolute and grinding despotism that the world ever saw," and that the despots are "the rulers of the country—the sovereign people," "all the free citizens" (184). Morton brings voice to the implicit logic of the text as a whole when he argues that the slaveholder is "but the instrument in the hands of despotism," and warns that "our nation is losing its character," a loss that is "the inevitable prelude to her destruction" (184). George Green, on trial for participating in a revolt, and told by the judge to speak freely, argues, " 'You tell me that I am to be put to death for violating the laws of the land. Did not the American revolutionists violate the laws when they struck for liberty? They were revolters, but their success made them patriots—we were revolters, and our failure makes us rebels. Had we succeeded, we would have been patriots too. Success makes all the difference' " (236). The white democrat mourns a nation lost to collective despotism, and the black revolutionary reminds that nation of its founding ideals, including the understanding that patriots create themselves by succeeding, and that their ideals become real only when their battles are fought successfully. Demystifying the logic that underlies history and national mythology, Brown here views events from the ground up, as it were, from the fields of secular history. And if from those fields we encounter a cynical view of the national ideals, we encounter also a revolutionary effort to restore those ideals to meaning.

This is also what Brown tries to do throughout *Clotel* in his reliance on the documentary complexity of his times to at once demystify history and to relocate the source of its possible authority. He works to "lay bare the institution" and thereby "cause the wise, the prudent, and the pious to withdraw their support from it, and leave it to its own fate." But he works as well to challenge the white reader's confidence in his or her claim to wisdom, prudence, and piety, for he shows that the institution of slavery is not limited by geography or local culture, where it might have been left to itself, but rather exists within each individual. One might well apply to

*Clotel* the interpretive approach Lindberg uses to *make* sense of Melville's *The Confidence-Man*. "Throughout this novel," Lindberg argues,

> Melville urges us to distinguish between the truth of a statement and the effects of it. Bypassing the problem of whether a given fabrication is true, we proceed *as if it is*. We must question why someone tells the story and what consequences it has. The dominant intellectual mode in *The Confidence-Man* is that of hypothesis or supposition, and the key question is, What *follows* from a given story? If we accept this narrative method, the meaning of the much argued concluding sentence becomes clear—"Something further may follow of this Masquerade." Melville does not need to tell us that something will follow *after* the Masquerade, for it is obvious that the Masquerade, which is simply our social experience, will itself continue. But if we are more willing than the barber to play with suppositions, something more than Melville has directly stated may follow *from* the Masquerade. (18)

Similarly, Brown brings together the various fragmented fabrications that constitute the social masquerade created by an uneasy reliance on and obfuscated devotion to the national system of slavery and racial domination. Brown knew well that one could not escape the masquerade; one could only learn to operate within it. Lindberg argues that "[t]o get at what follows from Melville's novel, we need to ask ourselves under what conditions this extensive masquerade could develop in the first place" (18); and, similarly, Brown looks to the underlying conditions of the social masquerade, locating its source in the fabricated identity of each reader. What does it mean, then, to withdraw one's support from the institution of slavery? It means that one must learn to look not only at one's world but also at oneself differently. *Clotel* offers the methods by which one can begin to do so. Still, as George Green argues, "success makes all the difference," and it is difficult to claim that Brown was successful, given the history not only of the United States but also of critical responses to this text. But *Clotel* waits beyond ethereal critical categories and narratives—waits in closer fields for those looking to construct more intimate and revealing histories, working this time from the ground up.

# 2

# God's Economy and Frado's Story
## Harriet E. Wilson's *Our Nig*

What is most immediately striking about Harriet E. Wilson's *Our Nig; or, Sketches from the Life of a Free Black* (1859) is that, quite simply, over one hundred years after the first edition appeared and disappeared, the book can be bought and read again.[1] The rediscovery of this book reminds us of the many books still unrediscovered: the many books long out of print and ignored, and the many more (no doubt) whose very existence remains unknown. But what is yet more striking about the publication of this delayed reprint is that, when we purchase this book, we fulfill, belatedly, the terms of its existence. For inextricably bound to Wilson's commentary on matters of gender, class, and race in the nineteenth-century northern states is her insistence on the book's status as a product for consumption in the marketplace. As Allida testifies in the Appendix, Wilson, having met with some success in selling a formula "for restoring gray hair to its former color," was forced by failing health to "resort to another method of procuring her bread—that of writing an Autobiography" (137).[2] Wilson herself, in the Preface, calls the book an "experiment which shall aid me in maintaining myself and child without extinguishing this feeble life" (3).[3]

This appeal for patronage was, of course, characteristic of many African-American publications in the nineteenth century, though Wilson's still stands out as something of an anomaly. In his study of pre-1860 African-American autobiographies, William L. Andrews notes that "more than a few slave autobiographies were published as fund-raisers for their narrators, and most were labeled so" (*To Tell a Free Story* 108). But Andrews notes as well that "in a society as hostile to blacks as the North was in the 1840s [and, of course, beyond], an ex-slave [or, I would add, a northern "free" black] who hoped for a good sale of his narrative was not likely to embarrass his white sponsors or contradict his audience's expectations" by presenting his or her subject "in an unsanctioned manner" (108–9). As Henry Louis Gates, Jr., has speculated, *Our Nig* might well have been ignored because it does in fact present an aggressively unsanctioned story that not only focuses on northern racism but is also critical of abolitionists themselves (*Figures* 137).[4]

Over 130 years after its initial appearance, one might say that the central critical question regarding *Our Nig* is not whether we should purchase it—both literally and figuratively—for we cannot help but celebrate the discovery of such an anomalous and unique literary treasure. Rather, the central critical question is what to do with our purchase, and how to understand the cultural value of this act of delayed exchange.[5] As it is impossible to provide the kind of patronage Wilson calls for, and as it is unjust to treat this sophisticated narrative merely as a historical document, inevitably we are moved to claim this text as a significant event in the developing narrative of African-American literary history, an African-American version of what Donald E. Pease, reconsidering the so-called American Renaissance, has called "global renaissance time—the sacred time a nation claims to renew when it claims its cultural place as a great nation existing within a world of great nations" (vii). It is not surprising, after all, that Gates would want to argue that this book marks a significant beginning of an African-American literary mode, a distinctive first in a century of firsts, the hidden root of an increasingly visible tradition.[6] By the logic of sacred literary history, what is significant is not only what Wilson does in this book but also that no one else had yet done it.[7] I would like to suggest that such critical approaches distort the relationship between book and reader and keep us from understanding the nature of Wilson's achievement. Ultimately, Gates's claims for *Our Nig* are simply the flip side of Lawrence Buell's evaluation of the book as "subliterary" (301): in sacred literary history, the goddesses and gods answer in accordance with the questions we ask of them. I wish to re-place this novel where Wilson places it: within the racial, gender, and economic matrix of secular history, as distinct from "sacred" literary history.

*Our Nig*, a blend of autobiography and fiction, tells the story of Frado, the child of a mixed-race marriage. The narrative begins with the story of Mag Smith, Frado's white mother, the victim of an upper-class seducer. As the story of her seduction spreads, Mag becomes increasingly desperate, and eventually crosses racial lines to marry "a kind-hearted African," Jim. When Jim dies, Mag lives with another black man, Seth Shipley; and when Mag and Seth can no longer care for Mag's children, they abandon Frado at the home of a white New Hampshire family, the Bellmonts, who take her in and claim her as "Our Nig," a domestic servant. Abused, primarily by Mrs. Bellmont and daughter Mary, befriended mainly by her dog Fido, Frado leaves the family at the end of her term of service.[8] In the narrative's closing chapter, readers learn that Frado's problems are augmented by her troubled marriage to a black sailor who claims to be a fugitive slave and who eventually dies of yellow fever in New Orleans. Looking to support the child of that marriage after a series of problems with both health and employment, Frado draws from the limited education she received during her term with the Bellmonts—an education continued under the tutelage of "a plain, poor, simple woman, who could see merit beneath a dark skin" (124). In the final chapter, as Gates notes, *Our Nig*'s third person narrator shifts to the first person as "the protagonist, the author, and the novel's narrator all merge explicitly into one voice to launch the text's advertisement for itself" (Introduction xlvii).

Depicting the life of a so-called "free black," showing that "slavery's shadows fall" even in the North, and including in her cultural testimony the experiences not only of the black laboring class but also of the white laboring class and lower middle class, Wilson conflates into a single ethical study racial, gender, and economic enslavement. In this light, the book's own status as product for sale takes on a heightened significance, for Wilson counters the culturally familiar proslavery critique of the evils of capitalism with an appeal for salvation by way of the marketplace. Indeed, Wilson reminds her readers that judgment on Frado's life is solely the province of God, and she frames her appeal for patronage as a "demand" for "sympathy and aid," by which acts black and white readers alike can both endorse and enact a system capable of translating what Martin R. Delany would later call "God's Economy" into human transactions. In other words, Wilson's self-advertisements are directed not merely towards her own elevation from poverty but also towards a program of mutual elevation based on a reconfigured marketplace, one that has been deconstructed and reenvisioned in the process of the narrative. In envisioning this reconfigured marketplace, however, Wilson does not gesture towards a possible harmony and trust between blacks and whites in the United States. Rather, she envisions a system that recognizes and *capitalizes* on racial tensions and mutual distrust, a new system of exchange and balanced conflict—a new economy of identity—that readers support by purchasing the book and in which they participate by reading it.[9]

### *"Silent Sympathy" and Cultural Understanding*

To speak of this project raises questions about Wilson's intended audience, and our answers to this, as to so many other questions about Wilson's life and work, can be only speculative. Although Wilson begins by appealing to her "colored brethren," this subject is more complicated than it might seem. Eric Gardner's recent research into the publishing history of *Our Nig* is valuable here, though his discoveries concerning Wilson's actual audience only emphasize the problem of determining her intended audience. Gardner argues that "ownership patterns . . . sustain the theory that Wilson was responsible for distributing the book herself—and that the distribution was limited to personal acquaintance with the author or her friends and agents" (240). Gardner notes as well that Wilson apparently was not able to market her book in Boston, where she would have found a large black community—though this, of course, does not mean that she did not want that community to purchase and read her book, for her son's death may have taken her back to Milford before she could fairly market the book in Boston. Many of the actual purchasers of the book, Gardner suggests, "either interpreted or deployed *Our Nig* as a book geared toward the moral improvement of young readers" (228). In her painstaking reconstruction of Wilson's biography, Barbara A. White identifies the "predicament" Wilson faced as she prepared to publish her narrative: "although it was necessary to receive the support of at least some 'good antislavery friends' to sell her narrative, she could not distribute it very widely without alerting" those "good antislavery friends" who had been the causes of many of her misfortunes. Ultimately, Wilson must have known that her story "could be received only by a small group, her 'colored brethren'" (White 40, 45). Similarly, Hazel Carby asserts that

"Wilson sought her patronage not from a white Northern audience but from her 'colored brethren.' Wilson attempted to gain authority for her public voice through a narrative that shared its experience with a black community which she addressed as if it were autonomous from the white community in which it was situated" (*Reconstructing* 43).[10]

Certainly, I agree that Wilson's "direct appeal to the black community marginalized a white readership" (Carby 44), but I think that her experience had taught her well that the black community was segregated but not autonomous from the white community, and that her task was to transform the dominant/subordinate relation to one of mutual dependence. The title of the work itself signals Wilson's awareness of her white audience, for her "colored brethren" would need no reminders that "Slavery's Shadows Fall" even in the North. Moreover, any "marginalization of a white readership" in the Preface is at least complicated by Wilson's handling of the first chapter, "Mag Smith, My Mother" (5). Presenting Frado's story as the sequel of a tale of love and seduction, and postponing the culturally significant identification of Mag Smith as a white woman, Wilson undermines any assumption that the relationship between narrator and reader can be defined according to the conventions of racial affiliation. Claudia Tate rightly distinguishes between Wilson's intended readers and "those readers who live outside the historical exigencies of Wilson's epoch, namely ourselves" (32). Focusing on Wilson's attempt to "re-create herself in a novelized form" (38), Tate implies that Wilson's first audience was both herself and the world which had constructed a restrictive selfhood for her. Both in the Preface and throughout the narrative, Wilson signals her awareness that this text might not be read only by her "colored brethren," and might in fact be both read and misread by those anxious to defend slavery (by comparing the relative condition of southern slaves and northern blacks), and anxious as well to dismiss African Americans by defining them as slaves, in effect, to their own "inferior" racial features.[11]

Wilson's concern, I believe, is not to reach an identifiable and coherent community of "colored brethren," but rather to contribute towards the creation of a reconfigured community of understanding. One can say of Wilson what Andrews has said of Henry Bibb, that he "dismisses the fictive reader as unreasonable and implicitly calls for a reader who can interpret his actions according to the standards that emerge dramatically and pragmatically in the narrative itself" (*To Tell a Free Story* 30). As

Andrews argues, "the act of reading autobiographies like Bibb's involves the reader in a decision about his own identity and his own position vis-à-vis the black and white categories of any socio-moral system of thought" (30). Similarly, Wilson appeals to an understanding "colored" by one's reading of *Our Nig*. That is, she appeals to an understanding generated by one's confrontation of the complex relations that have been reduced to the simple dichotomy of white and black, a simplification that can stand only with the support of an ever-increasingly contrived and corrupt ideological system. The legal and social codification of cultural simplifications is always complex, and *Our Nig*—a narrative that begins with an appeal to colored brethren and then begins again with a story of a white woman—draws its readers towards a recognition of that complexity.

Wilson begins by tracing Frado's identity to her white mother's experiences, establishing Frado as the most deliberately determined product of northern U.S. culture. That is, in her telling of Mag Smith's story, Wilson identifies the conceptual structures of cultural identity, structures that will later confine Frado even more tightly than they did her mother. As Mag successively crosses what one might call the concentric borders of cultural infamy, accumulating increasingly inflexible and restrictive cultural labels along the way, the system of values that distinguishes between acceptable and notorious identity, between cultural insiders and outsiders, becomes clear. Mag begins as a woman with a "loving, trusting heart" who has the democratic simplicity to believe that she can "ascend" to the social level of her duplicitous seducer and "become an equal" (5–6). The result, of course, is a reputation that follows her wherever she goes, leaving her with a "home . . . contaminated by the publicity of her fall" and "a feeling of degradation," yet still also with the hope that "circumspect" behavior might yet enable her to "regain in a measure what she had lost" (7). Finding the boundaries of morality carefully guarded, she is forced to remain in her assigned sphere of infamy; aggravated still further by the immigrant labor that altered so significantly the status of women in the workplace in the Jacksonian era, Mag is soon left "hugging her wrongs, but making no effort to escape" (8).[12] What follows is what the narrator calls "the climax of repulsion," Mag's interracial marriage to Jim, by which, the narrator notes, Mag "sunder[s] another bond which held her to her fellows," and "descend[s] another step down the ladder of infamy" (13). Her final step, into "the darkness of perpetual infamy," is the result of having "lived an outcast for years": her extramarital relationship with a second black man after Jim dies.

Had Mag set out deliberately to transgress the implicit boundaries of the dominant culture's standards, she could not have done a better job. The point here, though, is that her acts are not deliberate, and that in witnessing the consequences of seduction (for which the seducer himself receives only the admiration of his fellows), we witness the process by which collective cultural identity is maintained at the expense of individual moral character. After all, Mag's repentance does not prove to be the key that will reopen the cultural doors; she has been identified—and, clearly, she must remain—a cultural outsider, an example of moral transgression. Those doors closed to her, Mag marries and thereby comes to embody yet another cultural transgression, unacceptable intercourse between black and white. The product of these successive acts of transgression is the daughter Mag cannot support: Frado, the "titled" character of the narrative. Thus defined before birth, Frado's identity as cultural product is finalized when she becomes "Our Nig."

In identifying Frado as a cultural product, I refer to Clifford Geertz's conception of culture as "not so much the empirical commonalities in [human] behavior, from place to place and time to time, but rather the mechanisms by whose agency the breadth and indeterminateness of [one's] inherent capacities are reduced to the narrowness and specificity of [one's] actual accomplishments" (45). Wilson would amend this conception of the process of individuation by viewing it in specifically moral terms, and would thereby judge it. As Anna Julia Cooper would later put it in *A Voice From the South by a Black Woman of the South* (1892), "Our money, our schools, our governments, our free institutions, our systems of religion and forms of creeds are all first and last to be judged by this standard: what sort of men and women do they grow? How are men and women being shaped and molded by this system of training, under this or that form of government, by this or that standard of moral action?" (283). Arguing that the "value" of the individual is the value to which "all other values are merely relative," Cooper argues that the United States, "divinely ordered as we dream it to be," ultimately will be divinely judged by its ability, in relation to other forms of government, to "give us a sounder, healthier, more reliable product from this great factory of *men*" (282–83). Beginning the narrative with the story of Frado's birth and her eventual (and seemingly inevitable) creation as "Our Nig," Wilson takes her readers on a tour of the U.S. *factory*, and then centers the action, and the grounds for judgment, on this remarkable *product*.

It is Wilson's attention to the common cultural factory that complicates attempts to imagine that she wrote specifically for a community of black readers. For this particular cultural factory, it is clear, is incapable of producing stable, uniform grounds for trust. Instead, prevailing prejudices create the *appearance* of commonality by setting blacks apart and grouping them together as ideologically marked sites for political action in the form of charity. By such logic, all blacks are either physical or ideological fugitives in need of white protection, and all fugitives look alike. The resulting dangers for the artificially delineated black community become clear in Wilson's ultimate chapter, "The Winding Up of the Matter." Again, Wilson enters into delicate cultural territory, for she begins by alluding to "*professed* fugitives from slavery, who recounted their personal experience in homely phrase, and awakened the indignation of non-slaveholders against brother Pro" (126, my emphasis). Such false professions were an issue in both the North and the South. In newspapers and books, antiabolitionists warned potential fugitives that self-proclaimed representatives of the Underground Railroad could not be trusted; similarly, northern abolitionists and members of antislavery societies warned against free blacks who pretended to be fugitives to procure money and clothing from Underground Railroad sympathizers. The presence of false fugitives was simply a fact of antebellum life, as is suggested by the casualness of Frederick Douglass's claim, in discussing the character of the enslaved, that "[s]o uniformly are good manners enforced among slaves, that I can easily detect a 'bogus' fugitive by his manners" (*My Bondage* 164).[13] Wilson presents her protagonist as a victim of this kind of impostor; more importantly, though, she presents the cultural mechanism of this victimization: "Such a one appeared in the new home of Frado; and as people of color were rare there, was it strange she should attract her dark brother; that he should inquire her out; succeed in seeing her; feel a strange sensation in his heart towards her; that he should toy with her shining curls, feel proud to provoke her to smile and expose the ivory concealed by thin, ruby lips; that her sparkling eyes should fascinate; that he should propose; that they should marry?" (126). Wilson tells here a familiar story of courtship, love, and marriage. Doing so in a single sentence, she joins the sentimental associations readers would bring to it with the cultural divisions that make this particular love story seem like a series of nearly inevitable steps, one foregone conclusion leading to the next.

This conflation of the sentimental destinies of love and the limited destinies of cultural identity undermines the romance of it all, revealing the potential danger of innocent, unworldly love: its ability to shape one's understanding towards a naive belief in what eventually prove to be deceptive appearances. We have heard this story before, at the beginning of *Our Nig*: Frado's story echoes that of her mother Mag. But whereas Mag's love led her to the naive hope of transcending the divisions of class, Frado's *extends from* what proves to be an equally naive belief in the inherent community of race.[14] It is this belief—the product of "her own oppression"—that enables her to view his silence about his enslavement, when they are alone, as evidence that they are joined by a shared experience which is "painful to disturb oftener than was needful" (127). "There was a silent sympathy," the narrator emphasizes, "which Frado felt attracted her, and she opened her heart to the presence of love—that arbitrary and inexorable tyrant" (127). In the end, of course, the tyrant shows his face, as Frado's husband "[leaves] her to her fate . . . with the disclosure that he had never seen the South, and that his illiterate harangues were humbugs for hungry abolitionists" (127). Frado is the victim not merely of an oppressive culture, but also of her own prior experience as a victim. The oppressive culture she has come to know, and against which she has begun to develop strategic modes of defense, reveals yet another level of power. The sense of a community of silent sympathy among the oppressed becomes yet another dimension of the force of oppression, yet another layer of cultural identity as defined by others.

Unable to control the terms of her own cultural identity, and unable to trust others similarly defined, Wilson speaks both to and against those— black or white, male or female—willing to see her as a cultural type, a familiar product. That is, as has been noted by almost all critics of this narrative, Wilson signifies on her own culturally determined identity in her use of "Our Nig" as the title of both the book and its author. I think, though, that critics are sometimes led by their retrospective readings of an African-American literary tradition to a narrow understanding of the nature and terms of this act of signifying. Gates, for example, argues cogently that *Our Nig* "manifests . . . the transformation of the black-as-object into the black-as-subject" (Introduction lv), and certainly he is right. But as Wilson makes painfully clear, this particular "black-as-subject" still must face a culture eminently capable of retransforming her into "woman-as-object" and, into yet another concentric circle of identification, "worker-as-object." In other words, it is important to remember that Frado begins not only as a product of racist formulations, but also as a product of ethical, gender, and economic formulations. As this book demonstrates from the first page onward, troping one's way into black subjecthood affects only the color of the corner one has been backed into; one is still faced with the adjoining walls of social and economic objectification that limit the power and range of one's voice. To escape this corner and save her son, Wilson would need to transform her economic as well as her racial identities.

### "Slavery's Shadows" and the Politics of Labor

Wilson knew well the risks her project entailed, the risks not only of telling a story unsanctioned by northern abolitionists but also one sanctionable by northern and southern racists. Specifically, she ran the risk of undermining what Houston A. Baker, Jr., has called "the New England ideal so frequently appearing in Afro-American narratives," that of "free, dignified, and individualistic labor" (*Blues* 49). One thinks, for example, about one of the many proslavery responses to *Uncle Tom's Cabin*, W. L. G. Smith's *Life at the South: or "Uncle Tom's Cabin" As It Is; Being Narratives, Scenes, and Incidents in the Real "Life of the Lowly"* (1852), published in the North. Smith tells the story of a slave who escapes to the North only to experience unbearable hardships, and who, by the end of the novel, willingly returns to the plantation, having now recognized the value of the system and his "natural" place in it. This is but a strikingly direct representative of the many attempts to counter Stowe's portrayal of slavery by justifying a paternal system, one designed to prepare those of African origins for their destiny in "God's own good time" (vi). Indeed, in the mid-nineteenth century, southern attacks on northern capitalism often were grafted onto justifications of slavery, transforming the (northern) capitalist laborer into worker-as-object and the (southern) black slave into worker-as-subject, a formulation designed to transform a reified southern economic system into a national (and even universal) model.[15] Such arguments, like many nineteenth-century arguments dealing with slavery and labor, were complicated by the advocates' willingness to draw freely from a number of ideological and discursive systems—religion, science, politics, sociology, and economics—to dress up fundamental assumptions in new clothing. As Augustine St. Clare puts it in *Uncle Tom's Cabin*, "Planters, who have money to make by it,—clergymen, who have planters to please,—politicians, who want to rule by it,—may warp and bend language and ethics to a degree that shall astonish the world at their ingenuity; they can press nature and the Bible, and nobody knows what else, into the service" (261). The historian Laurence Shore has called this veiling of fundamental assumptions "the process by which 'elastic' men shaped and reshaped Southern ideology" (194).

The pervasive influence of these elastic proslavery/anticapitalist arguments is indicated by the number of antislavery authors who felt the need to respond to such arguments. When Miss Ophelia encounters such arguments in *Uncle Tom's Cabin*, she protests, "The English laborer is not sold, traded, parted from his family, whipped"—only to be assured by Augustine St. Clare that the two positions amount to roughly the same thing, a common condition that will eventually lead to a "mustering among the masses" and a millennial uprising (269–72), though not as quickly as that arranged by the protagonist in *Blake*, which I discuss in chapter 4. Understandably impatient for this eventual millennial uprising, William Wells Brown complains in *Clotel*, "Some American writers have tried to make the world believe that the condition of the labouring classes of England is as bad as the slaves of the United States." But Brown brings Clotel's situation to a point here to emphasize that "The English labourer may be oppressed, he may be cheated, defrauded, swindled, and even starved; but it is not slavery under which he groans. He cannot be sold; in point of law he is equal to the prime minister" (151).[16] Similarly, Harriet Jacobs looks at "the poorest poor" of Europe and finds "that the condition of even the meanest and most ignorant among them was vastly superior to the condition of the most favored slaves in America"; for although "Their homes were very humble, . . . they were protected by law" (184). And addressing the new twist in the familiar problem, Mr. Thomas, in Frances Harper's *Trial and Triumph*, speaks of the "unanimity of interest" between "the white people and the colored people of this country," and warns the white merchant Mr. Hastings, "You may protect yourself from what you call the pauper of Europe, but you will not be equally able to defend yourself from the depressed laborer of the new South, and as an American citizen, I dread any turn of the screw which will lower the rate of wages here" (222). Perhaps Harper here suggests the approach of the struggle Stowe envisioned; certainly, she points to one result of the long-sustained comparison between European laborer and American slave—a comparison which, of course, justified little change in policy or attitude on either side of the Atlantic.

Undaunted by visions of the coming struggle or by those who would emphasize the frail, saving grace of law enjoyed by European laborers, proslavery commentators seized upon the writings of such social theorists as Auguste Comte and Thomas Carlyle to present the slave system as not only effective but also entirely just and humane.[17] Two of the first American authors to use Auguste Comte's term "sociology" were proslavery advocates: George Fitzhugh, in *Sociology for the South, or the Failure of Free Society*, and Henry Hughes, in *A Treatise on Sociology, Theoretical and Practical*, both published in 1854. In *A Treatise on Sociology*, Hughes argued for what he called "warranteeism"—that is, a system that "warrant[s] the existence and progress of all." Hughes based the concept of warranteeism on his assertion that for the "healthy existence of all" in a given society, "three warranted or ordered systems are necessary": "the Political, the Economic, and the Hygienic." Slavery, by this logic, becomes simply "WARRANTEEISM WITH THE ETHNICAL QUALIFICATION." Another name for warranteeism, one learns, is "liberty labor," enabling Hughes to present, as a call for universal adoption of a system of government modeled after the American southern slave system, the slogan "LIBERTY-LABOR MUST BE THE SUBSTITUTE OF FREE-LABOR." The difference, Hughes argued, between warranteeism and "the Free-labor form of societary organization" is that in warranteeism "necessary association, adaptation and regulation are . . . not accidental: they are essential," and in the Free-labor system these necessities of social order "are not essential; they are accidental" (52, 55, 53).[18] Slavery thus may be seen as both the manifestation and the guarantor of social order, health, and justice.

Arguably the most forceful proponent of this argument was Fitzhugh, who draws from Carlyle insistently and often in his second book *Cannibals All! or, Slaves without Masters*, published in 1857, just two years before Wilson published *Our Nig*. Fitzhugh, with characteristically aggressive confidence, asserts in the latter work, "we not only boast that the White Slave Trade is more exacting and fraudulent (in fact, though not in intention) than Black Slavery; but we also boast that it is more cruel, in leaving the laborer to take care of himself and family out of the pittance which skill or capital have allowed him to retain" (15). Arguing that the precepts of Christianity and those of capitalism are mutually exclusive, Fitzhugh concludes that "it is impossible to place labor and capital in harmonious or friendly relations, except by the means of slavery, which identifies their interests" (31).

Fitzhugh is most effective in suggesting that southern slavery was too narrow a focus for debates on the ethics of economic systems; he situates such debates in the broader field of labor, bringing in European socialists for support. In fact, *Cannibals All!* quotes extensively from American and European socialist and anticapitalist tracts, some arguing for slavery as the solution to the oppression of the poor, regardless of race. For example, one self-professed English "Philanthropist" whose published essay Fitzhugh reprints in its entirety argues that "*slavery and content, and liberty and discontent, are natural results of each other.* Applying this, then, to the toil-worn, half-fed, pauperized population of England, I found that the only way to permanently and efficiently remedy the complicated evils, would be to ENSLAVE *the whole of the people of England who have not property*" (155). Similarly, the southern scientific agriculturist Edmund Ruffin seized upon socialist thought in 1853, arguing in "The Political Economy of Slavery" that "in their main doctrines, the socialists are right," and that the slavery system is the most effective means of securing the benefits of "the *association of labor*" (83, 82).

The consideration of slavery as a mode of organized labor provided not only convenient proslavery defenses against abolitionists but also powerful rhetorical tools for the organization of labor within a developing capitalist economy. David R. Roediger has demonstrated that the continuation of slavery in the United States shaped the development of an antebellum labor movement that was not only "exceptional in its rhetoric" but also "exceptionally militant as it critiqued evolving capitalist social relations as a kind of slavery" (66). As Roediger argues, "the comparison [between the white hireling and the black slave] could lead to sweeping critiques of wage labor as 'white slavery' but it also could reassure wage workers that they belonged to the ranks of 'free white labor'" (47). By way of the powerfully vague and inclusive phrase *white slavery*, "Abolitionists, free Blacks, bankers, factory owners and prison labor could, in sundry combinations, be cast as villains in a loose plot to enslave white workers" (73). Moreover, the emphasis on "whiteness" provided visible social contrasts, signaling the "possibility of social mobility" for the "white hireling" and highlighting (with clear, racialist logic) both the need for and progress towards improved labor conditions for white workers. In short, Roediger argues, "the growing popular sense of whiteness represented a hesitantly emerging consensus holding together a very diverse white working class" by enabling white antebellum workers to "displace anxieties within the white population onto Blacks" (97, 100).[19] As Frederick Douglass put it in 1855, "The impression is cunningly made, that slavery is the only power that can prevent the laboring white man from falling to the level of the slave's poverty and degradation" (*My Bondage* 330).[20]

Wilson could not assume that her story would tell its own moral, for many were waiting for stories like this with their own morals close at hand. The force of the tale would necessarily lie not in its events but in its telling, not in her overdetermined story but in the reconfiguring power of discourse. I am suggesting that Wilson's approach to the highly charged cultural politics that defined her position and restricted her options aligns with Foucault's conception of revolution as the reconfiguration of existing power relations. Striking reconfigurations had already taken place; according to Roediger, examination of "the labor and radical Democratic press of the 1840s shows that *white slavery* was the most common phrasing of metaphors regarding white workers' oppression with *slavery of wages* second and *wage slavery* a very distant third" (72). But while this common term that depended on racialized thinking could be used to codify racial divisions within the laboring class, it could be used also to name racially identified conditions that did not depend upon the race of those identified: "the term *white slavery*," Roediger notes, "was at times used even in articles speculating about the fate of free *Blacks* if abolition prevailed!" (72).[21]

The portrait of obstructed opportunities and possible responses that one encounters in *Our Nig* is a portrait in which racial attitudes cannot be separated from an intricate economic and social system. This is the vision of the U.S. economic system very frankly addressed by David Christy, the Ohio writer whose *Cotton is King* was widely used to redefine the nature of the argument between North and South. Addressing "the economical connections of slavery, with the other material interests of the world," Christy asserts the existence of a "*quadruple alliance*" supporting the system of slavery: "The Western Agriculturists; the Southern Planters; the English Manufacturers; and the American Abolitionists." Like England itself, Christy argues, American Abolitionists "[advocate] *Free Trade*, as essential to her manufacturers and commerce . . . not waiting to inquire into its bearings upon *American Slavery*" (266). And although Christy provided the South with its most prominent argument for (national) self-justification, he was not the only white Northerner reminding the nation that the economics of slavery ruled the North. Theodore Parker similarly reminded the country that "While the great mass of the people at the North, engrossed in direct productive industry, are really hostile to slavery, those absorbed in the large operations of commerce, taken as a whole class, feel little interest in the Idea of Freedom; nay, they are positively opposed to it." Noting that this class was once directly involved in the "African Slave-trade," Parker argues that "In all the great commercial cities" of the North "these men prevail, and are the 'eminent citizens,' overslaughing the press, the pulpit, the bar, and the court, with the Ideas of their lower law, and sweeping along all metropolitan and suburban fashion and respectability in their slimy flood" (Parker 14). As Frederick Douglass put it in discussing specifically southern white laborers in 1855, "The difference between the white slave, and the black slave, is this: the latter belongs to *one* slaveholder, and the former belongs to *all* the slaveholders, collectively" (*My Bondage* 330). Both the narrator and protagonist of *Our Nig* are also subjected to all slaveholders by way of an implicit national and international alliance; and Wilson's task, accordingly, is to remove from raw power the veil of authority provided by the mutually constituting systems of moral and civil law she means to endorse.

Wilson signals her awareness of the flexible logic of proslavery activists from the first page onward. Noting in her Preface her decision to omit "what would most provoke shame in our good anti-slavery friends at home," she carefully identifies Mrs. Bellmont with "*southern* principles," and asserts, "I would not . . . palliate slavery at the South, by disclosures of its appurtenances North" (3). Throughout *Our Nig*, which begins with a white woman displaced on the job market by "foreigners who cheapened toil and clamored for a livelihood" (8), Wilson approaches with particular deliberation and force the economic condition of African Americans, conflating the situations of the working class and the culturally enslaved— bringing together "white slavery" and the condition of the free black living under "Slavery's Shadows." Wilson's task was to transform herself from an object of charity to a laboring subject in an economy seemingly designed to exclude or deligitimize (or both) her labor. Increasingly, her only material for this transformation—the only material upon which she could perform as laborer—was the life that the culture itself had produced, and the only product she could offer was the narrative of that life.[22]

## Human Transactions and "God's Economy"

What one encounters in *Our Nig*, then, is similar to what Baker finds in Douglass's 1845 *Narrative*: "The tones of a Providentially oriented moral suasion eventually compete with the cadences of a secularly oriented economic voice" (*Blues* 43). Like Douglass, Wilson works to combine "literacy, Christianity, and revolutionary zeal in an individual and economically profitable job of work" (49). However, Wilson's experience had not offered her the kind of hope that Douglass's revolutionary self-creation *seemingly* had provided him in 1845, nor was Wilson writing under the auspices of an antislavery organization that would make it advisable to *represent* hope in the northern states. Rather, Wilson grounds her own hopes for an "economically profitable job of work" in a vision of what amounts to an eschatological interpretation of the existing economic system, a consideration of the market economy as the vehicle God has provided for the regulation and progression of human affairs. In 1879, Wilson's contemporary Martin R. Delany would speak of race as "a means in the providence of God's economy, to the accomplishment of his ends in the progress of civilization" (26).

The cultural politics that complicated notions of this providential progress are evident in the anonymous pamphlet entitled *Miscegenation*, a word this pamphlet introduced into the language. As George M. Fredrickson has noted, this pamphlet was "an ingenious hoax" created by "two Democratic journalists, David Goodman Croly and George Wakeman of the New York *World* . . . designed to discredit the Republican Party in the election of 1864." The pamphlet "was written from what purported to be the point of view of a Radical Republican or abolitionist," and "argued that mixed races were superior to pure ones and that racial amalgamation was the inevitable and desirable result of Republican doctrines" (Fredrickson 172). In this pamphlet, the authors present a vision of Providence that played into the fear at the racialist heart of white American culture. "Let the friends of humanity, then," the pamphlet announces, "understand that it is not by forwarding religious and educational institutions alone that they can bring about the Millennium. Churches and universities fill, of course, their appropriate spheres in ministering to the intellectual and moral wants of the race, but there are other, and apparently grosser agencies which will prove more effectual in ushering in the millennial man and woman" (Croly 33–34). The pamphlet calls for a new motto for "the great progressive party of this country": "Freedom, Political and Social Equality; Universal Brotherhood" (Croly 62–63). This vision of rights and common interests wedded to racist fears and racialist science offers a sampling of the world to which Wilson, writing a few years earlier about the product of a mixed union, had to respond, and the limitations she faced in looking for moral solutions to cultural problems.

The problem was to see the culture from a challenging perspective—and it was a problem because, as *Miscegenation* reveals, any perspective grounded in the culture inevitably served as a mirror for culture; appeals to the culture's official belief systems were quickly appropriated by the culture's unofficial convictions. Her recognition of this problem led Anna Julia Cooper to formulate in 1892 an understanding of a providentially ordered economy, an understanding that relied not on ideal visions of a world beyond or a millennial world ahead but rather on careful examinations of the world around. "You need not formulate and establish the credibility and authenticity of Christian Evidences," Cooper argues, "when you can demonstrate and prove the present value of CHRISTIAN MEN" (284). To judge a culture by its "productions," Cooper suggests, is to evaluate the extent of its adherence to moral law: "And this test for systems of belief, for schools of thought, and for theories of conduct, is also the ultimate and inevitable test of nations, of races and of individuals. What sort of men do you turn out? *How* are you supplying the great demands of the world's market?" (284). In 1859, Wilson looked with measured hope to the possibility of producing something that would enable her to enjoy the profits of God's economy.[23]

In this vision of economy, both wealth and poverty are moral terms, measured not by one's economic status but rather by one's character. Poverty, Gates has argued, is "the great evil in this book," "both the desperation it inflicts as well as the evils it implicitly sanctions" (Introduction xlvi); but I would suggest instead that "the great evil in this book" is not poverty itself but rather the will to dominate, which feeds upon cultural and personal vulnerability in whatever form it takes. After all, the one character in the narrative who views poverty as a disgrace and a dishonor is not Frado but one of the narrative's most visible villains, Mrs. Bellmont. It is Mrs. Bellmont who is unable to see that the chosen wife of her son (and Frado's favorite) is, as Jack Bellmont puts it to his mother, " '*worth a million* dollars . . . though not a cent of it is in money' " (112). It is Mrs. Bellmont also who insists that her daughter Jane marry Henry Reed, for Mrs. Bellmont has "counted the acres which were to be transmitted to an only son," and "she knew there was silver in the purse" (56). In each case, Mrs. Bellmont demonstrates, though in circumspect form, the same will to dominate that inspires her verbal and physical abuse of Frado. In each case, Mrs. Bellmont willfully distorts perceptions in her effort to either control or destroy those who threaten her ambitions. As the narrator phrases it in regard to Mrs. Bellmont's efforts to disgrace Jack's wife, once Jack is away and Jenny is "more in her own power," Mrs. Bellmont "wished to make [Jenny] feel her inferiority," and watched for acts "which might be construed into conjugal unfaithfulness" (113). In this instance, as in her response to Frado's attempts to understand and experience Christianity, Mrs. Bellmont demonstrates that literally nothing is sacred in the struggle for power, as the discourse of morality itself becomes a tool of domination.

Here and throughout *Our Nig*, Mrs. Bellmont draws readers' attention to the corruption of cultural discourse, its deliberate misuse, but that which the discourse is taken to signify remains unscathed. The narrator's clear disapproval of Mrs. Bellmont's motives for interfering with these relationships does not suggest disapproval of wealth itself. Jack's brother James does in fact marry a wealthy woman, a marriage the narrator clearly celebrates, but the telling difference is that James "did not marry her wealth"; rather, "he loved *her*, sincerely" (55). Similarly, when her father insists that she not be "compelled to violate her free choice in so important a transaction" (60), Jane's choice of George Means over Henry Reed is a choice of love over the eager accumulation of wealth for its own sake. Although Mrs. Bellmont tries to make George Means's name signify that he is, in fact, *mean*, Wilson shows that proper motivations inform the power of the cultural system, for this couple finds *means* enough not only to survive but also to maintain their "early love" beyond the end of the narrative.[24] The lesson is emphasized later in the narrative, in what seems like a pun on the other suitor's name, when the narrator notes that Mr. Bellmont "bowed like a 'bruised reed,' under the loss of his beloved son" (102). No longer the "reed" he once was, Mr. Bellmont begins to worry about his past actions—about the relationship between his professions and his practices, and about the preparation of his soul for "the celestial city" (102).

Mr. Bellmont's own subsequent attempt to reinvest discourse with meaning leads directly to the most striking turning point of the narrative, Frado's first direct act of resistance against Mrs. Bellmont's violence. Fearing for his own soul, Mr. Bellmont allows Frado to return to religious meetings; Mrs. Bellmont, afraid that word will get out about her beating Frado, tells Frado to "stop trying to be religious," threatening to "whip her to death" (104). Mr. Bellmont then acknowledges to Frado that "he had seen her many times punished undeservedly" (104), advising her "to avoid it if she could . . . when she was *sure* she did not deserve whipping" (104). "It was not long," the narrator notes pointedly, "before an opportunity offered of profiting by his advice" (105). In this confrontation, Frado, "the only moving power in the house" (62), recognizes the power of her position as laborer in an antagonistic relationship with her "employer"; essentially, she threatens to go on strike: " 'Stop!' shouted Frado, 'strike me, and I'll never work a mite more for you;' and throwing down what she had gathered, stood like one who feels the stirring of free and independent thoughts" (105). This is not only Frado's most direct and empowering act of resistance, it is also her most successful, for "[t]his affair never met with an 'after clap,' like many others" (105). The lesson is that, rightly perceived, the system works: moral self-government supports the principles of American political ideals. Those principles of liberty and independence so deeply ingrained in nineteenth-century national mythology but so often corrupted by practice are renewed, reenacted, in a natural chain of events that begins with Mr. Bellmont's attempt to align his professions and his practice.

` Indeed, all of Frado's economic opportunities are associated with a providential guidance over the marketplace. When she hears that "in some towns in Massachusetts, girls make straw bonnets," and that it is "easy and profitable," she is still left to wonder how "*she*, black, feeble and poor," could "find any one to teach her" (124). The answer is that "God prepares the way, when human agencies see no path" (124). The "way," in this case, is a woman who, guided by faith, is capable of seeing "merit beneath a dark skin," and who not only instructs Frado in the art of the needle but also "teach[es] her the value of useful books" (124). This lesson leads to a project of "self-improvement," as Frado comes to feel "that this book information supplied an undefined dissatisfaction she had long felt, but could not express" (124–25). Similarly, when she finds herself abandoned once again, towards the end of the narrative, "watched by kidnappers," and "maltreated by professed abolitionists," Frado once again finds help from a guiding hand: "In one of her tours, Providence favored her with a friend who, pitying her cheerless lot, kindly provided her with a valuable recipe, from which she might herself manufacture a useful article for her maintenance" (129). Episodes such as these inform the significance of her final claim that "[r]eposing on God, she has thus far journeyed securely" (130). Her reliance on God has been a progressive act of self-reliance; the rewards she has received for thus fulfilling her duty—her "steadfast purpose of elevating herself" (130)—have been the material means by which self-reliance is possible.

But lest one assume that Wilson promotes merely a naive acceptance of "the New England ideal" of "free, dignified, and individualistic labor" (Baker, *Blues* 49), Wilson presents a more complex perspective on the workings of "God's economy" in her depiction of the "courtship" of Mag Smith and Jim. Critics have focused on the signifyin(g) conclusion of Jim's appeal to Mag, when he asks her, "Which you rather have, a black heart in a white skin, or a white heart in a black one?" (12).[25] However, one should attend as well to the process that leads to that significant conclusion, for Wilson draws her readers' attention not only to economic contingencies but also to the marketplace logic that enables Jim to act upon his original inspiration to marry Mag. Knowing that Mag is out of wood, Jim asks, "How's the wood, Mag?" and when she admits it is gone, he says, "Too bad!" (12). The narrator, though, notes that "his truthful reply would have been, I'm glad" (12). Again, when Jim asks Mag about food, and is told she has none, "orally," we are told, he replies "Too bad!"—but "with the same *inward* gratulation as before" (12). His proposal itself does not even pretend to be romantic; Mag is desperate, and Jim, having forced her hand with good marketplace technique, simply presents himself as the last available source of supply: " 'Well, Mag,' said Jim, after a short pause, 'you's down low enough. I do n't see but I've got to take care of ye. 'Sposin' we marry!' " (12).

The significance of this episode lies not merely in the victory of a pure heart over a culturally derogated black skin, the victorious reversal of cultural associations; it lies also, and I think more fundamentally, in the process by which that victory is achieved, and in the economic system that enables this cross-racial exchange. After all, Wilson's final word on the grounds for Mag's acceptance is not that Mag has seen the light that enables one to look to the heart, but rather that "want is a . . . powerful philosopher and preacher" (13). But the sermon preached by want is not simply one on the virtues of economic gain. In a book that not only calls for the readers' "sympathy and aid" (130) but also dramatizes—in Frado's husband, and in the Bellmonts themselves—the possibility that sympathy can be used as a mask for self-serving deception, it is important to remember that Jim's efforts to help Mag (and himself) begin with pity. In this case, however, "pity" leads to genuine reciprocity, for Mag surrenders her hope to reenter the circle of cultural respectability, and Jim not only gets what he wants but also commits himself to give what he can. No simple act of charity, no simple attempt to purchase ideological self-definition, "pity" here becomes part of what might be called a system of sentiments, the initial point of exchange that provides entrance into God's economy, and that thereby promotes the development of "finer" sentiments. For "pity and love," the narrator summarizes, "know little severance. One attends the other. Jim acknowledged the presence of the former, and his efforts in Mag's behalf told also of a finer principle" (10).

This genuine reciprocity is the motive force of "God's economy," and Wilson is careful to contrast it to simple charity in narrating Frado's experiences when Frado is reduced by poor health and circumstances to a situation similar to that of her mother so many years earlier, and has finally "one only resource; the public must pay the expense" (122). She is left to two elderly maidens, who, the narrator notes with clear sarcasm, "had principle enough to be willing to earn the money a charitable public disburses" (122). When Frado falls ill, she is left to the appropriately named Mrs. Hoggs, who is "a lover of gold and silver," and who "asked the favor of filling her coffers by caring for the sick" (122). This move aggravates Frado's decline; and when Frado's health begins to improve and she begins to feel "hope that she might yet help herself," Mrs. Hoggs reports her to the authorities (123). Charity, in other words, diverts the motive power from the relationship between the principal parties to a third party, and instead of mutual exchange establishes a linear relationship, a chain of funds from the community to Mrs. Hoggs to Frado, a relationship that requires Frado's dependence to secure Mrs. Hoggs's position as a self-aggrandizing benefactor. In other words, the relationship must remain stagnant, with clearly defined and delimited roles.

Wilson was by no means alone in her complaints about charity as an approach to individual security in a racially charged culture, and she was not alone in turning to book production as a product and sign of labor. "There is something very beautiful about the charity of the poor," Frances Harper's narrator asserts in *Sowing and Reaping*, for "they give not as the rich of their abundance, but of their limited earnings, gifts which when given in a right spirit bring a blessing with them" (*MST* 126–27).[26] If Harper here values the blessings that come with charity from such as Wilson, she also criticizes the charity of the rich, those who, in their " 'dealings with . . . poor working people,' " as one character puts it, fail to do " 'what . . . religion calls for,' " often asking " 'so much work for so little money' " (130). Indeed, one struggling character in Harper's novel is praised for refusing charity, driven by a "spirit of self-reliance" (152). Symbolizing an individual voice that has risen from silence, the creation of a book is significant in part as an accomplishment that both requires and promotes self-reliance. One thinks, for example, of William Wells Brown before her, and of William Still after. Still was a black abolitionist prominently involved in the Philadelphia office of the Underground Railroad, and in the 1870s he published *The Underground Rail Road*, a record of that institution and of the fugitive narratives he encountered in his service. Larry Gara notes the significant claim Still made in compiling and marketing this book (and Still was a shrewd manager of both tasks). "In writing and distributing" the book, Gara notes, "Still proved that a Negro author could produce a creditable book and sell it on a large scale. . . . He hoped it would inspire other Negroes to greater efforts until they could exhibit such fruits 'of their newly gained privileges' as 'well-conducted shops and stores; lands acquired and good farms' well-managed, and 'valuable books produced and published on interesting and important subjects' " ("William Still" 50). Books offered potentially rich fields of labor—rich in material rewards, and rich in significance—and the writing, production, publishing, and marketing of books were all a part of the labor. Moreover, through books, one could transform the experience behind the "interesting and important subjects" into a powerful personal and communal tool—visible labor that could inspire others similarly to work with diligence and care. In other words, *Our Nig* should not be considered a token for charity; rather, it should be considered a significant product—the object of labor, a subject of culture.

Not an occasion for charity, *Our Nig* is designed to initiate a more active system of exchange, one based on mutual dependence and devoted to communal development. White has emphasized "the extent to which economic motives predominate in Wilson's narrative" (33), and she documents Wilson's struggle to support herself and, later, her son after her years with the family of Nehemiah and Rebecca Hayward, the models for the Bellmont family in *Our Nig*. Often dependent upon the town of Milford, New Hampshire, and at times forced to leave her young son either to the mercies of the "terrible conditions" at the county poor farm or to the publicly financed care of a local family, Wilson knew intimately the complex cultural labyrinth assigned to "free" black northern laborers, and she knew something about white charity also. Working against charity and towards a culture in which self-reliance might be possible, Wilson presents a vision of Christianity in which *redemptive* faith requires that one *redeem* one's resources in an economic management of selfhood. When James Bellmont "[finds] his *Saviour*," he wishes the same for Frado because that discovery will enable her to manage the "elements in her heart which . . . would make her worthy [of] the esteem and friendship of the world" (69). This projected "esteem" has not only social but practical significance: "A kind, affectionate heart, native wit, and common sense, and the pertness she sometimes exhibited, he felt if restrained properly, might become useful in originating a self-reliance which would be of service to her in after years" (69). However, such self-reliance can operate successfully only in a community of others who are similarly "transformed and purified by the gospel," for Providence operates in this narrative only through those who are attuned to its directives. One can receive only as others offer, and one can offer only as others are disposed to receive. And as Jim tried to expose Mag's need, so Wilson works to expose the depravation, the utter want, of her world, thereby indicating the still-unacknowledged demand for what only she, and others in her position, can supply: the products of experience, and the profits of a fully realized and hard-earned Christian perspective.

Wilson's strategy of exposure and exchange is neatly summarized in two episodes. In the first, Frado deals with one of the sheep she tends, a "willful leader, who always persisted in being first served," often throwing Frado down in his zeal (54). Frado entices the sheep with a dish, and "[calls] the flock to their mock repast," locating herself at "the highest point of land nearest the stream" (54). As expected, the "willful leader" "came furiously leaping and bounding far in advance of the flock," and as he leaps for the dish, Frado steps aside, causing him to tumble down into the river, and then to remain on the other side until the night, a sheepish victim of his own greed (54–55). The applicability of this lesson becomes clear later when Aunt Abby admonishes Frado for half-seriously wishing Mary Bellmont dead. Returning to the lesson she taught to one willful leader, and applying it to another, Frado says of Mary, "I'd like to try my hand at curing *her* too" (80). This episode echoes an earlier experience, when Mary tries to force Frado into a stream and, in the struggle, loses her footing and falls in herself. The eschatological implications of these stories of willful leaders and just desserts are underscored when Mary dies, inspiring Frado to say, "She's got into the *river* again" (107).

In the other of the two episodes, Frado is forced to eat from the plate from which Mrs. Bellmont herself has eaten. Annoyed at being "commanded to do what was disagreeable . . . *because* it was disagreeable," Frado has her dog Fido wash the plate, "which he did to the best of his ability," after which she eats from it (71). What makes this such a fitting image for Wilson's own strategies is not only Frado's symbolic victory over Mrs. Bellmont, but also the fact that Frado is paid a silver half-dollar by Mrs. Bellmont's own son for the pleasure of seeing his mother thus exposed and defeated. As James explains to his mother, "You have not treated her, mother, so as to gain her love; she is only exhibiting your remissness in this matter" (72). Mrs. Bellmont never learns the lesson, but it remains for others, an education that begins when one pays the price of this novel. Wilson's message is that exposure of a world of "remissness" must be recognized as a valuable service if the nation is to maintain its moral foundations. The exposure of willful leaders and tyrannical employers returns economic relationships to their moral grounds, there to be evaluated.

The value of a marketplace economy, then—and that which made it a practical entrance into "God's economy"—is that it depends not upon a hopeful cooperation but rather upon inevitable conflict. In this, Wilson anticipates Anna Julia Cooper, who viewed the "race problem" as a vital part of God's mode of governance, by which "eternal harmony and symmetry" are "the unvarying result of the equilibrium of opposing forces" (150). As Cooper would later argue, noting her preference for the troubled present over Edward Bellamy's utopian "grandmotherly government" in *Looking Backward*, "Progressive peace in a nation is the result of conflict; and conflict, such as is healthy, stimulating, and progressive, is produced through the co-existence of radically opposing or racially different elements" (151). Closer to Wilson's own time, in an essay of 1844 titled "On the Moral and Political Effect of the Relation between the Caucasian Master and the African Slave," a slavery advocate contends that the emancipation of female slaves would force them to rely on "cold charities," replacing "a *community* of interests" with "a *conflict* of interests" (339). Distrusting the community of interests, Wilson supports a renewed understanding of the dynamic exchanges between conflicting interests, for the interests that she knew were sure to conflict. But the conflicts, she suggests, may contain the terms of mutual dependence, the demands of collective survival—the recognition of which is the initial and fundamental step necessary for constructing a genuine and morally secure community of interests.

Throughout this narrative, Wilson argues implicitly that community can come only from the deliberate recognition of conflict, and that the nation can progress only by way of ongoing negotiations among antagonists who recognize that each has something the other needs to survive in a world governed ultimately by God. Baker, in his brilliant examination of the economic argument in Frederick Douglass's *Narrative*, has drawn our attention to the ways in which Douglass presents his life as a process by which he "eventually converts property, through property, into humanity" (*Blues* 49). Certainly, Wilson—addressing not slavery itself but rather its northern shadows—hopes to do the same. But as Douglass himself came to recognize after his initial optimistic vision of the New England economic system, the self-purchase necessary to African-American survival in the growing capitalist environment of the North required a communal self-purchase of all citizens. The ostensibly empowered must recognize that, like the physically enslaved, they too have been converted to property by the economic and political network that both supports and depends upon the slave system. Ultimately, the argument embedded in *Our Nig* is that communal self-purchase begins with this book; the story of the life produced by this culture serves as the catalyst for new cultural productions in the ongoing quest to convert disparate cultural property into a common humanity.

As this narrative conflates fiction and autobiography, bringing together not only Wilson and Frado but also the son in the Preface and the son in the ultimate chapter, Wilson draws the reader's attention to that other child of this cultural process, the book she has produced for sale. I return, then, to the question with which I began: What are we to make of our own purchase of this book? To claim it either as a great or a subliterary work (depending on the literary history one is constructing at the time) is simply to miss the point. Similarly, to make of it a significant beginning of an African-American literary tradition is also to miss the point. *Our Nig* insists upon its own status as a historically bound economic, cultural, and even moral production. Not only the story Wilson tells but also her mode of telling (often in sharp contrast to the works she alludes to in the chapter headings) are parts of this production, examples of the extent to which this culture "speaks" the subject—in its standards of morality, of class, of labor, of gender, and of racial difference. Karla F. C. Holloway has argued that "as long as [Wilson's] white audience is still an 'overseer,' the space she wants to diminish between them that would allow her to benefit from their empathy and financial expressions of support will not be bridged. They too are trapped by the logistics of the market metaphor that place them into positions of dominance and ownership rather than patronage and support" (136–37). As I have argued, though, Wilson builds into her text the exposure of that audience of "overseers," along with the appeal to a divinely governed marketplace by which such exposure should earn support—an approach by which she could earn money without selling self-respect. Although hers was a failed financial enterprise, I think it is a mistake to pronounce it a failed economic enterprise—for there are textual overseers still to encounter. By the terms of this economy, Wilson's production, *Our Nig*, stands not as a literary model to be either emulated or dismissed but rather as a mirror to be contemplated, the kind of mirror Wilson saw in her child, the kind that we—too late to save the child—can see in our cultural ancestors. There is beauty there, for those who know where to look, though others may find it an unattractive literary work. But "perfect" features, besides being in the eye of the beholder, are finally beside the point, for we find ourselves in our cultural family, and we acknowledge the relation. Or we don't. Wilson looks for her family in a community of distrust, and presents *Our Nig* not as a literary model but as an unadorned product of her culture. These many years later, the features are still recognizable.

3

# Reading the Fragments in the
# Fields of History

## Harriet Jacobs's *Incidents in the Life of a Slave Girl*

In 1837, at the Anti-Slavery Convention of American Women,[1] Mrs. A. L. Cox put forth a resolution proclaiming that "there is no class of women to whom the anti-slavery cause makes so direct and powerful an appeal as to *mothers*." Responding to this appeal, the resolution calls for women to "lift up their hearts to God on behalf of the captive, as often as they pour them out over their own children in a joy with which 'no stranger may intermeddle.' " The same resolution warns women to "guard with jealous care the minds of their children from the ruining influences of the spirit of pro-slavery and prejudice, let those influences come in what name, or through what connexions they may" (Sterling, *Turning* 17). The dual directive here—for hearts to be lifted upward to God's purifying realm, and for jealous care to be directed outward against humankind's *corrupting* realm—directs us in turn to what Jean Fagan Yellin calls the "double tale" in Harriet Jacobs's 1861 narrative *Incidents in the Life of a Slave Girl*. As Yellin notes, Jacobs dramatizes "the triumph of her efforts to prevent her master from raping her," but she also presents the story of "her failure to adhere to sexual standards in which she believed" (Introduction xiv). In other words, although Jacobs might hope that the story of her "triumph" would lift up her readers' hearts, she knew also that her "failure" would cause her readers to guard those same hearts with jealous care, and to turn God's realm against Jacobs in judgment.

It is this other double story, her white readers' inevitably dual response of approbation and judgment, that complicates Jacobs's attempt to "be honest and tell the whole truth,"[2] and that qualifies any common bond she might claim as a mother. Certainly, resistance to the institution of slavery required mothers to protest the habitual violation of an ideologically sanctified relationship—in effect, a matter of insisting upon the enslaved woman's right to the privileges and duties of motherhood. But Jacobs knew well that many antislavery white women, in their search for injustice, did not even think to look beyond the visible violation of the sacred relationship of mother and child. In other words, they saw only those horrors that threatened the ideological security of the domestic sphere, and from that sphere they judged such horrors. To maintain the sphere, the horrors (including both the act of violating and the act of being violated) must remain outside. As Robert B. Stepto argues, "The risks that written storytelling undertakes are . . . at least twofold: one is that the reader will become a hearer but not manage an authenticating response; the other is that the reader will *remain a reader* and not only belittle or reject storytelling's particular 'keen disturbance,' but also issue confrontational responses which sustain altogether different definitions of literature, of literacy, and of appropriate reader response" ("Distrust" 308). Thus distanced, Jacobs could not hope to "tell the whole truth" unless she could teach her readers to *hear* and understand the whole truth.

If Jacobs was to present something more than an object lesson in the horrors of slavery, she would have to inspire her readers to trace to their own homes the "ruining influences of the spirit of pro-slavery and prejudice," and to question not only their willingness but even their ability to fulfill the duties of motherhood in a culture that sanctions slavery. In other words, motherhood, as viewed from Jacobs's perspective, does not provide an unproblematic bond between narrator and reader, for Linda Brent, the pseudonymous author and subject of this story, cannot help but represent the most threatening and pervasive vice. No reader, no matter how sympathetic, can change Brent's cultural identity; the progression available to Linda Brent is that from a slave girl to a concubine to a slave mother to a fugitive slave to a "free black." Each new phase is a resounding echo of her previous condition: a restricted identity, the terms of which Brent can try to adapt to her needs but can never hope to control. Nor can Brent offer the dubious protection or comfort of a closing moral, for such closure was not available to her or to the larger community whose story she represents. Instead, the lesson of *Incidents* is that white mothers and daughters *cannot* identify with Brent, but that they must learn to do so if they are to achieve their own moral ideals, if they are to fulfill the terms of their own self-definition.[3]

*Incidents* directs itself towards this paradox, and operates in the space it at once opens and closes, thereby creating a need for the perspective that only Jacobs, and others like her, can offer. The choice for white women and mothers concerned about the immorality of slavery—the choice between taking the high moral ground of, say, an Esther and being the victim of a prophecy—cannot be accomplished by way of a sympathetic engagement in Brent's story, a self-assuring response to what Joanne M. Braxton terms "outraged motherhood."[4] Rather, this choice requires white women to learn from Brent not only a new language but also a new mode of understanding, one characterized not by a separation of subject and object but rather by a reciprocal relationship between two differently knowing subjects. Ultimately, Jacobs issues to her readers an epistemic challenge to change the nature of their knowledge by changing the way they look at and learn from African Americans.

## Motherhood Within the Gate

In *The Mother's Book*, her 1831 guidebook on domestic education (directed, as was *The American Frugal Housewife*, towards "the middling class"), Lydia Maria Child warns mothers to guard their children against the dangerous influence of seductive and deceptive popular novels, the kind that followed the pattern of sensationalist reform books wherein calls for reform provided a convenient guise for detailed descriptions of vice.[5] "Many readers, and writers too," Child notes, "think any book is proper for young people, which has a good moral at the end; but the fact is, some books, with a long excellent moral, have the worst possible effect on a young mind.—The morality should be *in* the book, not tacked upon the *end* of it" (90). Young minds, Child argues, are influenced by the experience of reading, leading her to "doubt whether books which represent vice, in any way, are suitable to be put into the hands of those, whose principles are not formed. . . . Familiarity with evil is a disadvantage, even when pointed out as an object of disgust" (91). Child cites *Charlotte*

*Temple* as an example of such a book, "written with the best intention," but still capable of doing "harm to girls of fourteen or fifteen" (91).

In the 1850s, Child continued her long and able service not only to antislavery efforts but also to the culturally defined institution of motherhood by editing the manuscript that would become one of the most striking African-American resistance narratives of the nineteenth century, Jacobs's *Incidents*. As Bruce Mills argues, Child's advice to Jacobs— particularly that a closing chapter on John Brown be omitted— "underscores her conviction that a female slave narrative would be most forceful if it invoked the sanctity of motherhood" (256). And Jacobs does indeed invoke motherhood, to the extent that, as Jean Fagan Yellin has noted, "motherhood is central to *Incidents*. . . . The evils of slavery are dramatized as the sexual abuse of women and the torture of mothers. The sketch of the childless cook, Betty, suggests that for a woman maternity is a prerequisite for full humanity; women black or white—Linda Brent, Grandmother, Aunt Nancy, Mrs. Flint—all are defined by the ways in which they respond to motherhood" (*Women & Sisters* 89).[6] But this particular book about motherhood, like some of Child's own fiction, would not pass Child's test of appropriate reading matter for young girls, for the young girl who is the subject and voice of this narrative cannot help but represent vice.[7] Her cultural identity is defined by the systematic vice of slavery; she discovers both the motive and the terms of her resistance to that system by willfully transgressing the culturally defined standards of virtue that proved inapplicable to her situation. In fact, Linda Brent, the book's pseudonymous author, cannot even offer the dubious protection or comfort of a closing moral—for such closure was not available to her or to the larger community whose story she represents.

Of course, *Incidents* is not intended for daughters and sons but for mothers and fathers. Still, there is reason to emphasize the distinction between what Child would want her children to read and the book she edited, for it reminds us that the nineteenth-century American institution of motherhood was not a monolithic enterprise. Fundamentally, the "incidents" one encounters in Jacobs's narrative remind us that the nineteenth-century American institution of motherhood was a racialized, class-based concept. As such, the concept of motherhood presented both possibilities and problems as a vehicle for social change. As Lori D. Ginzberg notes, "To those who worried that benevolent activities would weaken women's effectiveness in the home, reformers replied that benevolent work merely extended the job of motherhood" (16). However, the problem women faced in applying the concept of motherhood to new cultural contexts was that the ideology of motherhood carried with it its own contextualizing apparatus, and this could be turned back against reforming mothers. Not only men but many "benevolent women" themselves "were quite prepared," as Ginzberg demonstrates, "to use the ideology of femininity as a weapon against female organizing that served interests they thought too radical" (25). The potential force of this weapon is clear in Child's own summary of and subscription to the "ideology of femininity" in her 1827 guidebook for "middling class" women, *The American Frugal Housewife*: "There is no subject so much connected with individual happiness and national prosperity as the education of daughters. It is a true, and therefore an old remark, that the situation and prospects of a country may be justly estimated by the character of its women; and we all know how hard it is to engraft upon a woman's character habits and principles to which she was unaccustomed in her girlish days" (91). This relationship between the character of the nation and the character of its women means that habits and principles must be developed organically early in a girl's development instead of being engrafted late; and this relationship means also that mothers must devote themselves to overseeing this process of organic development. The question of a mother's duty in relation to social order was one of both praxis and principle. How one defined one's principles, in turn, defined one's representative identity as the individual embodiment of intermeshed political and religious ideologies.

Child's career might itself be viewed as an extension of the job of motherhood; but Child's own public entrance into the antislavery movement, the publication of *An Appeal in Favor of That Class of Americans Called Africans*, came at the expense of her position as a trusted guardian of the practice of motherhood, causing many mothers and fathers to cancel their subscriptions to the *Juvenile Miscellany*. Indeed, one review of Child's *Appeal* begins by reminding readers that Child is the author of *The Mother's Book*, and concludes with the lament, "It is . . . with regret that we see intellects like that of Mrs. Child, and pens like hers, which may be otherwise so agreeably and beneficially employed in urging on a cause so dangerous to the Union, domestic peace, and civil liberty, as the immediate emancipation of the slaves at the South" ("Slavery" 193). But the relationship between Child's early career and her antislavery work was yet more intimately problematic. With no culturally sanctioned way to negotiate the differences between class and caste and between reified womanhood and sexual exploitation, Child could hardly hope to apply to enslaved women the defense of middle-class motherhood that led her to argue in *The American Frugal Housewife* that "most of us could obtain worldly distinctions, if our habits and inclination allowed us to pay the immense price at which they must be purchased. True wisdom lies in finding out all the advantages of a situation in which we *are* placed, instead of imagining the enjoyments of one in which we are *not* placed" (106). Of course, Child wrote this early in her career and demonstrates a culturally delimited understanding of the possibilities of "wisdom" and the contingencies of social position. When Child writes of "a situation in which we *are* placed," she refers to fate, to the mysterious influence of divine Providence as enacted by human agency. Enslaved blacks, on the other hand, were placed in their situation by human hands that claimed the authority of divine agency and the power of fate while directing themselves towards the most vulgar of human motives. One encounters similar advice, in fact, in *Uncle Tom's Cabin*, when Mr. Wilson encounters George Harris, who has begun his journey north. " 'Yes, my boy,' " Mr. Wilson says with genuine sympathy but little understanding, " 'I'm sorry for you, now; it's a bad case—very bad; but the apostle says, "Let every one abide in the condition in which he is called." We must all submit to the indications of Providence, George,—don't you see?' " (134). For black women, who similarly were admonished by their lascivious so-called *protectors* and holders to not only abide in but realize the "advantages" of the "situation" in which they were placed, the brand of home-spun wisdom of which Child and Mr. Wilson speak would (and often did) constitute self-victimization at its most specific and, in general, a reminder of the multifarious degradation of enslavement.[8]

Motherhood, I am suggesting, was the essential condition of what I have called "reified womanhood," by which I mean the culturally determined attributes by which women could know themselves as Woman. These attributes are what Barbara Welter terms the "four cardinal virtues" of "True Womanhood": "piety, purity, submissiveness and domesticity" (152).[9] But it is important to remember that these virtues did not exist in an ideological vacuum, a separate sphere reserved for social constructions of gender. Rather, they existed in relation to the state—that is, they served both practical and ideological functions in the maintenance of social order and of national identity. Ideals of true womanhood, and the related reification of the woman's sphere of virtue in the home, at once worked to forestall social change and to place at the heart of American society an ideologically ahistorical realm, a world supposed to be untouched by the increasing complexities of material and political culture.[10]

In the context of its relation to the republican state, the effect of "True Womanhood" was to place women not only outside the realm of politics but outside of history itself. J. G. A. Pocock, among many others, has noted that theories of republicanism included the awareness of a republic's inevitable corruption, as government accumulates more power and shifts towards subtle new forms of tyranny, and as civic virtue—succumbing to the republic's own economic prosperity—is displaced by love of luxury. As Child puts it, "A luxurious and idle *republic*! Look at the phrase!—The words were never made to be married together; every body sees it would be death to one of them" (*The American Frugal Housewife* 99). In effect, what was most threatening to the stability of a republic were the effects of its own material success upon the character of individual citizens. As John Grammer has argued, republicanism "amounted to a theory of entropy, believing that republican societies generally tended toward tyranny, and that only a virtuous citizenry, always ready to turn the nation back toward its republican traditions, could interrupt that tendency. Because government tended over time to become tyrannical, time itself could seem an enemy of republican order" (11).

Outside the realms of the public institutions and events that defined human history, and inside the home, women's virtue served as the ideological womb of civic virtue.[11] In an 1853 essay in *Putnam's Monthly* on "Woman and the 'Woman's Movement,'" the writer argues that the woman's life "is always a present one"; and "Hence the first woman was named *Eve*, that is, LIVING" (287). Woman therefore stands as "the expressive type or symbol of that lustrous life which shall one day redeem him [her husband] from earth, and ally him with divinity" (287). Through the republican woman, the republican man maintains an intimate relationship with the eternal. As it is idealized in the essay "The Homes of America The Hope of the Republic," which appeared in *The United States Democratic Review* in 1856, home "is a place, apart from and beyond the world"; "the spirit of home is the pervading spirit, which lends high aim and purpose to our lives, and makes an aggregate of virtue sufficient to sustain a pure form of republicanism" (296–97). It was the republican duty not only of domestic education but of motherhood itself both to ennoble and to protect, but not to participate in, the political sphere. To redefine womanhood as historical agency released the ideologically ahistorical anchor that secured what many women took to be their historical roles. Deliberately private, representing a simplicity of faith and virtue that belies the complexity of life, the culturally constructed domestic sphere served the most public of purposes. To many women as well as men in the antebellum United States, for women to leave the home and enter the political arena was a matter not of leaving the private sphere to enter the public, but rather of redefining one's role in the public sphere, for women were thought to serve distinctively public roles by holding to private spheres. Child, for example, presents good republican philosophy in *The American Frugal Housewife* when, in demonstrating her sense of the extent of the mother's responsibilities, she notes that "Nations do not plunge *at once* into ruin—governments do not change *suddenly*—the causes which bring about the final blow, are scarcely perceptible in the beginning; but they increase in numbers, and in power; they press harder and harder upon the energies and virtue of a people; and the last steps only are alarmingly hurried and irregular" (91). Motherhood was both a condition and a duty, both noun and verb; it was the ongoing, delicate negotiation of the relationship between the historical and the ahistorical by way of domestic education. True womanhood involved the embodiment of timeless virtues; true motherhood was the expression of womanhood in history, the preparation of children for lives in the world.

In 1859 one of the many attacks on the increasing public prominence of women was an article published in the *Southern Literary Messenger* on the "Intellectual Culture of Woman," an article designed ultimately to argue that it is the mother's role, within the context of domestic education, to defend the institution of slavery. Asserting that "it is no slight duty . . . to which woman is called, in the discharge of her offices to society," the author strategically amplifies the implicit responsibilities inherent in the ideology of femininity, arguing that "the social problems which are the subject and the origin of laws, the manners and customs of the people which originate and produce these laws, are the product, directly or indirectly, of the women" (329). As this appropriation demonstrates, the ideology of motherhood—like religion itself, like law, like republican philosophy—proved infinitely flexible. Whether or not a woman accepted the role of a true woman, the task of applying this generalized role to the concerns of the day was unavoidably political. To be a mother in opposition to law and custom was to announce an ideological reconstitution of motherhood.

At the 1837 Anti-Slavery Convention of American Women, for example, agreements about the public efficacy of Christian virtue and sympathetic motherhood were more easily reached than agreements about attendant redefinitions of woman's social role. On the second day of the convention, Angelina Grimké offered the following resolution relating to such redefinitions of woman's sphere:

> RESOLVED, That as certain rights and duties are common to all moral beings, the time has come for women to move in that sphere which Providence has assigned her, and no longer remain satisfied in the circumscribed limits with which corrupt custom and a perverted application of Scripture have encircled her; therefore that it is the duty of woman, and the province of woman, to plead the cause of the oppressed in our land, and to do all that she can by her voice, and her pen, and her purse, and the influence of her example, to overthrow the horrible system of American slavery. (Sterling, *Turning* 13)

According to the convention notes, this resolution, and the suggested amendments that followed, "called forth an animated and interesting debate respecting the rights and duties of women. The resolution was finally adopted, without amendment, though *not anonymously*" (13). On the next day, the minutes record that "L. M. Child in consideration of the wishes of some members, who were opposed to the adoption of the resolution on the province of women, moved that the same be reconsidered. The motion was seconded by A. W. Weston, but after discussion was lost" (17). Twelve women asked that their opposition to the resolution be recorded, with their names, in the minutes.

Grimké had directed a similar argument—and had demonstrated a careful awareness of the tensions it creates—toward a much less receptive audience in her "Appeal to the Christian Women of the South," which appeared in *The Anti-Slavery Examiner* in 1836. Noting that southern women are likely to wonder what they, who lack political and legislative power, can do, Grimké argues that they can do "four things": read, pray, speak, and act on the subject (16–17).[12] The first three things Grimké explains in three paragraphs; the fourth occupies much of the rest of the essay—not merely because there was so much to be done, but because

Grimké had to justify and situate ideologically the concept of action by women against the state. What follows is a history of heroic women, grounded ultimately in the example of the male apostles, beginning with biblical women and proceeding to Protestant women in the time of Catholic Inquisitions; and then to English women who worked for "the great and glorious cause of Emancipation"; and finally to "The Ladies' Anti-Slavery Society of Boston" (18–24).

In effect, Grimké presents a brief history of activist women in order to *dehistoricize* the concept of activism, placing the concept, with good abolitionist logic, within an eschatological framework. Referring to the courage of the apostles Peter and John to preach the gospel regardless of the threat of persecution, Grimké argues that "*Consequences*, my friends, belong no more to *you*, than they did to these apostles. Duty is ours and events are God's" (19). Duty thus becomes a matter of stepping outside of human history and entering into providential history. Specifically, it becomes the moral human agency by which biblical prophecies will be fulfilled on earth. Beginning with the prophecy of Psalm 68:31 ("Ethiopia shall stretch forth her hands unto God") Grimké proceeds to the prophecy of judgment near the end of the book of Daniel (12:4): "Many shall run to and fro, and *knowledge* shall be increased."[13] Grimké then concludes this section of her essay significantly by alluding to another prophecy, from the book of Isaiah—that book that warns against luxury and fashion, a country under peril of judgment, and that prophecizes that "a virgin shall conceive, and bear a son, and shall call his name Immanuel" (7:14). The verse Grimké quotes is one of communal hope, of Isaiah's prophecy of a messianic kingdom (11:9): "They shall *not* hurt nor destroy in all my holy mountain" (27). Having placed slavery in this Old Testament prophetic framework, Grimké argues that "*Slavery, then, must be overthrown before* the prophecies can be accomplished" (27). Womanhood, in other words, can justify an activist stance not by abandoning the "cardinal virtues" of true womanhood but rather by tracing these virtues to their theological roots. By this formulation, womanhood is not ushered into history, nor is it separated from its relation to the state, nor is the relationship between womanhood and the state provided a new ideological configuration. Rather, the existing ideological configuration for defining the relationship between womanhood and state is intensified, urging women to serve not the historical state but the philosophical state, the nation viewed as a potential fulfillment of providential history, a nation blessed by God (and therefore open to particularly harsh judgment if it should fail in its mission).

The need for this transition from the domestic to the biblical sphere is central to *Incidents in the Life of a Slave Girl*, but Brent (and Jacobs) cannot claim the cultural authority of motherhood; she can only struggle to call into question her readers' own claims to authority. Jacobs's self-representation undermines the ideological foundation by which woman-hood can be comfortably reconfigured, offering no entrance into biblical womanhood except by way of an unprotected entrance into social and political history. As Hazel V. Carby reminds us, at the end of her narrative Brent remains "excluded from the domain of the home, the sphere within which womanhood and motherhood were defined. Without a 'woman's sphere,' both were rendered meaningless" (*Reconstructing* 49).[14] However, the unspoken assertion behind Jacobs's self-presentation is that her white motherly readers themselves cannot claim the power of reified woman-hood because the ideological vessel of that power is falsely constructed. Accordingly, as Brent promises not "to try to screen [herself] behind the plea of compulsion of a master" (54), so Brent's female readers must learn to step out from behind their own ideological screens. To do so means to confront the actual conditions and events of their world, in all their disturbing and disruptive ideological contradictions, and, more to the point, to acknowledge responsibility for these contradictions. The screens themselves, woven of coarse ideological threads, provide a unified public diorama to cover the many private stories that would reveal the nation's failure to live up to its professed ideals. And as Jacobs knew well, yet another screen—in some ways, the most deceptive of all, and most capable of undermining the individual sense of moral responsibility—was the abolitionist belief in the possibility of understanding the "monstrous features" of slavery once the "veil" of propriety is "withdrawn," as Child puts it in her introduction to the narrative (*Incidents* 4). For the "monstrous" is always the Other; and as the Other, Jacobs would have no real voice, no way to penetrate the screen between narrator and reader. White readers would need to learn to see the monstrous at home before Jacobs could extend her own cultural identity beyond that of a representa-tive and victimized site of monstrous exchanges.

By all cultural standards, ideological motherhood in *this* narrative of national life has been violated and corrupted, and Jacobs argues that it is only by acknowledging and studying the terms of that violation and corruption that motherhood can be restored to integrity. After all, *Incidents'* central character, Linda Brent, has no living mother, and can look for her maternal guidance only from her grandmother. Indeed, Brent notes early in the narrative that "if I knelt by my mother's grave, [Flint's] dark shadow fell on me even there" (28). Instead of providing the moral entrance into history, motherhood in this narrative marks the violent intrusion of history into a woman's life. For Brent, the state does not await the performance of motherhood; rather, the state has become sexually implicated in the condition of womanhood and the conception of motherhood. When telling of her attempt to avoid Flint's demands by submitting herself to relations with a future statesman,[15] Brent notes significantly that without slavery she would have nothing to confess. Asserting that her own deliberate moral transgression was the only avenue for self-determination, Brent reminds the reader again that "the condition of a slave confuses all principles of morality, and, in fact, renders the practice of them impossible" (55). Her grandmother's own rejection of Brent after this transgression emphasizes the strictness with which American Christianity defines that which it creates, forcing Brent outside the moral sanctuary of the domestic sphere.

Banished from that culturally determined domestic sphere, Brent leaves her grandmother's house, and as the gate closes behind her—"with a sound I never heard before" (57)—she enters into a new stage in her relation to her grandmother, history, and selfhood. Jacobs's readers seemingly are left within the gate, with little more to offer than sympathetic echoes of the grandmother's lamentation after the two are reconciled: "Poor child! Poor child!" (57). Brent herself is left with the experience that will produce the children who will motivate her eventual escape from the South. But the internal logic of *Incidents* comes to a point here, as Brent completes her identity as a highly determined product of the American Christian slave culture, literally embodying its moral and social contradictions in the children she soon carries. Jacobs's task is to draw her readers themselves beyond the gate, to show that they reside there already, and thereby to make Brent their representative and her quest theirs as well.[16]

### Silent Understanding and Locked Eyes

To perform this task, Jacobs must re-educate her readers, teaching them to see the invisible by giving voice to the unspeakable, forcing them beyond the gate of moral security and into a realm where all is uncertain, and where nothing can be addressed directly. What is needed is not merely the familiar argument that slaves and whites alike are taught in the "school of slavery" to accept and participate in the moral corruption of the system. Although Jacobs indeed works to reveal the baseness of these lessons learned in school, she argues further that the mode of thought one acquires in this school is inadequate to change the course of these lessons. Whereas Harriet Beecher Stowe argued that her readers should *"feel right"* (515), Jacobs (perhaps fortified by her own disillusioning experience with Stowe, and certainly by her attenuated enslavement as a "free black" in domestic service)[17] begins with the assumption that it will matter little if readers "feel right" if they do not also challenge fundamentally the nature and terms of their self-definition. Drawing her readers into an awareness of their own identities as U.S. citizens, Jacobs challenges the reader's ability even to know whether he or she does "feel right." If one is produced by this culture, then "feeling right" is a matter of aligning one's behavior (both physical and intellectual) with one's conception of moral law. As Stowe argues through her characterization of Marie St. Clare in *Uncle Tom's Cabin*, if one's conception of moral law is distorted, then so too is one's "conscience," and feeling right will mean simply that this dual distortion is perfectly aligned.

Jacobs could not simply appeal to a true application of Christian precepts, for the "all-pervading corruption produced by slavery" (51) made such appeals, in and of themselves, worthless. The dominant culture's ability even to understand those precepts was itself in question. Moreover, the many "Christian" slaveholders and proslavery ministers throughout both the northern and southern states demonstrated daily that such appeals could easily be redirected back at the enslaved. Well versed in the multifarious ways in which slavery is capable of "[perverting] all the natural feelings of the human heart" (142), Jacobs has little hope of appealing to that heart for justice. She knows that the justice of the heart can only echo, even at its best, the conceptions of justice defined by culture and habit. The ideological system that both requires and sustains the figurative heart would be the interpretive filter through which any appeal must pass. As Carby argues, not only white southern women but also the northern women "who formed Jacobs's audience were implicated in the preservation of this [ideological] oppression" (*Reconstructing* 55). Unable to trust in relationships engendered by the fundamental commonalities of women's condition and experiences, Jacobs needed to reshape the ways in which women relate their individual experience to the concept of gendered commonality.

The problem was that many, blinded by custom, could not see what they were doing to blacks; in fact, many were incapable of imagining that the dominant culture's ethical standards could even apply to blacks. Early in *Incidents*, Brent notes that her otherwise solicitous and kind original mistress had taught her "the precepts of God's Word: 'Thou shalt love thy neighbor as thyself,'" and "'Whatsoever ye would that men should do unto you, do ye even so unto them'" (8). The mistress commits her "one great wrong" (bequeathing Brent to her sister's daughter) not because she fails to believe in the "precepts of God's Word," but rather because she does not recognize Brent as her neighbor in the moral sphere (8). Brent's later mistress, worried about Dr. Flint's interest in the girl, forces her to act as a moral agent by swearing on the Bible and "before God" to tell the truth; but this episode is fundamentally similar to the earlier one, for Brent's account simply leads Mrs. Flint to "[pity] herself as a martyr." Brent adds pointedly that Mrs. Flint "was incapable of feeling for the condition of shame and misery in which her unfortunate, helpless slave was placed" (33).

Certainly, Jacobs writes in the hope that the exposure of immorality will inspire in her readers a renewal of moral character, leading to reformative actions. At its most basic level, *Incidents* follows the signifyin(g) strategy of motivated repetition and exposure that Linda Brent had learned from her grandmother. When Dr. Flint informs "Aunt Marthy" that, out of respect for her feelings, he will sell her at a private rather than a public auction, Brent's grandmother realizes that "he was ashamed of the job," not only because he was selling her, but also because "every body who knew her respected her intelligence and good character" (11). She had, in other words, become visible to the community, and the ethical transgressions inherent in slave auctions had accordingly become visible as well. Grandmother uses this visibility to advantage, standing on the auction block, leading observers (who otherwise were willing participants in this socioeconomic ritual) to remark, "Shame! Shame! Who is going to sell *you*, aunt Marthy? Don't stand there! That is no place for *you*" (11). Finally, she is purchased by one who recognizes that "she had been defrauded of her rights," a "maiden lady" who can sign the bill of sale only with a cross (11–12). This pivotal morality play, in which the dominant culture refuses to apply to one the corrupt standards it willingly applies to others, is central to *Incidents* as to other slave narratives. Indeed, Jacobs presents American Christianity and American slavery as symbiotic ideological systems, mutually dependent for ideological integrity. She presents American Christianity not as the system that enables her to *see* her wrongs, but rather as the system that forces her to *commit* her wrongs—a closed system that requires transgression, thereby making visible the terms of moral self-definition. Like the Inquisition to which she compares it, American Christian slavery requires a conspicuous institutional emphasis of moral standards, a public ritual that all but requires sins that must be punished, and that veils the sins of the institutional body itself, the "secrets of slavery" (35). Although there are many, Brent reminds her readers, who "are thirsting for the water of life," "the law forbids it, and the churches withhold it" (73). These many are assigned instead to "inferior" roles in which moral self-awareness cannot lead to repentance. Comparing the life of a "favorite slave" to that of a "[felon] in a penitentiary," Brent notes that the felon "may repent, and turn from the error of his ways, and so find peace," while for the slave "it is deemed a crime in her to wish to be virtuous" (31).

Jacobs signals her awareness also that this effort to reform by exposing wrongs relies on a rather tenuous hope. Christian "precepts" can be applied to African Americans for the purposes of intellectual and spiritual colonization, but the flexible logic by which those precepts are applied belongs to the dominant culture, the members of which determine—at times consciously, at times not—which aspects of black bodies and black lives shall be visible. Dehumanized enough to be viewed as a slave, Brent was still human and woman enough to be the object of Flint's lust; still invisible, however, remained the human heart and divine soul that would make it impossible for Flint to fulfill his desires without sacrificing his community standing. Jacobs had long been in the North when she wrote *Incidents*, and Northerners, she notes through Linda Brent, are all too ready to "satisfy their consciences with the doctrine that God created the Africans to be slaves" (44). And those who could see more than a slave often had trouble seeing more than a servant. Jacobs knew that exposure simply uncovered one layer of black invisibility, one more dimension of the fullness of human experience that whites had not learned (or did not care) to recognize in blacks.

At issue is not only *what* knowledge the reader gains from this text, but also *how* the reader conceptualizes the acquisition of that knowledge. In *What Can She Know?*, Lorraine Code joins many looking to construct a feminist epistemology in arguing that "the subject-object relation that the autonomy-of-reason credo underwrites is at once its most salient and its most politically significant epistemological consequence" (139). In traditional approaches to knowledge acquisition, Code argues, "the subject is removed from, detached from, positions himself at a distance from the object; and knows the object as other than himself" (139). This subject/object relation characterized the nineteenth-century relationship between white reader and black author. In this highly politicized relationship, the black author served as the ostensibly self-voicing object of knowledge. However, the tenor and quality of that voice was itself an object of knowledge, obliged to obey the demand that Thoreau complains of in *Walden*: "that you shall speak so that they can understand you" (216).[18] The conventions of cultural communication carry with them the cultural assumptions and prejudices that can undermine true communication between white and black. As Karen Sanchez-Eppler argues compellingly, the "moments of identification" that characterized the feminist/abolitionist alliance led easily and invisibly to "acts of appropriation" (31). Jacobs's task was to redefine the terms of this identification by reappropriating the authority to define the experience of oppression.

She approaches this task by redefining knowledge—replacing, in effect, the gaze as the central perspectival figure for acquiring knowledge, drawing instead on the visual mode sometimes referred to as "locking eyes." As Lorraine Code notes, "direct eye contact between people" is "a symmetrical act of mutual recognition in which neither need be passive and neither in control. Such contact is integral to the way people position themselves in relation to one another and signify the meaning of their encounters. Through it, they engage with one another, convey feelings, and establish and maintain, or renegotiate, their relationships" (144). The most familiar experience of "locking eyes" might be the intimate contact that two people can discover through love—a discovery both revealed and developed when each discovers her or his ability to look into the eyes of the other, to meet intent look with intent look. Out of this symmetrical act of mutual recognition, the two create something more than the sum of one-plus-one. And if the relationship thus formed fails to develop or is not sustained, the unavoidable sign of the failure is the couple's inability to look each other in the eye.[19] Locking eyes is also, I would suggest, what Thoreau refers to in *Walden* when he meditates on the possibility of encountering someone who is fully awake: "To be awake is to be alive," he asserts, adding, "I have never yet met a man who was quite awake. How could I have looked him in the face?" (61). In that exchange, Thoreau suggests, he would have to encounter the evidence of his own remaining sleepfulness; he would not be able to meet that look with equal understanding, to make of the exchange something truly symmetrical and reciprocal. One encounters a pointed example of an imbalanced and revealing exchange also in William Wells Brown's *Narrative* when Brown's master and "near relative" Dr. Young informs Brown that he has decided to sell him. "I raised up my head," Brown writes, "and looked him full in the face. When my eyes caught his he immediately looked to the ground" (55). What is most eloquent here is what Brown doesn't write but instead indicates in this exchange: the mutual understanding that Dr. Young cannot acknowledge and yet does by resisting eye contact. And this eloquence is echoed painfully a few pages later, when Brown and his mother are captured during their attempt to escape. Brown's mother, whom he has convinced to make this attempt, "looked me in the face, and burst into tears. A cold chill ran over me, and such a sensation I never experienced before, and I hope never to again" (60). The exchange here speaks of a world of mutual knowledge and unspeakable emotions—and son and mother are forced to acknowledge the difference between the relationship they have imagined, with each serving her or his role in relation to the other, and that which they are allowed to have.

Throughout *Incidents*, working behind the screens of their official relationship, Jacobs looks to establish intimate and reciprocal contact with her women readers, which requires that she first break through their subject/object mode of knowing. If this project seems most clearly de-limited by Jacobs's cultural position, Jacobs actually works on the assumption that those closer to the cultural center—the white northern women she and Child appeal to in *Incidents'* Preface and Introduction—are yet more delimited. In this, Jacobs acts upon a recognition that is associated today with feminist standpoint theory. "The starting point of standpoint theory," as Sandra Harding explains,

> is that in societies stratified by race, ethnicity, class, gender, sexuality, or some other such politics shaping the very structure of society, the *activities* of those at the top both organize and set limits on what persons

who perform such activities can understand about themselves and the world around them. . . . In contrast, the activities of those at the bottom of such social hierarchies can provide starting points for thought—for *everyone's* research and scholarship—from which humans' relations with each other and the natural world can become visible. . . . These experiences and lives have been devalued or ignored as a source of objectivity-maximizing questions—the answers to which are not necessarily to be found in those experiences or lives but elsewhere in the beliefs and activities of people at the center who make policies and engage in social practices that shape marginal lives. (54)

Certainly, this is a just description of the cultural field by which Jacobs's experiences are contained and defined—and Jacobs can only work in that field. But as she cannot hope to have any readers actively value her "standpoint," she must work towards a fundamental breakthrough in the ways in which knowledge about this field is grounded and constructed.

To initiate such a breakthrough, Jacobs must rely upon the power of the stories *suggested* by the stories one tells. By saying indirectly that which she cannot communicate directly, Jacobs deflects the reader's attempt to acquire knowledge from her text; she disrupts the subject/object dynamic of the gaze, and locks eyes, if only momentarily, in a quiet glance of mutual understanding. Through this indirect mode, Jacobs accomplishes what might be called *deferred* discourse, a suspended communication that first addresses unspeakable bonds, formed of common experiences, between (black) narrator and (white) reader, so that later the task of truly reciprocal discourse might be possible. These unspeakable bonds, formed of the gendered experiences for which women have no recognized public language, provide Jacobs with a possible mode of communication beyond the words contained and defined by the dominant, patriarchal culture, as if to exchange knowing looks with those female readers gazing at her pages.

Consider, for example, Brent's brief sentimental plot about a "young lady" who inherits both a fortune and seven slaves, a mother and her six children. Brent presents her as one of the conspicuous exceptions to the rule of cruelty, one for whom "religion was not a garb put on for Sunday," as "there was some reality in her religion" (50). Caught in the contradictions of the system, the lady tries to act according to her beliefs, and tries to inculcate those beliefs by example as well as by word. However, she falls victim to love, marrying a man who is interested in her wealth. Before her marriage, she offers to manumit her slaves, "telling them that her marriage might make unexpected changes in their destiny" (50), but the enslaved family does not know enough of the world of slavery to seize the opportunity. When her new husband assumes control over the slaves—who had "never felt slavery," but were now "convinced of its reality"—the lady can only admit to the "free" patriarch of the enslaved family, "I no longer have the power I had a week ago" (50). Power lost to marriage, including the power to act upon one's moral beliefs, was, of course, a prominent concern of feminist/abolitionists who drew from the rhetoric of enslavement. The sequel to this story, in which the young lady cannot but recognize that "her own husband had violated the purity she had so carefully inculcated" (51), provides an embodied reminder that one cannot negotiate a privileged moral relationship within the system of slavery. The face of the child reveals the unspoken bonds that characterize the system's invisible community. In this story, the wife finds herself "locking eyes" with the product of the system and the evidence of her own implication in that system.

In the silent reciprocity of locked eyes, Jacobs could speak through the stories she tells and, yet more powerfully, through those untold and untellable stories she implicitly draws from her readers. In the most intimate chapter of *Incidents*, under the decidedly objectified title "A Perilous Passage in the Slave Girl's Life," Brent argues that the reader cannot understand the "deliberate calculation" by which she chose to take Mr. Sands as her lover (54). Certainly, her readers will want to stand at a distance from such calculated transgressions of the ideology of moral relations between the sexes. And yet, as Brent explains *why* they cannot understand her motives, her language echoes not only feminist/abolitionist rhetoric but also the rhetoric and plot of many a sentimental romance:[20] "Pity me, and pardon me, O virtuous reader! You never knew what it is to be a slave; to be entirely unprotected by law or custom; to have the laws reduce you to the condition of a chattel, entirely subject to the will of another. You never exhausted your ingenuity in avoiding the snares, and eluding the power of a hated tyrant; you never shuddered at the sound of his footsteps, and trembled within hearing of his voice" (55). This passage can change depending on whether one approaches it after having read other slave narratives or after having read sentimental or seduction fiction—literature also replete with ominous footsteps and threatening voices.[21] Jacobs's appeal for understanding, that is, sends a covert message to the many women who have either read about or experienced the stratagems of a "hated tyrant," and who have felt the consequences of being "unprotected by law or custom," "subject to the will of another." Her readers' unspoken, responding narratives are likely to begin in sympathy when Brent confesses "I know I did wrong," and to extend in empathy when she claims, "No one can feel it more sensibly than I do" (55). Critics looking at this passage have noted the assertion that ends the paragraph—"I feel that the slave woman ought not to be judged by the same standards as others" (56)—and have rightly argued that Jacobs suggests that such standards are inadequate to account for the reality of the black subject's life.[22] In this regard, of course, Jacobs simply echoes Douglass's own assertion, voiced by Madison Washington in "The Heroic Slave," that " 'Your moral code may differ from mine, as your customs and usages are different' " (50); and Douglass is yet more direct when he speaks in his own voice in *My Bondage and My Freedom*: "The morality of *free* society can have no application to *slave* society. Slaveholders have made it almost impossible for the slave to commit any crime, known either to the laws of God or to the laws of man" (248). Jacobs, who might emphasize the word "almost" here, takes the point still further, indicating not only the inapplicability of the morality of free to slave society but also that of patriarchical society to women's actual lives. The moral codes of this culture—by which men idealize white women while dominating, restricting, and generally holding to a double standard the actual women around them—are inadequate to account for the reality of *any* woman's life. Seeing their own experiences behind the veil of this confession, Jacobs's white female readers could see also the failure of their own culture to provide them with a sense of moral closure, let alone justice.

Moral closure, in the form of mutual understanding and a truly reciprocal relationship, comes when Brent confesses a second time, not to the presumably Christian reader but rather to her daughter Ellen. This time, in the brief chapter entitled "The Confession," Brent addresses herself to someone who neither needs nor wants to hear the confession, someone who understands the world that necessitated and shaped Brent's decision. The reader gazes on as an informed spectator, waiting, perhaps, to see Ellen's reaction. But Brent and the reader alike discover that the confession is unnecessary—at least as an *informative* act. Ellen knows of her mother's past, and she knows who her father is. But Brent's confession still has value as a *moral* act, the act of confessing one's sins for the sake of those who listen. Ellen's experience has provided her with a different knowledge of the world than that known by Brent's white readers, and therefore with a different standard for judgment. "I thanked God," Brent tells us, "that the knowledge I had so much dreaded to impart had not diminished the affection of my child" (189). Ellen, after all, knows the world well enough to say of her former belief that a father should love his child, " 'I was a little girl then, and didn't know any better' " (189). In this case, Brent's confession makes possible the reciprocity of trust: "I had not the slightest idea she knew that portion of my history. If I had, I should have spoken to her long before; for my pent-up feelings had often longed to pour themselves out to some one I could trust. But I loved the dear girl better for the delicacy she had manifested towards her unfortunate mother" (189). Reading this chapter, we see Ellen's reading of her world, an understanding born of experience that strengthens her relationship with her mother. Far from endangering the relationship, Brent's confession signals an unspoken understanding between mother and daughter that both had suspected but not fully realized. Through this exchange, the two give voice, and a shared consciousness, to the history of a relationship that might otherwise have seemed always imminent, always unfulfilled.

Jacobs's point is that different standards of judgment, capable of accounting for the actual lives concealed behind the moral and behavioral screens of reified womanhood, will not come from the dominant culture; they can come only from "the knowledge that comes from experience" in slavery (17). Certainly, Jacobs's readers still do not know any better than to hold to a belief in the natural love of a parent for a child, a love to be expressed according to established cultural codes of behavior. Transgression of the codes constitutes transgression of parental duty and love. Even Brent's own grandmother warns her that her plans to escape constitute a double blow to motherhood, damaging Brent's role and reputation as a mother, and hurting her grandmother in the bargain. " 'Nobody,' " her grandmother informs her, " 'respects a mother who forsakes her children' " (91). Aware of this, and in spite of the rewards of her confession to her daughter, Brent still hesitates when the time comes to tell the reader. She knows that the white reader's judgment, even when directed at the system of slavery, necessarily encompasses herself as well. But as Brent, writing "only that whereof I know," describes the "all-pervading corruption produced by slavery," her readers may find themselves encompassed by their own standards of judgment, wondering who has forsaken whose children. For the sins enabled by slavery are both individual and systemic, extending beyond individual families to pervert the roles and relationships that give meaning to the *concept* of family: "It makes the white fathers cruel and sensual; the sons violent and licentious; it contaminates the daughters, and makes the wives wretched" (52). Clearly, history has invaded not only Brent's life but those of her readers as well. Brent's point is that she is valuable to those contained by the ideological American home precisely because she stands outside that home and therefore knows it differently than those inside.

### Reading the Fragmented Text

It is here, in this moral realm born of her struggles, that Jacobs works to transform herself from the object of knowledge to a subject of mutual understanding. In this narrative that is celebrated for its frank depiction of the experiences of enslaved women, Brent works to train her readers to read their world and themselves indirectly. For as experience shapes knowledge, so knowledge, in turn, shapes experience; that is, her white readers' "knowledge" of themselves and their world tells them what to see in Brent's story, and how to understand it. White readers must learn to read their way out of the self-fulfilling prophecies of racialized knowledge and into the world of Brent's experience. This, of course, requires a heightened state of self-consciousness, which Brent encourages by emphasizing the necessity of considering one's response to Brent's confessions. For example, when she meets with Mr. Durham in Philadelphia, Brent "frankly" tells him of her life, noting that "it was painful for me to do it; but I would not deceive him" (160). Mr. Durham's response is significant, the last word of which burns Brent "like coals of fire": " 'Your straightforward answers do you credit; but don't answer every body so openly. It might give some heartless people a pretext for treating you with contempt' " (160–61). As Jacobs makes painfully clear, this advice still stood as she wrote this narrative.

Equally clear was the extent to which apparently straightforward discourse could prove threatening. When Brent looks to recover her daughter, who is staying with Mrs. Hobbs, she makes a point of noting that she had to contrive a story to present in her note. It was important, she emphasizes, that no one know that she had recently arrived from the

South, "for that would involve the suspicion," she explains to the reader, "of my having been harbored there, and might bring trouble, if not ruin, on several people" (165). And having thus presented this reading of the cultural text, Brent explains the necessity of deception in her response to this text: "I like a straightforward course, and am always reluctant to resort to subterfuges. So far as my ways have been crooked, I charge them all upon slavery. It was that system of violence and wrong which now left me no alternative but to enact a falsehood" (165). Straightforwardness may be best, but experience has taught her when to practice it and when to avoid it. In a system based on deception, straightforwardness can be dangerous, opening one not only to contempt but also to violence. All that is stated directly in such a system is held to the logic of the dominant ideology, in which anything Brent might say is held to be either inconsequential or threatening to the standing order. Brent's security, and the security of her extended community, depends upon careful reading, and equally careful narration.

Appealing to the deferred narratives of women's actual lives, the encoded stories that they can whisper to one another but not reveal to the world,[23] Jacobs draws her female readers into an unspoken realm contained and silenced by the ideological boundaries of cultural womanhood, a realm with its own mode of discourse (for communication both behind and across gender lines) and of knowledge. Wounded and sexually violated by Mr. Flint's words, Brent is "made . . . prematurely knowing, concerning the evil ways of the world" (54); in writing *Incidents* she uses the conventions of sentimental discourse to suggest the evil beneath the smooth patriarchal veneer. But she learns also that the subterranean realm of the actual "ways of the world" has its own silent codes, its own system of relations—the sensual vortex not only of the "secrets of slavery" but also of the secrets of women's experience. The second Mrs. Flint, Brent notes, "possessed the key to her husband's character before I was born," and "she might have used this knowledge to counsel and to screen the young and the innocent among her slaves" (31). Instead, Mrs. Flint carries her struggle to the visible cultural apparatus for assigning guilt and maintaining order: she punishes the female slaves and watches her husband "with unceasing vigilance" (31). Mr. Flint himself, when under his wife's eye, simply takes his violations to the subterranean realm of communication: "What he could not find opportunity to say in words he manifested in signs. He invented more than were ever thought of in a deaf and dumb asylum" (31). Jacobs knew the power of this mode of discourse not only as a slave but also as a "free" black in the North where she lived daily with unspoken signs of prejudice. If *Incidents* was to be transformative, this is the realm it would need to transform, and this the discourse it would need to appropriate.

*Incidents* offers its readers ample opportunity to practice Brent's mode of interpretation—that is, to reread apparently straightforward discourse, to question and interpret the cultural text guided by the hermeneutical map of Brent's narrative. Consider, for example, this one of many examples, towards the end of the narrative, when Brent receives a letter from her former enslavers. Brent copies the letter, and then comments on it, though telling her readers nothing they could not have determined from the letter itself:

> The letter was signed by Emily's brother, who was as yet a mere lad. I knew, by the style, that it was not written by a person of his age, and though the writing was disguised, I had been made too unhappy by it, in former years, not to recognize at once the hand of Dr. Flint. O, the hypocrisy of slaveholders! Did the old fox suppose that I was goose enough to go into such a trap? Verily, he relied too much on "the stupidity of the African race." I did not return the family of Flints any thanks for their cordial invitation—a remissness for which I was, no doubt, charged with base ingratitude. (172)

Note that before she reprints the letter, Brent hints that it is a veiled text, a letter "which purported to be written by her younger brother," but she does not tell the reader that "though the writing was disguised" she "recognized at once the hand of Dr. Flint" (171–72). The reader guesses the identity of the writer, and sees through the feigned affection and cordiality of the letter, simply noting these characteristics associated with the mythology of the paternalistic southern system. Brent simply affirms this reading after she presents the letter, and adds at the end her own ironic rendition of formal courtesy, concerning their "cordial invitation," as an inside joke for the reader to enjoy.

But however threatening Flint's duplicitous letter may be, yet more threatening are those whose straightforwardness serves as simply the most direct example of a well-trained, restrictive perspective, as when Mrs. Hobbs, a northern woman and mother, looks Brent "coolly in the face" to inform her that Ellen has been "*given*" to Hobbs's eldest daughter

(166). In so doing, Mrs. Hobbs exemplifies the limited hopes one could place in the justice that might come of *enraged* motherhood. If Jacobs had hoped to appeal to mothers through this narrative, this experience certainly reminded her how tenuous the power of that appeal might be. As Brent puts it, questioning the very bond of motherhood that she seems to count on for understanding elsewhere in the narrative, "How *could* she, who knew by experience the strength of a mother's love, and who was perfectly aware of the relation Mr. Sands bore to my children,—how *could* she look me in the face, while she thrust such a dagger into my heart?" (166). A partial answer, of course, is that Mrs. Hobbs's experience is insufficient for understanding the very injustice of which she is aware. One could say that she is fundamentally incapable of looking Brent in the face, for she can *look into* only the face her experience has prepared her to see. She lacks the knowledge that comes from the experience of slavery, and she *cannot attain* this knowledge. As Brent puts it when she is reunited with her son Benjamin, "O reader, can you imagine my joy? No, you cannot, unless you have been a slave mother" (173).

Brent's experience has trained her differently; she is able to recognize Mrs. Hobbs's gaze for what it is, even though she is astounded to encounter it. More significantly, Brent's experience enables her to read the broader cultural text from an informed rather then a merely theoretical perspective. Consider Brent's discussion of the relative condition of American slaves and the European laboring classes, a comparison that dominated debates about slavery, and that was therefore a standard feature of many slave narratives. Brent ends by emphasizing that she will address only the relative condition of the two groups, and not the actual experience of European laborers. She does so to contrast her account of the laborers from uninformed accounts of slavery in America: "I do not deny that the poor are oppressed in Europe. I am not disposed to paint their condition so rose-colored as the Hon. Miss Murray paints the condition of the slaves in the United States. A small portion of *my* experience would enable her to read her own pages with anointed eyes" (184–85). Without such experience, one lacks the eyes to read not only Brent's experience but also one's own pages, one's *own* experience. And can we imagine? No, we cannot. At best, we can recognize that we are incapable of reading our world without the "small portion" of Brent's experience that we gain by reading this narrative. We need Brent's help if we are to read "with anointed eyes" not only the system of slavery but also the broader system that has informed our identities.[24]

Brent underscores this need for a "small portion" of her experience not only by reminding her readers that the act of interpretation is a moral act but also by emphasizing the fragmentation of the cultural text. One might take as the symbol of this text the letter that Mr. Thorne writes to Dr. Flint, informing him of Brent's whereabouts. Thorne tears up the letter, and Ellen retrieves the fragments, telling Mrs. Hobbs's children that Thorne is out to expose her mother. The children do not believe that she can be right until they "put the fragments of writing together, in order to read them to her" (179). Similarly, Brent argues throughout *Incidents* that we are faced with a fragmented cultural text, and that we cannot read it until we reassemble the fragments. Moreover, we cannot put the fragments together without Brent's help. Earlier in the narrative, when William accompanies Mr. Sands to Washington and then runs away, Brent presents us with varying accounts of William's escape. She presents the reader first with William's letter to his family; next with Mr. Sands's account to Brent's Uncle Philip; and, finally, with William's unwritten account to Brent herself when later they meet. The first is a conditioned account, for one could not afford to assume that the letter would be read only by one's intended audience. The second is a version of the dominant culture's interpretation of the event. The third is a frank account—to one who knew how to read the situation, one who had experienced enslavement—that deconstructs the authorized explanation. The true account of this event is not the last but the combined implications of all three. Brent presents the reader with a series of conditioned readings, each of which works to encompass, undermine, or otherwise account for the others. The fragmented text, in other words, is not simply a puzzle waiting to be pieced together; rather, it is a series of overlapping pieces that together form no single picture but indicate pictures that must be envisioned.

If Linda Brent cannot claim the knowledge of cultural privilege and education, she can claim the knowledge that forms the contours of her readers' lives, the knowledge gained from moral and ideological transgression, the transgression by which the dominant culture defines the enclosing boundaries of social order. Ostensibly, *Incidents*, like other works produced and endorsed by the abolitionist movement, argued that stories of experience will arm empowered white readers with the knowledge they need to struggle for the right. Brent herself acknowledges this possibility of empowering knowledge, noting that "never before had my puny arm felt half so strong" as when she understood Flint's implicit demand that she was "made for his use, made to obey his command in *every* thing" (18). But Brent shows also the limited value of this forearming knowledge when she becomes the victim of knowledge. Resolving "never to be conquered," able to "read the characters, and question the motives, of those around me" (19), she resists Dr. Flint by taking up with Mr. Sands (whose motives she also reads and understands). Thus she accepts the same situation she had tried to resist, with only the comfort of knowing that she had deliberately chosen, from a strictly limited field, her sexual partner. As the object of knowledge, Brent embodies the significations of both official cultural discourse and the more intimate subterranean codes, both order and its underlying chaos. Public discourse defines her; private whispers surround her. She is the Other that embodies the unspeakable experiences of the Self. In short, she is the fully determined product of the will to know—so determined, in fact, that she stands at the other side of the gate of knowledge, where the imminence of sexual and social violation is brought not only to consummation but also to public display. And it is from this public platform that she gazes back at the reader, locking eyes to begin the mutual task of re-forming knowledge, discourse, and community.

Perhaps, then, the absent specter of John Brown to which Mills has drawn our attention can be found in the envisioned pictures conjured by Brent's narrative. At the end of the narrative, Brent completes the spiritual community by returning to her grandmother. Brent notes that "it has been painful . . . to recall the dreary years I passed in bondage" (201), but she notes as well that "with those gloomy recollections come tender memories of my good old grandmother, like light, fleecy clouds floating over a dark and troubled sea" (201). Her grandmother herself has changed, learning to accept and aid in Brent's mission, and her uncompromising sense of moral justice and rectitude remains to highlight the "dark and troubled sea" that lingers beyond the end of the narrative, a reminder of Brent's need to tell her story after the events were long in the past. Toward the end, Brent outlines her own perspective on this ongoing mission in her account of her stay with Mrs. Bruce at the Pavilion at Rockaway. Not freedom but prejudice marks the "climax" of this narrative, for Linda, surrounded by nurses "of a great variety of nations," is treated as if her "presence were a contamination," and exclaims to the reader, "This was the climax!" (176). Her response to this situation suggests the envisioned picture this narrative means to frame, the implied text hovering above the troubled sea of the world of her experience:

> My answer was that the colored servants ought to be dissatisfied with *themselves*, for not having too much self-respect to submit to such treatment; that there was no difference in the price of board for colored and white servants, and there was no justification for difference of treatment. I staid a month after this, and finding I was resolved to stand up for my rights, they concluded to treat me well. Let every colored man and woman do this, and eventually we shall cease to be trampled under foot by our oppressors. (177)

Rights find their expression in a commercial economy, where equal value requires equal treatment. Power comes with an economic assertion of rights, the combined effect of an only temporarily fragmented community. Brent frames a vision of a day when "every colored man and woman" learns to speak from history, from experience itself, instead of accepting the proffered positions of an ideology devoted increasingly to manipulating human history in an effort to keep divine history, and justice, at bay. *Incidents* indicates the blessed contours of that community, the bonds of which are formed and reinforced by oppression.

# 4

## *The White Gap and the Approaching Storm*
### Martin R. Delany's *Blake*

A deeply ambitious man with good reason to feel ambitious, Martin R. Delany would no doubt feel both annoyed at the scant attention he has received from literary scholars and vindicated by the growing interest in his life as an early example of black nationalism. As a devoted Freemason, he would no doubt be pleased also that his life remains something of a mystery, a series of sometimes inexplicable events, incomplete manuscripts, lost documents, and apparent contradictions.[1] The list of Delany's accomplishments in his long life has become something of a litany among those relatively few historians and literary critics who have written on him. Delany was a political leader who led the call to form a black nation in either Central America or Africa; he was a practicing physician who was admitted to Harvard (and then was asked to leave after a single semester when the white students protested the presence of black students in the class);[2] he formed and edited a newspaper *The Mystery*, and then became Douglass's co-editor for *The North Star*; he was a major in the United States army; and the list goes on, shaping the contours of one who with good reason believed himself a natural leader. Still, in her revisionary biographical sketch of Delany, Nell Irvin Painter argues that this man who is commonly associated with the beginnings of black nationalism held to "an elitist, not a democratic, creed," in which "the masses" were "no more than a mute, docile work force to be led by their betters—their *black* betters, but their betters nonetheless" (170). One of Delany's "favorite concepts throughout his life," Painter notes, was "Elevation," and "the most common adjective in Delany's vocabulary" was "intelligent" (152, 156). Certainly, this is true; but certainly also one must join Painter in giving Delany his due for a life's devotion to what were often unpopular and unrewarding causes. "Never seeking material gain in politics," Painter notes, Delany "lived up to his ideals of a gentleman in public life" (171).

Of his many accomplishments, one that virtually disappeared from his own accounts of his life was his novel *Blake: or the Huts of America; A Tale of the Mississippi Valley, the Southern United States, and Cuba*. Never published in book form until Floyd J. Miller published in 1970 what is believed to be an incomplete version, many chapters from *Blake* first appeared in serial form in *The Anglo-African Magazine* in 1859, and then in *The Weekly Anglo-African* in 1861–1862. A complex novel divided into two parts with many interweaving narrative lines, encompassing life and politics in the United States, Cuba, and Africa, *Blake* responds to the romantic racialism and cautiously attenuated depictions of *Uncle Tom's Cabin* with emphatically hard depictions of the life of the enslaved. Delany's huts are more threatening than Stowe's idealized cabins, the sites of sexual violence, dangerous alliances, traitorous fellow slaves, and even a general darkness that hides the "large black house roaches" that partially fill the bowls of hasty pudding ("Sumpen heah mighty crisp in dis mush an' milk!" proclaims Daddy Joe, who later loses his supper). Readers of this novel witness a child called to perform for white men, forced by a cutting whip to move through various stereotypical traits of black character—alternately forced to " 'whistle, sing songs, hymns, pray, swear like a trooper, laugh, and cry, all under the same state of feelings,' " as is announced by Captain Grason, who adopts the role of "a ringmaster in the circus" (67). This scene, of course, echoes the one readers encounter in the first chapter of *Uncle Tom's Cabin*, in which young Harry performs his role of Jim Crow for Mr. Shelby and the slavetrader Haley, picking up the "prize" of raisins thrown on the floor; dancing to and singing what the narrator refers to as "one of those wild, grotesque songs common among the negroes"; walking like "old Uncle Cudjoe, when he has the rheumatism"; and then showing how "old Elder Robbins leads the psalm"

(13–14). But whereas in *Uncle Tom's Cabin* Harry proves to be pitiable but charming, so that Haley decides he wants to purchase him, and whereas Stowe's narrator seems disturbed by the performance but an inadvertent subscriber to the stereotypes being performed, in *Blake* the result of the performance is that "the poor boy Reuben, from hemorrhage of the lungs, that evening left time for eternity" (68). This is an eternity unlike any that Stowe's Uncle Tom or Eva could know, and a time that Stowe could barely indicate.

The story itself resists neat summary, for if it is impressive in its range and variety, its overall unity remains elusive, perhaps because we still lack the final chapters, perhaps because Delany himself was unsure of how to tie together the novel's various narrative threads, and perhaps (as I will suggest) because Delany devoted the narrative above all to a determined mystery. Delany alters and conflates historical events, recasts historical figures, and he either finished, added to, or revised portions of the novel after returning from what must have been a life-changing journey to Africa and a highly publicized trip to England. Parts of the novel simply don't make sense, as when Henry Blake and his wife fail to recognize one another in Cuba;[3] and then, once they do recognize one another and we discover that Maggie understands as well as Henry that money is the key to liberation, Henry's bond with Maggie quickly drops to the background of the novel. Joined partly by this thin marital thread and partly by suggestions of an organized body of blacks preparing to strike against slavery, the relation between the first half of the novel (set mainly in the United States) and the second half (set primarily in Cuba and Africa) still is not entirely clear and remains unresolved—providing chapter 74, the last chapter by default, with a Melvillian, ominous ending: "Woe be unto those devils of whites, I say!" (313).

The novel's general design and purpose, though, are clear enough, and were announced at the initial publication of a few of its chapters in *The Anglo-African Magazine* in January 1859:[4]

> This work differs essentially from all others heretofore published. It not only shows the combined political and commercial interests that unite the North and South, but gives in the most familiar manner the formidable understanding among the slaves throughout the United States and Cuba. The scene is laid in Mississippi, the plot extending into Cuba; the Hero being an educated West India black, who deprived of his liberty by fraud when young, and brought to the United States,

in maturer age, at the instance of his wife being sold from him, sought revenge through the medium of a deep laid secret organization. (20)

In this prospectus, we have a vision of the novel that is decidedly suggestive and ambiguous—appropriate enough for an advertisement. The teasing promise of "the formidable understanding among the slaves throughout the United States and Cuba" and of "a deep laid secret organization" capture well the spirit of this novel. For what is finally most striking about the work is its air of mystery, of secrets suggested but untold, and of an organization powerful because it is, in fact, and will remain, a secret. My purpose here is not to try to guess at those secrets but rather to examine the cultural strategies behind Delany's assertion of secrecy, and the philosophical framework that informs those strategies.

In this novel, Delany creates a world that doesn't yet exist, a unified black community committed to a coherent philosophical framework. The materials for this framework he draws from the dominant culture itself: the loosely constructed and unstable ideological and discursive structures used to both justify and obscure the pervading presence and influence of the system of slavery. In *Blake*, Delany responds to a nation, as he puts it in *The Condition, Elevation, Emigration, and Destiny of the Colored People of the United States* (1852), "untrue to her trust and unfaithful to her professed principles of republican equality," a nation that has transformed "a large portion of her native born countrymen" into "nonentities among the citizens, and excrescences on the body politic—a mere dreg in community" (*The Condition* 14). But Delany does not advocate a simple resistance to clear injustice, for he recognizes that the power structure is all-encompassing and has influenced the minds and self-perceptions of the black community itself. What must be recognized, he argues, is not only the dominance of this culture but also the fact that it works, that it creates the individuals it perceives. "The degradation of the slave parent has been entailed upon the child," he argues, "induced by the subtle policy of the oppressor" in "a system of regular submission and servitude, menialism and dependence, until it has become almost a physiological function of our system, an actual condition of our nature" (*The Condition* 47–48).[5] To argue against the oppressors that surround is one thing; and to work against the influence of oppression within is another.

Accordingly, Delany's strategy in this novel is similar to that of his protagonist Blake, who declares, "I'll do anything not morally wrong, to gain our freedom; and to effect this, we must take the slaves, not as we wish them to be, but as we really find them to be" (*Blake* 126). This is not merely the rhetoric of communal unity, for when Delany himself looks beyond the slaves to the northern "free" blacks in *The Condition*, he also takes them as he finds them to be, and the news is not good:

> White men are producers—we are consumers. They build houses, and we rent them. They raise produce, and we consume it. They manufacture clothes and wares, and we garnish ourselves with them. They build coaches, vessels, cars, hotels, saloons, and other vehicles and places of accommodation, and we deliberately wait until they have got them in readiness, then walk in, and contend with as much assurance for a "right," as though the whole thing was bought, paid for, and belonged to us. (*The Condition* 45)

In the face of such material forms of domination, Delany argued, "moral theories" and "speculations" are not enough; "the *practical* application of principles adduced," he argued, "the thing carried out, is the only true and proper course to pursue" (*The Condition* 41). Although he holds to an intricate moral framework informed by belief and submission to a deity, Delany argues that professions of religion and moral convictions do not fundamentally alter the position of the consumers, and do not sufficiently address the intricate structure of power and material dominance blacks faced in the United States. Indeed, what is most striking about Delany's view of the white culture of dominance is that though its motives and ends may be wicked, its means are moral. "These are the means by which God intended man to succeed," he argues, and this explains, therefore, "the white man's success with all of his wickedness, over the head of the colored man, with all of his religion" (*The Condition* 45). To struggle against this wickedness, one must adopt God's intended means. "We live in society among men," Delany reminds his readers in *The Condition*, "conducted by men, governed by rules and regulations. However arbitrary, there are certain policies that regulate all well organized institutions and corporate bodies" (*The Condition* 41). The key word here is *arbitrary*, for Delany's purpose is not to resist the rules but to play the game as it exists, exposing the inability of the rules as formulated to account for, much less organize, the world as it is. In this world, Delany suggests, the rules are fictive, a gloss of coherence over a text of contradictions; and by drawing out the complex reality that the rules both control and resist,

Delany indicates a new configuration of the cultural game, one in which black Americans are essential players.

I am suggesting that *Blake*, fiction though it may be, is Delany's own practical application of principles adduced; this novel is "the thing carried out." In *The Condition*, Delany lists the various accomplishments of white America, and among them includes "literary attainments," by which white authors contribute to and manipulate "literature, science, law, medicine, and all other useful attainments that the world now makes use of" (*The Condition* 45). *Blake* enters this field (the protagonist is introduced as a "man of good literary attainments" [17]), and takes print discourse as its battleground, arguing for the necessity of a new conception of literary realism—that is, one that extends beyond descriptions of material conditions to the realities of cultural attitudes, the power of literary representations, and the moral logic of American Christian capitalism. This is, after all, a novel that treats the "shining gold eagle" coin as the "emblem of [the] country's liberty" (135), and argues for the enslaved that "money will obtain them everything necessary by which to obtain their liberty. The money is within all of their reach if they only knew it was right to take it" (43). Redefining what is "right," exposing the inverted values of the dominant culture, drawing power from the contradictions of the discourse of dominance and enslavement, Delany devotes his efforts to his belief that society is "governed by mind" (*The Condition* 41). In *Blake*, he works to create a new government of mind by creating a community of readers capable of challenging and negotiating the complex cultural terrain in which they find themselves, and which they find *within* themselves. He draws his black readers through the discursive interstices created by the dominant culture's divided loyalties and conflicted views, and leads them towards a reconfigured government of mind.

## Premises, Conclusions, and Communities

If, as Nell Irvin Painter suggests, Delany's favorite adjective was "intelligent," his favorite noun was "economy" (156). Informing all his work is a notion of what he would later refer to as "God's Economy" (26), a vision of a providential design within which all human life is contained. In *The Condition* Delany argues that God "has means for every end," and "God's means are laws—fixed laws of nature, a part of His own being, and as immutable, as unchangeable as Himself." Accordingly, "nothing can be accomplished but through the medium of, and conformable to these laws" (*The Condition* 38). There are three laws, Delany posits, defining three spheres of possible activity: the spiritual, the moral, and the physical. "That which is Spiritual," he explains, "can only be accomplished through the medium of the Spiritual law," that is, through prayer. That which is moral requires one to "exercise" one's "sense and feeling of *right* and *justice*"; and that which is physical requires physical labor. This tripartite division enables Delany to assert that "The argument that man must pray for what he receives, is a mistake, and one that is doing the colored people especially, incalculable injury" (*The Condition* 38–39).

Delany thus resituates what he viewed as the misapplied religiosity of the black community and frees himself to focus on his most frequently mentioned subject, political economy—a concept that involves the land, population, and resources essential to national identity and that refers fundamentally to "a knowledge of the wealth of nations; or how to make money" (*The Condition* 194). As he puts it in "Political Destiny of the Colored Race on the American Continent," his manifesto on black national self-determination, "it is neither the moralist, Christian, nor philanthropist whom we now have to meet and combat, but the politician, the civil engineer, and skilful economist, who direct and control the machinery which moves forward, with mighty impulse, the nations and powers of the earth" (204). *Blake* operates in this realm, and looks to realign it to Delany's vision of God's moral design. Focusing on those who rule the "physical" realm, where "success in life" depends upon "the physical laws governing all earthly and temporal affairs, [benefiting] equally the just and the unjust" (*The Condition* 39–40), Delany portrays a world of complex realities and conflicting economies.[6]

Delany argued often that in the "physical" realm of struggle the black race had the decided advantage of being a sturdy and adaptable labor force with a proven record of investing in and profiting from the American economic work force. As he argues in *The Condition*, the black worker is capable of "enduring fatigue, hunger and thirst—enduring change of climate, habits, manners and customs, with infinitely far less injury to their physical and mental system, than any other people on the face of God's earth," qualities that make them, Delany argued, "a *superior race*" (56, 202). Although this is the kind of assertion for which Delany is famous as a prototypical black nationalist, it was not a new line of argument. In 1838, for example, the white Ohio abolitionist Charles Olcott argued that "*In a state of freedom*, one black laborer would be worth more than two white ones, in the hot regions of the south; because black laborers only can endure the climate; and because they have far more skill in the kind of labour required" (52).[7] On the same page, Olcott speaks against colonization schemes, "[t]he ostensibly benevolent pretense, of furnishing the negroes with 'a home' on the wild shores of Africa, their 'native' country as it is foolishly called." Referring back to the argument he presents in the first lecture in the volume, Olcott argues that "By the laws of God, every innocent person has a Divine right, to a secure and permanent 'home' of his own choosing, ANY WHERE he pleases on the whole globe, wherever chance or choice may direct his domicil. . . . Our black countrymen are Americans; not Africans; and as such are entitled to an American 'home'; where God has given them a right to stay and reside as long as they choose" (52). Delany similarly argues that "[o]ur common country is the United States," and that "[w]e are Americans, having a birthright citizenship—natural claims upon the country—claims common to all others of our fellow citizens—natural rights, which may, by virtue of unjust laws, be obstructed, but never can be annulled" (*The Condition* 48–49). Delany's argument echoes Olcott's in many particulars, as when he notes that though whites may say that the black "race" is inferior, they rely on blacks to do labor they cannot bear to do themselves. Reapplying the theories of biological determinism used to speculate on God's intentions, Delany argues that this adaptability to labor and climates "proves our right and duty to live wherever we may *choose*; while the white race may only live where they *can*" (202).

But if Delany could find white men and women who believed in the ability of African Americans to prove themselves in the fields of business, industry, and finance, he knew also that color prejudices ran deep, and that the black success story in the hands of white narrators often took a peculiar twist. Consider, for example, James Freeman Clarke, who argued in 1859 that the power of labor provided the best response to the degradation of black Americans and the best strategy for both effecting systemic change and challenging prejudices. "Colored people," Clarke asserts bluntly, "ought to make money." But as Clarke continues, he reveals the kind of prejudice that marks the limitations of this strategy: "A colored man who makes a thousand dollars, does more to put down prejudice, than if he made a thousand moderately good speeches against prejudice, or wrote a thousand pretty fair articles against it. No race in this country will be despised which makes money. If we had in Boston or New York ten orangoutangs worth a million dollars each, they would visit in the best society, we should leave our cards at their doors, and give them snug little dinner-parties" (263–64).[8] Delany—who had been asked to leave Harvard Medical School and who was barred from securing a patent for an invention[9]—recognized that, high society cynicism aside, money will not talk to those who can so easily dismiss "moderately good speeches" and "pretty fair articles" while waiting to celebrate orangutan millionaires. In *The Condition*, Delany presents an impressive list of successful black businessmen, mechanics, soldiers, literary and professional men and women, scholars, and citizens, only to note that these success stories came, finally, to very little in the struggle against prejudice and for rights. If a few doors had opened, the system itself remained closed.

*Blake* begins by addressing this closed system, the circular logic it endorses and the injustices it perpetuates. The opening chapter, "The Project," places the story in Baltimore "during a contest for the presidency," and the narrative begins (as does *Uncle Tom's Cabin*) by introducing the reader to "gentlemen" engaged in a business discussion. Although they are described as "men of intelligence," these gentlemen are, the narrator notes, "little concerned about the affairs of the general government"; instead, "their time and attention appeared to be entirely absorbed in an adventure of self-interest" (3). For the moment, the subject of their transactions remains a mystery, though one that the reader can easily guess at. What is clear is that large political concerns are subsumed by economic self-interest and extralegal transactions, and this is the theme that drives *Blake*'s plot. The relation between governance and economics is soon made clear in a pair of statements, the first explaining the justice of Colonel Franks's decision to sell his wife's favorite maidservant, and the second explaining why a northern judge might in good conscience own a slave.

The first of these statements has to do with Colonel Franks's decision to go against his word and sell Blake's wife Maggie, who has annoyed him by being "true to her womanhood" (8). Summarizing the slaveholder's position, the narrator notes that Colonel Franks "was affectionate and indulgent," but that he must punish a disobedient slave or "be disrespected by his own servants." And beyond this specific, ostensibly practical response, the narrator notes, is a general principle of rights and governance: "The will of the master being absolute, his commands should be enforced, let them be what they may, and the consequences what they would. If slavery be right, the master is justifiable in enforcing obedience to his will; deny him this, and you at once deprive him of the right to hold a slave—the one is a necessary sequence of the other. Upon this principle Colonel Franks acted, and the premise justified the conclusion" (13–14). As is clear, this justification of the will to dominate supports conclusions in order to question principles; at issue is not the *condition* of slavery but rather the *premise* of the system itself.

Ten chapters later the reader encounters another argument that uses premises to justify conclusions. In this case, the premises are those of the Northerner Judge Ballard, who had "for years . . . been the partner in business with Colonel Stephen Franks," and who had come south to "examine the country, purchase a cotton farm, and complete the arrangements of an interest in the 'Merchantman' " (59). Chided for displaying a more direct and open interest in the slave trade—that is, for being "a proselyte, and heretic to the teachings of his Northern faith" (59)—the Judge responds with clear and, by this point, familiar logic: " 'It is plain that the right to buy implies the right to hold, also to sell; and if there be right in the one, there is in the other; the premise being right, the conclusion follows as a matter of course. I have therefore determined, not only to buy and hold, but buy and sell also. As I have heretofore been interested for the trade I will become interested in it' " (60). In this case, the conclusion justifies the premise, which in turn extends the application of the conclusion: the slave system not only maintains its own foundation but facilitates its extension, encouraging "heresy" to a faith never really held. And while one might view this as at least an end to hypocrisy, it is also the end of those ideal ethics that have the power of marking certain actions, however acceptable in practice, as disreputable or unethical. After all, the Judge discovers here the nerve to do openly and extensively what before he had done in more private and limited ways. Delany here presents truth as the mere expression of an exclusive power. Objects for enslavement are transformed into logical conclusions. As Delany put it in his response to the Fugitive Slave Bill, which reified the implicit logic of a nationally sanctioned slave system, "The *will* of the man who sits in judgment on our liberty, is the law. To him is given *all power* to say, whether or not we have a right to enjoy freedom" (*The Condition* 155). To him is given also the power to use the slave as the conclusion for ever-flexible premises.

Placing the problem of slavery and black self-determination within a closed system of policy and law, Delany identifies the need for a unified political economy beyond the boundaries of the U.S. system. Himself arguing "from premise to conclusion," Delany contends in *The Condition* that "To imagine ourselves to be included in the body politic, except by express legislation, is at war with common sense, and contrary to fact" (157). In that text, Delany concludes that African Americans must form their own body politic; in *Blake*, he works to create the specter of that organized body, building on his belief that the materials for that body already exist, and that they await a structuring framework. Observing in *The Condition* the historical pattern of domination by one class over another, Delany notes the national cast this domination often assumes: "That there have in all ages, in almost every nation, existed a nation within a nation—a people who although forming a part and parcel of the population, yet were from force of circumstances, known by the peculiar position they occupied, forming in fact, by the deprivation of political equality with others, no part, and if any, but a restricted part of the body politic of such nations, is also true" (*The Condition* 12). Building upon his belief in the superiority of the black race, Delany looks to identify the contours of this nation within a nation. In effect, Delany disputes Clarke's assertion that talk will lead nowhere; for as Delany has shown the power of argument to extend political and economic domination, so he works to use the power of argument to create an effective response to that domination. In telling this story of a gathering black social, political, and military force, he hopes to work from fictive conclusion to actual premise—from the representation of a unified black nation in fiction to the assumption of its existence in fact.[10]

We see this promised transformation in Madame Cordora's response to her education on Africa late in the novel. Madame Cordora's confusion begins when the poet Placido argues that "colored persons, whatever the complexion, can only obtain equality with whites by the descendants of Africa of unmixed blood" (260). Madame Cordora complains that this constitutes "a positive admission that the mixed bloods are inferior to the pure-blooded descendants of Africa," and thereby replicates the very position—inequality based on blood—"colored persons" are "contending against" (261). And in Placido's explanation Delany presents again a consideration of cultural logic, of premises and conclusions: " 'The whites assert the natural inferiority of the African as a race: upon this they premise their objections, not only to the blacks, but all who have any affinity with them. . . . Now how are the mixed bloods ever to rise? The thing is plain; it requires no explanation. The instant that an equality of the blacks with the whites is admitted, we being the descendants of the two, must be acknowledged the equals of both'" (261). But what secures Madame Cordora's transformation is Placido's challenge to the assumption that Africa is "unadapted to useful cultivation or domestic animals, and consequently, the inhabitants savage, lazy, idle, and incapable of the higher civilization and only fit for bondmen, contributing nothing to the civilized world but that which is extorted from them as slaves" (261). Placido proceeds to portray the African race as "among the most industrious people in the world," and argues that the "race and country will at once rise to the first magnitude of importance in the estimation of the greatest nations on earth" (261–62). And when Madame Cordora wonders whether there "are really hopes of Africa becoming a great country," Placido responds that these are "not only 'hopes' but undoubted probabilities," and voices what would become Delany's standard definition of political economy: "The foundation of all great nationalities depends as a basis upon three elementary principles: first, territorial domain; second, population; third, staple commodities as a source of national wealth" (262).[11] Africa, possessing a firm foundation, can only be destined for greatness. And with this reconfigured perspective on Africa and the black race, Madame Cordora's transformation is complete: "'although I thought I had no prejudices, I never before felt as proud of my black as I did of my white blood. I can readily see that the blacks compose an important element in the commercial and social relations of the world. Thank God for even this night's demonstration, if we do no more. How sensibly I feel, that a people never entertain proper opinions of themselves until they begin to act for themselves'" (262). Here a challenge to premises proves a challenge to prejudices, and leads Madame Cordora to a new pride in her racial identity and a fuller sense of the relationship between experience and perspective, between the determination to act for oneself and the ability to entertain "proper opinions" of oneself.

In this way Delany works throughout *Blake* to achieve a revolution of the mind by way of a fictional representation of an envisioned black political economy—an economy that begins by investing in new premises. As Eric Sundquist has noted, Delany compresses and freely alters historical events and characters, laying "several spheres of action upon one another" and telescoping at least two decades of activity "into the much shorter time frame of the novel," to "create a fictive world in which Cuban and American slavery are yoked together in historical simultaneity" (184). Through the fictive world of the novel, Delany "projects not just revolution but the founding of a modern black state of the sort [he] envisioned in his political writing" (204). This projection serves as premise, as capable of producing action as the premises that encourage Colonel Franks's sale of Blake's wife and those that encourage Judge Ballard to become more actively involved in the slavery system. In *The Condition*, Delany complains that African Americans, "as a body, . . . have been taught to believe, that we must have some person to think for us, instead of thinking for ourselves"—to the point that "the most ordinary white person, is almost revered, while the most qualified colored person is totally neglected" (190). In *Blake*, Henry recognizes the problem, noting that "we must take the slaves, not as we wish them to be, but as we really find them to be" (126). If for Blake this means accepting a position as "High Conjuror" because the position "makes the more ignorant slaves have greater confidence in, and more respect for, their headmen and leaders" (126), for Delany it means conjuring a new vision of communal identity, one capable of ushering into existence the revolutionary communal bond of black nationalism.

It must be, of course, a nation in control of its own political economy; the purpose of creating an imagined nation based upon a fictive world is to establish the necessary foundation for a communal investment in self-liberation from constraints both real and imagined, both psychological and habitual. When Blake helps his wife attain her liberty, Maggie encourages him to end his revolutionary struggles, arguing that "as we are now both free and happy, let us attend to our own affairs" (191), and arguing also that "our people had better . . . be satisfied as we are among the whites, and God, in His appointed time, will do what is required" (192). Blake responds with a lesson—domestically patronizing—on what might be called the economy of liberty and rights: " 'My dear wife, you have much yet to learn in solving the problem of this great question of the destiny of our race. I'll give you one to work out at your leisure; it is this: Whatever liberty is worth to the whites, it is worth to the blacks; therefore, whatever it cost the whites to obtain it, the blacks would be willing and ready to pay, if they desire it. Work out this question in political arithmetic at your leisure' " (192).[12] Here Delany draws from the discourse and logic of the practical sphere to redefine the moral. Expenditure and profit, struggle and liberty: this is the economy in which one must operate; this is the means by which God expects humanity to "do what is required." Accordingly, white history can be read typologically to determine the divine destiny of the African race. As he puts it in "The Political Destiny of the Colored Race," "That the continent of America was designed by Providence as a reserved asylum for the various oppressed people of earth, of all races, to us seems very apparent" (221). And that Providence seemed to favor the black race seemed equally apparent. As he asserts in *The Condition*, "God has, as certain as he has ever designed any thing, has designed this great portion of the New World, for us, the colored races; and as certain as we stubborn our hearts, and stiffen our necks against it, his protecting arm and fostering care will be withdrawn from us" (*The Condition* 183). Calling for a united effort by blacks to join together in a new colony and new nation, Delany promises, "Heaven's pathway stands unobstructed, which will lead us into a Paradise of bliss. Let us go on and possess the land, and the God of Israel will be our God" (*The Condition* 208). Like many other African Americans, Delany found in the biblical story of Moses the original type of African destiny; in white American history, he found the practical type, the divinely ordained means by which to fulfill that destiny.[13]

The discourse of commercial exchange that Blake uses in his domestic lecture to his wife ("worth," "cost," "pay") provides a framework for envisioning and justifying self-liberation; it indicates also a strategy for undermining the dominant economy. Blacks, in effect, must purchase the liberty owned by the whites, and they can do so best by capitalizing on the dominant culture's bankrupt moral economy. As Blake transforms commercial discourse to speak for a moral economy, so Delany makes clear that the dominant culture's own moral economy has been reduced to purely commercial interest. When the U.S. fugitives begin the journey north to Canada, they encounter a skiffman who refuses to provide passage across the Arkansas River, refusing written passes "peremptorily on any pretext" (135). Henry presents a more valuable pass, "a shining gold eagle," "at the sight of which emblem of his country's liberty," the narrator notes with clear irony, "the skiffman's patriotism was at once awakened, and their right to pass as American freemen indisputable" (135). Soon the fugitives "become so conversant with the patriotism and fidelity of these men" that they offer money as a matter of course, thus encouraging their ferrymen and boatmen to fulfill their moral duty by acting "contrary to the statutes" of their nation. At one point, in fact, the fugitives' pursuers threaten a ferryman with guns, at which point Blake hands the man twenty-five dollars and says, " 'your cause is a just one, and your reward is sure; take this money, proceed and you are safe—refuse, and you instantly die!' " (140). The ferryman, thus caught in the congruence of physical and moral judgment, exclaims " 'Then I be to do right,' " and takes the fugitives and the money to the opposite shore (140–41). In a more promising example of the congruence of the physical and moral realms, Henry explains, as he sends a couple on their journey north,

> With money you may effect your escape almost at any time. Your most difficult point is an elevated obstruction, a mighty hill, a mountain; but through that hill there is a gap, and money is your passport through that White Gap to freedom. Mark that! It is the great range of White mountains and White river which are before you, and the White Gap that you must pass through to reach the haven of safety. Money alone will carry you through the White mountains or across the White river to liberty. (84)[14]

Sampson, the husband, replies to this literal and figurative map to liberty, "Brother, my eyes is open, and my way clear!" (84). So, too, should *Blake*'s readers note Delany's opening of the White Gap of money in the mountainous racial struggle ahead.

The beauty of this revelation is that it enables the enslaved to operate within the closed circle of the dominant culture, to use the enslavers' own premises and conclusions against them. As Henry advises his initial co-conspirators, Charles and Andy,

> Keep this studiously in mind and impress it as an important part of the scheme of organization, that they must have money, if they want to get free. Money will obtain them everything necessary by which to obtain their liberty. The money is within all of their reach if they only knew it was right to take it. God told Egyptian slaves to "borrow from their neighbors"—meaning their oppressors—"all their jewels"; meaning to take their money and wealth wherever they could lay hands upon it, and depart from Egypt. So you must teach them to take all the money they can get from their masters, to enable them to make the strike without a failure. (43)

As Douglass argues in *My Bondage and My Freedom*, slaves cannot steal, they can only take their lost wages[15]—and so Blake takes "some of the earnings due me for more than eighteen years' service to this man Franks" (31), and then reinvests it in his own liberty. The dominant culture provides, in effect, the capital black Americans need to purchase their liberty. *Blake* reverses the terms of the dominant culture's commercial investments, taking money from the practical realm and applying it to the moral.

## The White Gap: Discourse and Paranoia

This transformation of commercial discourse into a vehicle for revolutionary moral reform is characteristic of Delany's strategies throughout *Blake*. One might say that what other antislavery commentators identified habitually as a fundamental disjunction between discourse and practice Delany characterizes as a discursive White Gap—the passage to the reinvention of power by way of the appropriation of moral discourse and authority. In his efforts to encompass symbolically what one of his biographers called "the days when Slavery held her carnival over the land" (Rollin 51), Delany enters into the carnivalesque world of the novel, that heteroglot realm where official discursive practice confronts the evidence of its own artifice. As Allan D. Austin has noted, in *Blake* Delany presents a rich and varied discursive world:

> Except, perhaps, for his hero, who is a special case, most of the speaking characters in *Blake* are given remarkably individual linguistic attention. Their attitudes, subject matters, tones, and even rhetorical and lexical qualities are surprisingly vivid from one to another and consistent within themselves. Classes of slaves are differentiated from one another, as are classes of Whites from ferrymen to the Cuban Captain-General, by their speech. Delany also attempts to differentiate slave dialects geographically. (11)

Delany's representation of what Bakhtin calls "the Tower-of-Babel mixing of languages" enables him to interrogate the official language of national unity—that is, to examine the conventional patterns of dominant culture social exchange against the "background," as Bakhtin has it, of "contradictory opinions, points of view and value judgments" (278, 281). The assumption of national unity implies the threatening presence of a possible disunity; the defense or tolerance of slavery makes sense only because other views seem both possible and imminent.

Delany draws his readers into this imminent world in his portrayal of New Orleans during Mardi Gras, viewed beneath a Hawthornian moon, "the influence of whose soft and mellow light seems ever like the enchanting effect of some invisible being, to impart inspiration" (98). Here, even after the daily warning signal "admonishing the slaves as well as free blacks to limit their movement," black, white, and "Creole quadroons" all pass "fearlessly along the public highways, in seeming defiance of the established usage of Negro limitation" (98). That is, here "Freedom seemed as though for once unshielded by her sacred robes and crowned with cap and wand in hand, to go forth untrammeled through the highways of the town" (99). But this unusual freedom takes place against the background of the "men of sorrow," the "black slave-boatmen of the Mississippi river" who were "fastened by the unyielding links of the iron cable of despotism," singing songs "of apparently cheerful but in reality wailing lamentations" (100).[16] Significantly, it is here too that Blake's plot is discovered, having been inadvertently but recklessly betrayed by one Tib, "evidently bent on mischief," who has insisted upon immediate action, and begins "shuffling, dancing, and singing at such a pitch as to attract attention from without" (104, 106). Tib runs from the house exclaiming, " 'Insurrection! Insurrection! Death to every white!' "; and the response by the white community is quick, energetic, and notably discursive, as the fear of insurrection breaks to the surface of the communal consciousness and then breaks into the pages of the official media: "The commotion thus continued till the morning; meanwhile editors, journalists, reporters, and correspondents, all were busily on the alert, digesting such information as would form an item of news for the press, or a standing reminiscence for historical reference in the future" (107). The clear contrast of freedom and enslavement that Delany presents in this chapter serves, in other words, to highlight the ways in which official discourse defines itself against the threat of insurrection. Against the vision of "Creole, male or female, black, white or mixed race" all joining in unified reverential praise of God and "all fondly interchanging civilities" (99–100), the debasement of slavery becomes pronounced, and the organized power of domination and discursive control over information and over history becomes more visible.

And as Delany presents New Orleans as a world of domination under the guise of freedom, so he presents Arkansas as a world of freedoms taken under the arbitrary authority of domination. Indeed, one might say

that, in this novel, Arkansas is the negative image of New Orleans (the
two scenes presented in sequential chapters), though both are images of
the same reality. In Arkansas, as in New Orleans, there is a deep blend of
race and culture that belies the clear social categories used to justify racial
oppression. As one rough colonel in Arkansas puts it when asked whether
he has implied that "white men can't live without niggers," " 'I'll be
hanged, gentlemen, if it don't seem so, for wherever you find one you'll
all'as find tother, they's so fully mixed up with us in all our relations!' "
(96). But whereas cultivated New Orleans during Mardi Gras provides a
startling vision of freedom, Arkansas—"the roughest, apparently, of all
the states"—provides images of open oppression and naked power:

> Armed with bowie knives and revolvers openly carried belted around
> the person, he who displays the greatest number of deadly weapons
> seems to be considered the greatest man. The most fearful incivility and
> absence of refinement was apparent throughout this region. Neither the
> robes of state nor gown of authority is sufficient to check the vengeance
> of awakened wrath of Arkansas. Law is but a fable, its ministration a
> farce, and the pillars of justice but as stubble before the approach of
> these legal invaders. (88)

Freedom here, not "unshielded by her sacred robes" as in New Orleans,
walks nakedly about, though it is the freedom of some taken by exerting
power over others, and it is the freedom to define or ignore those social
relations accordingly. We are not all that far away from New Orleans.

Working in the White Gap between the social carnival of New Orleans
and the legal fable of Arkansas, Delany relies on a strategically ominous
silence, presenting the specter of black insurrection while also refusing to
embody that specter in words. For while *Blake*'s plot is unified by Blake's
propagation of his plan (continually referred to as "the secret") in various
states and into Cuba, the reader is never let in on the secret, though the
reader witnesses again and again the ritual passing of this secret throughout the novel. As Sundquist suggests, "Perhaps the lesson of [Nat]
Turner's 'Confessions' that Delany most absorbed was that the propaganda of proslavery—its claims of affection and benevolence—was a
strong ground on which to build a counterstructure of African American
conspiracy and terror" (194). Thus Delany emphasizes "a plan for a general
insurrection of the slaves in every state, and the successful overthrow of
slavery" (39), "a deep-laid scheme for a terrible insurrection" (85), a plan

to avenge "the general wrongs of our people, by inducing the slave, in his might, to scatter red ruin throughout the region of the South" (128). The plan itself, though, Delany veils in a ritualistic silence, a conversation that readers can observe but not hear. Indeed, Blake's first presentation of this plan to Charles and Andy early in the novel is postponed first by Blake's own emphasis of the plan's simplicity ("It is so simple that the most stupid among the slaves will understand it as well as if he had been instructed for a year"), a presentation characterized by a religious call and response exchange with his two friends (" 'Amen!' responded Charles"), and postponed second by a prayer. And only then, "whilst yet upon their knees," does Henry impart "to them the secrets of his organization," as the reader looks on, unable to hear (39–40).[17]

As David Brion Davis has noted, "It is an indisputable though neglected fact that by the 1850's conspiratorial imagery had become a formalized staple in the political rhetoric of both North and South, appropriated by eminent statesmen and journalists as well as by fanatics" (7). No stranger to this imagery, Delany was fully aware of its power to create a community by both inclusion and exclusion, distinguishing between those within the circle of secrecy and those without. For example, in the *Official Report of The Niger Valley Exploring Party*, the record of his 1859–1860 trip to Africa between the beginning and ending of his publication of *Blake*, Delany notes with obvious relish the white community's reaction to the 1854 Emigration Convention in Cleveland. Speaking of the convention's "Secret Sessions" and its plans for "checking the abominable Slave Trade," Delany suggests that the convention had done much simply by discussing plans to emigrate to Central and South America and to launch expeditions in Africa. As Delany puts it with characteristic overstatement, the convention's "great gun was leveled, and the first shell thrown at the American Continent, driving a slaveholding faction into despair, and a political confusion from which they have been utterly unable to extricate themselves" (*Official Report* 33). As evidence of the "alarm" sounded throughout "the political pro-slavery press," Delany then quotes an article from the Pittsburgh *Daily Morning Post* on "A Grand Scheme for the Colored Race." The portions of the article that Delany quotes largely concern Delany himself and his "Political Destiny of the Colored Race on the American Continent," presented at the convention. In that report, Delany envisions "a united and powerful body of freemen, mighty in politics, and terrible in any conflict which might ensue, in the event of an attempt at the disturbance of our political relations, domestic repose, and peaceful firesides" ("Political Destiny" 235). The *Daily Morning Post* article, in turn, points to the efforts of the American Colonization Society—which Delany refers to elsewhere as a "monster" that "was crippled in its infancy, and has never as yet recovered from the stroke" (*The Condition* 31)—as the proper channel for black dreams of "all the advantages of civilization and freedom," and denounces "the delusive dream of conquest and empire in the Western Hemisphere" as "an absurdity too monstrous and mischievous to be believed" (*Official Report* 35–36). For Delany, the dream, however much still deferred, was powerful in and of itself, and in *Blake* he works to shape that dream to *alarming* designs.[18]

Delany's belief in the power of a secret organization with its own rituals of communication was deeply rooted in his devotion to Freemasonry. His 1853 pamphlet, *The Origin and Objects of Ancient Freemasonry*, is virtually an abstract of the ideas presented in most of his other writings, including an Afrocentric vision of history.[19] Indeed, as Blake emphasizes that his plan is so simple that even "the most stupid among the slaves will understand it," so Delany presents Freemasonry as a system by which mysteries could be comprehended by the uneducated:

> Whether Gentiles, Greeks or Jews, all taught the same as necessary to his government on earth—his responsibility to a Supreme Being, the author and Creator of himself. But the mythology of those days, not unlike the scientific theology of the days in which we live, consisted of a sea of such metaphysical depth, that the mass of mankind was unable to fathom it. Instead, then, of accomplishing the object for which this wise policy was established, the design was thwarted by the manner in which it was propagated. Man adhered but little, and cared less, for that in which he could never be fully instructed, nor be made to understand, in consequence of his deficiency in a thorough literary education—this being the exclusive privilege of those in affluent circumstances. All these imperfections have been remedied, in the practical workings of the comprehensive system of Free and Accepted Masonry, as handed down to us from the archives at Jerusalem. (22)

For Delany, Freemasonry was a system of moral and practical governance, the means by which the three realms of human existence—the spiritual, the moral, and the physical—were unified into a practical guide for behavior and social interaction. The secrecy of the organization was part of its appeal, for Delany recognized that strategically managed secrecy provided leverage in a world where power was otherwise all too explicitly defined. Indeed, in *The Origin and Objects of Ancient Freemasonry* as in *Blake*, Delany intimates the existence of a significant secret in order to emphasize the existence of the community that exists beneath that veil of secrecy, revealing enough to draw attention to all that cannot be known by those outside the organization: "Must I hesitate to tell the world that, as applied to Masonry, the word—*Eureka*—was first exclaimed in Africa? But—there! I have revealed the Masonic *secret*, and *must stop!*" (40). Not for nothing was Delany's first significant publishing venture, his newspaper, called *The Mystery*, a word that both provokes curiosity and distances those not in on the secret, a word that signifies by withholding the world of understanding to which it refers.

Delany knew the value of mystery as an element in the art of persuasion. In her celebratory biography, Frances A. Rollin quotes (from conversations) Delany's story of his attempt to see Lincoln. Told that such an interview would be impossible, Delany answers with assurance, drawing heavily from the rituals and discourse of Freemasonry:

> the mansion of every government has outer and inner doors, the outer defended by guards; the security of the inner is usually a secret, except to the inmates of the council-chamber. Across this inner lies a ponderous beam, of the finest quality, highly polished, designed only for the finest cabinet-work; it can neither be stepped over nor passed around, and none can enter except this is moved away; and he that enters is the only one to remove it at the time, which is the required passport for his admission. I can pass the outer door, through the guards, and I am persuaded that I can move this polished beam of cabinet-work, and I will do it. (163)

Once Delany does indeed succeed in meeting with Lincoln, he switches to another discourse equally enshrouded with mystery and myth, that of the Underground Railroad. Delany advises Lincoln on the desirability "of the full realization of arming the blacks of the South, and the ability of the blacks of the North to defeat it by complicity with those at the South, through the medium of the *Underground Railroad*—a measure known only to themselves" (166–67). If this is the proposal Delany presented to Lincoln, it was, to put it mildly, extravagant in its claims, but revealing in its strategy.[20]

Delany's mysteries and secrets played into the very fears of organized black resistance and mystified black identity against which the dominant culture's discourse of power drew its meaning. In *Blake*, these mysteries exist in the "White Gap" of official discourse, in the carnivalesque realm where the usual social codes are disrupted and redefined, a realm of underlying realities and indirect modes of communication. Delany portrays a nation whose culture has become dysfunctional, veiling its realities beneath an increasingly artificial system of social control, and losing its ability to ensure stable social communication and social interaction. There are two major lines of communication in this novel. The first is what I have called the discourse of power, or what might be called "official discourse," which functions through control over the media. The second is *unofficial* discourse, represented by illegal economic exchanges (as in the *Merchantman* deal that opens the novel), joking acknowledgements of actual social and extralegal relations (as in the conversations among the whites in Arkansas), and—perhaps most tellingly—gossip. For example, the plan to have Henry purchased by a friendly agent so that he can find his wife in Cuba is revealed through a string of conversations: "Having heard the conversation between her mistress and Henry, Ailcey, as a secret, informed Van Winter's Derba, who informed her fellow servant Biddy, who imparted it to her acquaintance Nelly, the slave of esquire Potter, Nelly informing her mistress, who told the Squire, who led Franks into the secret of the whole matter" (28). Shortly later, the narrator traces a similar line of gossip, this time concerning Mrs. Van Winter's alleged involvement in the slaves' escape. Mrs. Van Winter "was by all regarded as a friend to the Negro race," and was therefore "the subject of strong suspicion among the slaveholders of the neighborhood"; accordingly, this "strange story . . . spread through the city as a statement of fact" (56). The lines of unofficial discourse take on the force of reality.

Victims of the White Gap between official and unofficial discourse, African Americans were potentially skilled manipulators of that Gap—and this is the skill that Delany himself foregrounds and draws from in this novel. For slaves, Delany argues, this skill already is an essential tool of survival: "The slaves, from their condition, are suspicious; any evasion or seeming design at suppressing the information sought by them frequently arouses their greatest apprehension. Not unfrequently the mere countenance, a look, a word, or laugh of the master, is an unerring foreboding of misfortune to the slave. Ever on the watch for these things, they learn to read them with astonishing precision" (11). Moreover, Delany demonstrates that the slaves have learned to manipulate this skill, as when Judy avoids answering Colonel Franks's questions about little Joe's absence by playing to the hilt the stereotypical role the culture has assigned her. When Colonel Franks assures her that she shouldn't be frightened to tell all she knows, she responds zealously: " 'No maus Stephen, I's not feahed; ah could run tru troop a hosses an' face de debil! My soul's happy, my soul's on fiah! Whoo! Blessed Jesus! Ride on, King!' " (45). Similarly, Henry is able to use the White Gap in his own service; for Colonel Franks, afraid to admit to his wife that he has arranged for Henry to be sold, gives Henry a pass to go to the secret purchaser Dick Crow and plans to tell his wife that Henry has run away. Henry naturally uses the pass to escape. Further, when the mutinous slaves from the *Vulture* are to be sold, Placido works to "covertly [depreciate] the value of the slaves by the circulation of 'postscripts' from the 'press,' giving full particulars of the mutiny at sea." Prices for the captives are thus "reduced . . . to a minimum," placing them "in the reach of small capitalists, for whom they were purchased by agents, who pretended themselves to be spectators." These agents, "among the fairest of the quadroons," arrange for the captives to go directly "into black families or their friends" (238).

In his commentary in *The Condition* on African Americans' deference to and preference for white opinion, Delany complains that "In religion— because they are both *translators* and *commentators*, we must believe nothing, however absurd, but what our oppressors tell us" (191). In *Blake*, Delany works to undermine this commentary by retranslating scriptures to serve the needs of the enslaved.[21] As Henry explains to Charles and Andy, " 'You must make your religion subserve your interests, as your oppressors do theirs! . . . They use the Scriptures to make you submit, by preaching to you the texts of "obedience to your masters" and "standing still to see the salvation," and we must now begin to understand the Bible so as to make it of interest to us' " (41). "Stand still and see the salvation" becomes an ongoing refrain in *Blake*, a motto of careful planning for the coming insurrection.[22] Echoing here Moses at the parting of the Red Sea, *Blake* draws its readers to another parting, the parting of the White Sea of moral authority. Interpretation becomes a vehicle for self-definition and power, a heightened and organized version of Judy's zealous deceptions, the pass through the White Gap to self-liberation. In *The Condition*

Delany notes with pride that "[t]he colored races are highly susceptible of religion," but laments that "they carry it too far," for it leads them to rely upon unfounded hope, and "consequently, they usually stand still" (38). Certainly, Delany argues, "[t]o depend for assistance upon God, is a *duty* and right; but to know when, how, and in what manner to obtain it, is the key to this great Bulwark of Strength, and Depository of Aid" (38). When, how, and in what manner—these are the goals of the interpretative journey one takes in *Blake*; this is the true Canada of this novel.[23]

## Closing the Gap: The Black Renewal of Meaning

Essential to this interpretive task is the determination to "know God, that is understand His nature and purposes, in order to serve Him" (*The Condition* 38), and the black community can approach this tall order, Delany argues, by avoiding the temptation to "expect Him to do that for them, which it is necessary they should do themselves" (38). That is, Delany capitalizes on the discursive instabilities of the dominant culture. Ultimately, he works to close the White Gap with what might be called a black renewal of meaning; he works to restore discursive integrity by realigning the relations between the physical, moral, and spiritual realms. When his wife is sold, and he is told to put his trust in the Lord, Blake asks indignantly, "What's religion to me?" and one might say that the novel is directed towards raising and answering that very question.[24] But Delany does not look to a conventional faith; rather, he looks to reconfigure religion and recontextualize faith by reconceptualizing moral duty. Henry Blake does indeed assert, "I have altogether lost my faith in the religion of my oppressors"; but he asserts also "I do trust the Lord as much as ever, but I now understand him better than I use to" (21, 20). The shift in understanding is caused by Henry's entrance into the cultural White Gap; as he pursues his revolutionary goals, he pursues also the search for divine guidance and sanction for those goals. What is required is the development of a mode of religious interpretation that extends beyond the purely spiritual realm, one capable of reading the world.

Although he denounces the U.S. institution of religion, Delany does not look beyond Christianity for this mode of religious interpretation; as Sundquist has noted, "Delany clearly puts little stock in visionary prophecy or conjure" (195). At one point, Delany separates the narrator's and protagonist's perceptions to argue against an easy prophetic interpretation of the natural world. Blake observes a meteor, a comet, a "brilliant planet," and "a blazing star whose scintillations dazzled the sight, and for the moment bewildered the mind," vibrating "in a manner never before observed by him" (124). Blake is "disposed to attach more than ordinary importance" to such sights, and to think that they have "an especial bearing in his case"; the narrator, though, notes that "the mystery finds interpretation in the fact that the emotions were located in his own brain, and not exhibited by the orbs of Heaven" (124).[25] But one must interpret this split between narrator and protagonist as cautiously as Delany would have his readers interpret the heavens. Sundquist rightly sees the narrator's rationalization of Blake's experience as "a clear transfiguration of the millenarian signs of Turner's revolt" (195); but *Blake* later presents its readers with unmistakable signs that can in fact be read and trusted. What is required is a stable and dependable mode of interpretation for reading such signs—and even for distinguishing between true and false prophecies.

Blake's renewed search for spiritual understanding begins with the recognition of his responsibilities in the moral and physical realm. At the beginning of his journey, on his approach to the Red River, having killed one would-be "assailant" and facing "dangers . . . staring him in the face at every step," Delany is forced to confront the enormity of his self-assigned task and his inability to fully define his own role:

> Here for the first time since his maturity of manhood responsibilities rose up in a shape of which he had no conception. A mighty undertaking, such as had never before been ventured upon, and the duty devolving upon him, was too much for a slave with no other aid than the aspirations of his soul panting for liberty. Reflecting upon the peaceful hours he once enjoyed as a professing Christian, and the distance which slavery had driven him from its peaceful portals, here in the wilderness, determining to renew his faith and dependence upon Divine aid, when falling upon his knees he opened his heart to God, as a tenement of the Holy Spirit. (68–69)

His training has not prepared him to conceive of his responsibilities in this revolutionary venture, and his duty seems beyond his abilities. Having lost the relative safety and comfort of institutional religion, he enters into his errand into the wilderness with a determination to renew his relationship with God, but with no sure guidance as to how to do so. Perhaps, though, the tone of his prayer suggests not only his determination but also his path: "Arm of the Lord, awake! Renew my faith, confirm my hope, perfect me in love" (69). Blake must become, in effect, the arm of the Lord; a militant and practical Christianity must replace the earlier comfort of professions.

The prayer is soon answered in an episode that should be considered as the interpretative companion to Blake's attempt to read meteors and comets prophetically. When he reaches the Red River, and while considering how he will cross it, Blake ducks into a cove to escape the notice of an approaching steamer, and there he finds himself "amidst a squad of huge alligators" (69). Unable to retreat without being seen, and tempted to "surrender himself to his fate and be devoured," Blake seizes "the fragment of a limb which lay in the cove, [beats] upon the ground and [yells] like a madman," while giving the alligators "all possible space," and manages to frighten them away (70). He thus escapes not only death but capture, and the escape serves "to strengthen his fate in a renewed determination of spiritual dependence" (70). He still faces the task of crossing the river, and "while gazing upon the stream in solemn reflection for Divine aid to direct him, logs came floating down," and he thereby crosses. In striking contrast to the skepticism in the other "prophetic" episode, the narrator here notes that Blake's "faith was now fully established, and thenceforth, Henry was full of hope and confident of success" (70). Interpreting the heavens (for which there are rational explanations) is a false mode of interpretation. In this episode, the interpretive difference is Blake's active role in securing his fate, his physical involvement in the natural *text*.

This interpretive lesson is repeated when Blake fulfills one of his major goals, his reunion with his wife in Cuba. She liberates herself (by purchasing her freedom), and they settle into their new home. That evening, as they tell each other their stories, "the Omnipotence of God was satisfactorily verified and established to depart from them 'no more forever,' in the living reality" (190). And as the narrator summarizes Blake's telling of his story—the story of the novel thus far—the moral is clear:

> Maddened to desperation at the tearing away of his wife during his absence from her child and home, he had confronted his master at the hazard of life, been set upon the auction block in the midst of an assemblage of anxious slavetraders, escaped being sold, traversed the greater part of the slaveholding states amid dangers the most imminent;

been pursued, taken, and escaped, frequently during which time, he, too, had his faith much shaken, and found his dependence in Divine aid wavering. But God to them, however their unworthiness, had fully made manifest Himself, and established their faith in His promises, by again permitting them to meet each other under circumstances so singular and extraordinary. (191)

This narrative within the narrative serves as a guide for discovering *Blake*'s lessons. As Henry explains shortly after this episode, "I still believe in God, and have faith in His promises; but serving Him in the way that I was, I had only 'the shadow without the substance,' the religion of my oppressors" (197). What is needed is an active expression of faith, the recognition that promises from the spiritual sphere require action in the moral and physical spheres.

This is a religion beyond the "discipline" of official commentary (197). When the Cuban conspirators form "a provisional organization" with its own "Army of Emancipation" (Blake is Commander in Chief), their meetings include prayer, and this practice meets with resistance from the Catholic members of the group. Blake explains that the group is and must be transdenominational, joined by "a faith in a common Savior as an intercessor for our sins" (257–58). "No religion," Blake asserts, "but that which brings us liberty will we know; no God but He who owns us as his children will we serve" (258). Accordingly, the organization's ceremonies must be " 'borrowed from no denomination, creed, nor church: no existing organization, secret, secular, nor religious; but originated by ourselves, adopted to our own condition, circumstances, and wants, founded upon the eternal word of God our Creator, as impressed upon the tablet of each of our hearts' " (258). Following the dictates of the tablets impressed within, and following no dictates impressed from with-out, the group must form its own identity, its own discursive practices, and its own mode of religious interpretation. The task—the mode of interpretation—requires the harmony of spiritual inspiration within and action without. Whereas once, Blake explains, " 'faith and hope were our only dependence, expecting God to do everything for us, and we nothing for ourselves, now with the same faith and hope and dependence on God we have learned and know what He requires at our hands, and stand ready in obedience to this divine command to do it' " (284). God, one might say, makes Himself manifest when one makes one's own moral responsibilities manifest. To read God's will as written within is to do, to act in the world; and it is in acting that one refines one's ability to read the text within.

Appropriate moral action closes the White Gap, restoring the correspondence of word and deed, of professions and practice, of human history and divine Providence. This is what the novel builds to; this is the lesson of the struggles aboard the ship first encountered at the beginning of the novel (the *Merchantman* now appropriately renamed the *Vulture*) as a storm approaches and the slaves in the hold get loose and begin to resist. As with New Orleans and Arkansas, the slave ship provides an isolated metonym where the dominant, opposing cultural forces can be highlighted and the will to dominate unveiled. On the middle passage the ship enters into a realm beyond the geographical boundaries that contextualize and normalize the will to dominate, and those on the ship must confront the resisting text of their indeterminate surroundings. During a momentary calm that emphasizes the contrast of the "beautiful crimson sky" and the "black and gloomy gulf beneath," the imposing scene both invites and resists interpretation:

> It was then that the vastness of Omnipotence was felt and realised in all its grandeur; it was then the human heart manifested its most delicate sympathies; it was then that the soul poured forth from its hidden recesses those gifts of God to man; the Divine sentiment of benevolence, philanthropy and charity in tender accents of compassionate regard in Christian solicitude. The soul then dives into the mysteries of godliness or soars to the realms of bliss, when the reflector, for the time, is lost entirely to external objects. (205–6)

The scene, in other words, draws forth the spiritual "gifts" that should guide moral behavior. Those gifts, for those who can read, should identify clear moral roles. The ship, of course, is the manifestation of broad misuse of those gifts, distortions that provide another text to read as the storm approaches: "The black and frowning skies and raging hurricane above; the black and frowning slaves with raging passions below, rendered it dreadful without, fearful within, and terrible all around" (234). This newly restored text of moral significance is glimpsed first by the "young American passed midshipman" Spencer, struck by the sight of the slave Mendi:[26] "Terrible as they might have been, the storm and hurricane above had not produced the trepidation in the young American as did the storm of silent vengeance deeply concealed amidst the fires of the troubled soul of this outraged son of Africa" (235). Struggling between the corresponding texts of the storm without and that within, the White Gap of (non)meaning is transformed into an eschatologically charged version of what Charles W. Chesnutt terms in *The Marrow of Tradition* "a moral 'pocket' " (267), a line of reasoning that forces one beyond one's desired conclusions as one finds oneself enclosed by the consequences of one's own deceptions. The hurricane around is but the figurative gloss God has provided for the moral hurricane the white slavers must face.[27]

Delany extends the view from the slave ship to the world at large, drawing his readers into a revitalized moral economy of actions and consequences, of moral misreadings and divine retributions. As *Blake*'s plans develop, its fictive world presents the citizen reader with a text to read, while also arguing that the established cultural system lacks the interpretive practices necessary to interpret that text: "Already the atmosphere of sentiments began to change, the weather of prospects to alter, the sunlight of promise grow dim, the day of anticipation darker, and clouds of the downtrodden were seen in specks, to gather throughout the island. The signs of the public zodiac were warningly significant of an approaching storm, though a great way off, yet the calculation of the political calendar paid no attention to it" (257). Delany here refers to the Army of Emancipation, but one might take this as the unifying storm of *Blake* as a whole. The dispersed elements of what seems a loosely constructed text are gathered in an image that provides the novel with discursive coherence, joining its local patterns of resistance and its conspiratorial undercurrents into a threatening cloud of significance.

Delany's visions not only of political economy but also of moral justice are joined in the simplicity of Blake's plan—an organization that operates according to the laws of the economy of nature. When he first tries to impress upon Andy and Charles the simplicity of his plan, Blake stresses that the world around will clarify it to even "the most stupid among the slaves": " 'So simple is it that the trees of the forest or an orchard illustrate it; flocks of birds or domestic cattle, fields of corn, hemp, or sugar cane; tobacco, rice, or cotton, the whistling of the wind, rustling of the leaves, flashing of lightening, roaring of thunder, and running of streams all keep it constantly before their eyes and in their memory, so that they can't forget it if they would' " (39).[28] As Sundquist suggests, although "Blake's 'secrets' of organization are never spelled out . . . they are no doubt consistent with the natural rights philosophy alluded to in [this] claim"

(193). But *Blake* is concerned with practical responsibilities as well as abstract rights and argues that the one cannot be comprehended without the other, for understanding in this novel *follows* as well as precedes action. And following the action of reading the novel, one might say that Blake's secret is no more complicated than the scriptural admonition that "as you sow, so shall you reap."

In effect, Delany presents this secret as a lesson not only of moral justice but also of practical action: as the enslavers sow, so must the oppressed, having learned from the dominant culture's methods. As Blake explains to the general council of revolutionaries, "Nature, after all, in uncorrupted purity, is the best and most reliable friend of man" (293). At the same council, Blake returns to his earlier natural imagery, explaining that the time for combined, organized action is finally approaching:

> The time, he impressed them, was fast elapsing, and Nature being exact and regular in her fixed laws, suspended nor altered them to suit no person, circumstance, nor thing. That the time to strike was fast verging upon them, from which, like the approach of the evening shadow of the hilltops, there was no escape. It would overtake them whether or not they desired it, though in accordance with its own economy, would be harmless and unfelt in its action and progress. This period was familiar and regular action of nature which suggested the occasion and proffered the auspices. (292–93)

Nature will take its course, and Delany joins his fictional double in waiting for the outcome. Gathering storms and approaching harvests: trusting in the economy of nature, Delany, like his protagonist, is one "whose hints and suggestions have never, until recently, been comprehended" (293). And in creating this fictive world of conspiratorial hints and suggestions, Delany, like his protagonist, sows "the seeds of future devastation of ruin to the master and redemption to the slave" (83). And the harvest will belong to the just.[29]

When discussing in *The Condition* the hope of some that the Fugitive Slave Law would be resisted by the white population, Delany notes the love Americans feel for their country and their laws, asserting that "Their country is their Heaven—their Laws their Scriptures—and the decrees of their Magistrates obeyed as the fiat of God" (156).[30] In *Blake*, Delany works to envision a different heaven, identify different scriptures requiring different modes of interpretation, and looks for a new country obedient not to human designs but to God's. Unable to change the world, Delany reconfigures the terms by which one perceives and understands the world, placing heaven back where it belongs and finding moral duty in combined action. Unable to create the black community necessary for such action, Delany imagines it, and provides those participating in this act of imagination with a new ethical discourse speaking of a new historical testament that follows the course of vengeance of the old. In his call for black Americans to colonize the Americas and form their own nation, Delany promises that the spirit and conviction that shape collective plans also determine collective successes: "If we but determine it shall be so, it *will* be so; and there is nothing under the sun can prevent it" ("Political Destiny" 206). What did prevent it is that not all agreed with Delany. Perhaps in *Blake* we see Delany following his own advice, determining that it shall be so, making the world he envisioned out of the resisting materials of the world in which he lived.

# 5

# The Education of Othello's Historian

## The Lives and Times of Frederick Douglass

Perhaps one of the most well-known, seemingly representative, and ideologically contested sentences from Frederick Douglass's 1845 *Narrative* is his promise to his readers, "You have seen how a man was made a slave; you shall see how a slave was made a man" (60). In this sentence—placed, as Henry Louis Gates, Jr., has noted, "at the structural center" of the *Narrative* (*Figures* 94)—one can see a perfect embodiment of the carefully balanced eloquence for which the *Narrative* is justly admired. As Robert B. Stepto observes, in sentences like this Douglass "fashions language as finely honed and balanced as an aphorism or Popean couplet, and thereby orders his personal history with neat, distinct, and credible moments of transition" (*From Behind the Veil* 21). The perfect symmetry of the sentence represents Douglass's transformation of what Gates has termed the ethical and cultural "binary oppositions" represented in the *Narrative* into a cognitive and interpretive method. The *Narrative*, Gates argues, "attempts with painstaking verisimilitude to reproduce a system of signs that we have come to call plantation culture." In this reproduction, "[w]e see an ordering of the world based on a profoundly relational type of thinking, in which a strict barrier of difference or opposition forms the basis of a class rather than, as in other classification schemes, an ordering based on

resemblances or the identity of two or more elements" (*Figures* 88–89).[1]
For some, this play of oppositions by which Douglass signals his transformation epitomizes a specifically masculine paradigm of liberation and
selfhood. The grounds for the confident eloquence of Douglass's promised
transformation from slave to man is the central episode in the *Narrative*,
his fight with Covey, a physical victory that Douglass presents as "the
turning-point in [his] career as a slave" (*Narrative* 65). As Valerie Smith
has argued, "by representing themselves as isolated heroic subjects, male
slave narrators also defined their humanity in the terms of prevailing
conceptions of American male identity" (xxvii).[2] Douglass moves, that is,
from an identity defined by difference (based on position) to one defined
by resemblance (based on gender).

But although this episode remains a significant "turning-point" in his
later versions of his life, Douglass no longer promises the reader who has
"seen how a man was made a slave" that he or she will "see how a slave
was made a man." The wonderful balance and eloquence of the original
sentence is replaced by what nearly seems deliberate stylistic clumsiness.
This is how Douglass phrases his promise in the 1855 *My Bondage and My
Freedom* and in the 1881 *Life and Times of Frederick Douglass*: "You have,
dear reader, seen me humbled, degraded, broken down, enslaved, and
brutalized, and you understand how it was done; now let us see the
converse of all this, and how it was brought about; and this will take us
through the year 1834" (*My Bondage* 270; *Life and Times* 575).[3] His
emphasis on the "converse of all this" aside, in abandoning the stylistic
balance of the original sentence, Douglass seems to abandon as well his
emphasis of the binary oppositions that in 1845 informed his mode of
reading and that constituted the relational ethics of his identity as a slave
and then as a fugitive; and the apparent abandonment is only emphasized
by his strange trailing off at the end of the sentence, in which Douglass
seems to go out of his way to deemphasize the singularity of this episode
by presenting it as one among many, one that will simply "take us through
the year 1834."

This revised sentence epitomizes important changes in Douglass's construction of his public identity. Most significantly, it indicates Douglass's
attempt to move beyond a perspective based on binary oppositions. But
it indicates as well the complexities of self-representation enlarged by such
a move.[4] As William L. Andrews has argued, in *My Bondage and My
Freedom* "Douglass [gives] evidence of his intellectual and artistic matura-

tion beyond the boundaries of binary thinking that govern his 1845 *Narrative*" (*To Tell a Free Story* 231). But Andrews follows Douglass in recognizing that to move beyond these boundaries is not to move into a free realm, for Douglass still lived within the restrictive boundaries of cultural identity that he hoped his self-representation might help to change. Resisting what Wilson J. Moses calls the "literary box" within which Douglass was confined in 1845, the more "magisterial" role Douglass assumes in his later autobiographies was still restricted by the fact that "[h]is development as an artist and intellectual was circumscribed by the time and place in which he was born" (67, 66). Further, Douglass's development as artist and intellectual was circumscribed by the very terms of his success in these roles and by his ascension to public prominence. As Houston A. Baker argues,

> the expressive, married, economically astute self at the close of Douglass's work represents a convergence of the voices that mark the various autobiographical postures of the *Narrative* as a whole. The orator whom we see standing at a Nantucket convention at the close of Douglass's work is immediately to become a *salaried* spokesman, combining literacy, Christianity, and revolutionary zeal in an individual and economically profitable job of work. Douglass's authorship, oratory, and economics converge in the history of the *Narrative's* publication and the course of action its appearance mandated in the life of the author. (*Blues* 49)

The question is the extent to which Douglass could control the terms of this convergence. Each of these roles—authorship, oratory, and economics—would constantly refer Douglass back to his relational position, to his reliance on others to support the terms of his public identity, and to his limited ability to define on his own terms the "job of work" he wanted to do.[5] As Gates has noted, there is significant evidence that "Douglass took wide liberties with the order and narrating of the 'facts' about his experiences as a slave," evidence that "reinforces a more subtle reevaluation of Douglass as a language-using, social, historical, and individual entity" (*Figures* 115). I agree with Gates that "[a]nyone . . . who writes more than one autobiography must be acutely aware of the ironies implicit in the re-creation of successive fictive selves, subject to manipulation and revision in written discourse" (116). Among those ironies is Douglass's attempt to write into existence a historian who takes liberties with the facts and who is his own subject; a sociologist who is his own field; and an individual entity whose identity is not wholly his to define.

In the relationship he constructs between narrator and reader(s), Douglass necessarily focuses on what is at once the most intimate and the most public manifestation of his cultural identity, his identity as defined in relation to the (white) Other. As Andrews argues, in *My Bondage and My Freedom* Douglass refuses to align himself with a wholly comforting Christic vision, making of himself instead a "manifestation of the trickster," and thereby "refusing to identify himself wholly or finally with either the insider or outsider but only with the freedom to move back and forth across the margin" (*To Tell a Free Story* 231). In this way, Andrews suggests, Douglass "turns the tables on his readers and gives them the same untenable choices between binary oppositions that the black autobiographer traditionally had to make. Thus the turning point of *My Bondage and My Freedom* becomes as much a matter of what choice the reader turns to, once faced with the savior/satan duality in Douglass, as it is a matter of the choices Douglass himself made at Covey's and Freeland's in 1833–34" (231). The reader, thus positioned, faces not only a discomforting choice but also the recognition that the choice is artificially restrictive, for what Andrews calls "this Douglass-doubling" involves the binary opposition of two fictive selves, two stereotypical versions of the black response to oppression. Douglass is a presence both beyond and within each of these specters—a complex self represented by neither but involved in the representation of both.

To say this, though, draws out another dimension in Douglass's post-1845 versions of public selfhood, the inadequacy of any available paradigm for the representation of a complex (black) selfhood, and this inadequacy is, I believe, what is finally epitomized in Douglass's revised version of self-transformation. As I will argue, in *My Bondage and My Freedom* and *Life and Times* we see an increasingly conflicted relationship between the (moral and cultural) representative and (complex) represented self, in which Douglass extends beyond "Douglass-doubling" to an identity contained by multiple discourses. One might say that instead of a vision of Douglass as neither insider nor outsider, these later autobiographies show Douglass as *both* insider and outsider—and the same shifting that proves telling for the white reader proves threatening to the black narrator. In his revised version of his promised transformation, Douglass emphasizes the multiple cultural forces that together constitute the process by which, in 1845 terms, "a man was made a slave." In 1855, Douglass emphasizes that legal enslavement is only part of the process of making a slave; involved also are the ingrained cultural and religious perspectives by which he is "humbled," the technologies of social management by which he is "degraded," and the physical discipline by which he is "broken down," all of which precede the state of enslavement, which is the final stage of the combined result of being "brutalized." In emphasizing the various categories of his condition and reminding the reader that he or she has learned how each of these effects was achieved, Douglass draws attention to the multiplicity of the enslaving world and indicates his attention to that world's multiple discourses of brutalization. In his closing phrase—"and this will take us through the year 1834"—Douglass claims the ultimate authority of the autobiographer/historian, containing the multiplicity of his world in his narrative of the continuous history of his life. I am thinking here of Michel Foucault's discussion of continuous history in *The Archaeology of Knowledge*, in which he argues that

> Continuous history is the indispensable correlative of the founding function of the subject: the guarantee that everything that has eluded him may be restored to him; the certainty that time will disperse nothing without restoring it in a reconstituted unity; the promise that one day the subject—in the form of historical consciousness—will once again be able to appropriate, to bring back under his sway, all those things that are kept at a distance by difference, and find in them what might be called his abode. (12)

Douglass, I suggest, would find particularly seductive the promise of gathering together everything that has eluded him into a reconstituted unity. Working through his various fictive selves in his autobiographies, he looks to make something continuous of the increasingly dispersed terms of identity.

It is in this role of autobiographer/historian that Douglass looks to reconcile the conflict between his self-representation and his role as representative self.[6] The clear spheres of a moral suasionist perspective provided a unitary model of liberation in which Douglass could present himself as the constructed Other whose identity embodies the moral contradictions of a world professing devotion to the "Christianity of Christ" while corrupting that profession in its construction of the "Christianity of this land" (*Narrative* 97). But beyond that unitary model lies a world of multiple discourses that do not add up to a clear oppositional sphere of identity, and even Andrews's model of the trickster is inadequate to account for the many forces working both with and against each other to construct and maintain a vision of race based primarily on the priorities of power. Beyond 1845, Douglass faces the task of claiming authority over multiple discourses—legal, political, social, moral, scientific—affiliated only by the common assumption of racial domination. Douglass the historian of public identity claims the authority of a synthetic analysis in the name of representative selfhood. Ultimately, though, the self one encounters in 1855 and beyond is representative in its *inability* to provide a center that can hold against the conflicting pressures of the many discursive fields it contains. The implicit narrative of Douglass's successive narratives, in other words, involves the movement away from a clear economy of selfhood to the expanding economy of an ungovernable public identity.

### The Construction of Identity

In the 1845 *Narrative* Douglass presents what might be called a simple constructionist model of society. That is, although Douglass subscribes to the ideal moral order that motivates the Christian religion, his fundamental assumption is that culture shapes individuals, be it in accordance with the ideal order or against it. As Douglass narrates the story of his life, he narrates the process by which he was brought into the cultural system of slavery; when he passes through "the blood-stained gate, the entrance to the hell of slavery" (*Narrative* 18), he enters a system designed to transform him into a slave. His point, of course, is that though the system works, it works only by keeping its products within the gate, where they cannot develop the moral perspective necessary to question the terms of their identities or even recognize the terms of their production as slaves. The central model for culture that drives the 1845 *Narrative*, then, is the circle we encounter in Douglass's discussion of slave songs. Noting the profound meaning of those "words which to many would seem unmeaning jargon" (*Narrative* 23)—words that carry a potential instruction greater "than the reading of whole volumes of philosophy on the subject" could achieve—Douglass notes also that the instruction was virtually lost on him at the time. "I did not, when a slave," he confesses, "understand the deep meaning of those rude and apparently incoherent songs. I was myself within the circle; so that I neither saw nor heard as those without might see and hear" (*Narrative* 24). That is, the constructed self within the gates of slavery cannot understand his or her own condition; within the circle, the experience and training that provide and shape one's modes of interpretation and understanding render the words of the slave songs incoherent, its melodies affective but inarticulate.[7] Only outside the circle can one understand. In the simple constructionist model, in other words, one has a tightly contained identity, and the limitations of that identity are clear, which of course suggests the hope of transcending that containment. Indeed, the songs themselves suggest that not all is contained by the circle of slavery, for the songs give voice to meaning even if no one can understand. One's moral self remains uncontained and uncontainable, at odds with and obscured by one's constructed identity, but not lost. The gates of slavery imprison selfhood and lock out morality, making the central question of the *Narrative*, Are you inside the circle of slavery or outside?

Concerning those we encounter within the gates, the answers Douglass presents to this question are clear and well defined. The central representative of the national system of slavery is Mr. Gore, "a man possessing, in an eminent degree, all those traits of character indispensable to what is called a first-rate overseer" (*Narrative* 28–29). The central mediator between slaveholder and slave, the system's essential manager and enforcer, the overseer was the embodiment of the *system* of slavery, its institutional center. And Gore was the center of the center, the perfect candidate for this cultural office: "He was just the man for such a place, and it was just the place for such a man" (*Narrative* 29). This perfect correspondence of character and culture serves as a social constructionist ideal against which all other characters in the *Narrative* are measured, the gravitational center towards which all others are drawn. When Sophia Auld begins her moral descent from "angelic" to demonic character (*Narrative* 37), she is drawn towards a cultural force that leads ultimately to Gore. Indeed, in a system seemingly based on deception and hypocrisy, Gore is the one who stands true to his mutually supporting codes of conduct, identity, and systemic order. "He did nothing reluctantly," Douglass notes, "no matter how disagreeable; always at his post, never inconsistent" (*Narrative* 30), in sharp contrast to the difference between Mrs. Auld's initial appearance and her eventual character. In his *Life and Times*, Douglass praises Lucretia Mott's character and heroism, asserting that "[i]n her there was no lack of symmetry—no contradiction between her thought and act" (*L&T* 903); in 1845, Gore seems to represent the dark other side of this sort of symmetrical accomplishment, for "[h]is words were in perfect keeping with his looks, and his looks were in perfect keeping with his words" (*Narrative* 29). Throughout the *Narrative*, Gore stands as the ominously perfect cultural product, the "ideal" overseer who is defined by and defines in turn those other cultural roles (slaveholder, slave) upon which his identity depends. It is, I would argue, impossible to understand Gore without understanding the fundamental institutional logic of the system of slavery, and (to borrow a stylistic turn from Douglass) it is impossible to understand the system of slavery without understanding Gore.

It is significant, then, that ten years later in *My Bondage and My Freedom* Douglass again revises the elegant and seemingly appropriate stylistic symmetry *out* of his narrative of the past. Noting of Gore that "[u]pon this individual I would fix particular attention," Douglass admits also, "I hardly know how to bring this man fitly before the reader" (*My Bondage* 199). And at first, Gore no longer seems the perfect embodiment of private and public correspondence: "He was, it is true, an overseer, and possessed, to a large extent, the peculiar characteristics of his class; yet, to call him merely an overseer, would not give the reader a fair notion of the man" (*My Bondage* 199). Breaking Gore from his perfect relation to his environment, Douglass opens for himself the cultural space to step in as sociological commentator:

> ·I speak of overseers as a class. They are such. They are as distinct from the slaveholding gentry of the south, as are the fish-women of Paris, and the coal-heavers of London, distinct from other members of society. They constitute a separate fraternity of Park lane bullies in New York. They have been arranged and classified by that great law of attraction, which determines the spheres and affinities of men; which ordains, that men, whose malign and brutal propensities predominate over their moral and intellectual endowments, shall, naturally, fall into those employments which promise the largest gratification to those predominating instincts or propensities. The office of overseer takes this raw material of vulgarity and brutality, and stamps it as a distinct class of southern society. (*My Bondage* 199)

To paraphrase, overseers are just the men for such a place, and the slave system provides just the place for such men: Douglass here simply amplifies the cultural concept implicit in his original depiction of Gore, extending it to emphasize his understanding of the function of culture in relation to human nature. One thinks of Clifford Geertz's meditation on culture: "One of the most significant facts about us may finally be that we all begin with the natural equipment to live a thousand kinds of life but end in the end having lived only one" (45). Douglass here meditates on the process of individuation—the cultural system that gives point and definition to laws of attraction by providing outlets for some human affinities and not for others—by which the "raw material of vulgarity and brutality" is authorized by a system seemingly designed to churn out Gores. But instead of the perfect exemplar of this systemic operation, Gore instead now stands out as something of a transcendent individual, somewhat unaccountable even by Douglass's explanatory model: "He was an overseer; but he was something more" (*My Bondage* 200).

Both contained and uncontainable by Douglass's 1855 model of cultural individuation, Gore becomes, I would suggest, more dangerous than he was in 1845, and in ways and for reasons that speak ominously about Douglass's own revised self. As Andrews has argued, the 1845 *Narrative* "had pictured its protagonist in slavery as a heroic loner whose relationship to his environment was largely adversarial"; in 1855, "a sense of [Douglass's] complex relationship . . . to his environment"—"largely missing from the *Narrative*"—"is infused into *My Bondage and My Freedom*" (*To Tell a Free Story* 218). But Gore enters into that complex relationship in problematic ways, for as Douglass looks beyond a moral suasionist portrayal of the slave system into a political engagement with the national system, he enters into Gore's world. The point of the 1845 *Narrative* is largely that those within the "hell" of slavery, those within its systemic circle, would naturally be corrupted. Douglass could oppose the system on simple moral grounds, calling on readers to reject the system that will inevitably shape their character. Gore represents the ultimate product of this system, the one that helps to explain the other white figures in the system. For the others are not perfect embodiments of that system; their transformation is not yet complete. Thus they provide the grounds both for moral warning and for eventual hope, on the suasionist model. Their partial complicity in a system they cannot wholly embody or endorse provides points of entrance. One thinks, for example, of Covey, who, although a major benefactor of the slave system, participates in that system largely by conforming "everything he possessed in the shape of learning or religion . . . to his disposition to deceive" (*Narrative*

57), to the point that "[h]e seemed to think himself equal to deceiving the Almighty" (*Narrative* 57). Of course, he cannot deceive the Almighty, as Douglass's struggle with him demonstrates; and his "disposition to deceive" proves an advantage to Douglass, for, as Douglass speculates, when Covey's profitable reputation as "first-rate overseer and negro-breaker" is threatened, he cannot afford to punish Douglass (*Narrative* 65–66). His disposition to deceive is turned against the management of the slave system itself, thereby exposing one of the many systemic fractures—the tensions between professions and practices, between appearances and realities—that serve as foundation for a moral suasionist argument against the system.

In 1855, the system remains the great evil, but instead of emphasizing the nation's implication in the system, Douglass seems to go out of his way to portray the world of slavery as a world apart, untouchable "[i]n its isolation, seclusion, and self-reliant independence" by the outside world (*My Bondage* 160). "The plantation," he asserts, "is a little nation of its own, having its own language, its own rules, regulations and customs. The laws and institutions of the state, apparently touch it nowhere" (*My Bondage* 160). In 1855, what is evil about the system is its inability to shape properly or otherwise rein in human nature; that is, what is evil about the system of slavery is the absence of civilization: for "[g]rim, cold, and unapproachable by all genial influences from communities without, *there it stands*; full three hundred years behind the age, in all that relates to humanity and morals" (*My Bondage* 160).

Douglass's purpose in emphasizing this isolation is not to envision a world of clear insiders and outsiders, but rather to emphasize his own representative role as the embodiment of the possibilities for systemic change. Emphasizing the relationship between environment and character—demonstrating with self-conscious authority time and again that "a man's character greatly takes its hue and shape from the form and color of things about him" (*My Bondage* 171)[8]—the 1855 Douglass presents himself as the product of this system:

> Civilization is shut out, but nature cannot be. Though separated from the rest of the world; though public opinion, as I have said, seldom gets a chance to penetrate its dark domain; though the whole place is stamped with its own peculiar, iron-like individuality; and though crimes, high-handed and atrocious, may there be committed, with almost as much impunity as upon the deck of a pirate ship,—it is,

nevertheless, altogether, to outward seeming, a most strikingly interesting place, full of life, activity, and spirit; and presents a very favorable contrast to the indolent monotony and languor of Tuckahoe. Keen as was my regret and great as was my sorrow at leaving the latter, I was not long in adapting myself to this, my new home. (*My Bondage* 160–61)[9]

In his attraction to this world that excludes civilization but not nature, Douglass emphasizes both the power of culture to shape adaptable natures and the extent to which Douglass himself had internalized the larger struggle he examines in 1855. Both in and of this world, Douglass's struggle to escape bondage is less a moral or political struggle than a contemporary replication of a larger historical struggle, that of civilization over barbarism.[10] Douglass becomes a national representative, fighting not only for its moral and political principles (as he does in the 1845 text) but for the very civilization that served as foundation for the development of those principles.

The central concern in 1855, then, is not morality or politics or even cultural constructions of selfhood, but rather the potentialities of human nature itself, and as Douglass both embodies and transcends his cultural role and training, so must Gore. Other overseers merely fulfill their cultural office; Gore embodies the principles inherent in that office. As the world of the plantation itself is isolated and independent, so "[t]here was an easy air of independence about" Gore, who consciously upheld the "maxim" that others "practically maintained" (*My Bondage* 200); in the "[g]rim, cold, and unapproachable" world of slavery, Gore "was always the cold, distant, unapproachable *overseer* of Col. Edward Lloyd's plantation, and needed no higher pleasure than was involved in a faithful discharge of the duties of his office" (*My Bondage* 160, 200). And in a world where "crimes, high-handed and atrocious, may . . . be committed, with almost as much impunity as upon the deck of a pirate ship," Douglass argues, "[a]ll the coolness, savage barbarity and freedom from moral restraint, which are necessary in the character of a pirate-chief, centered, I think, in this man Gore" (*My Bondage* 160, 201).[11] Still very much the man for such a place, Gore becomes something more by being something less—for he is no longer just the man for such a *time*. Carrying traces of a barbarous age, the 1855 Gore is the embodiment not of the system but of human nature uncontained by a civilizing system.

Douglass's changing portrayal of Gore is emblematic of a broader complexity he faced after 1845 in identifying and drawing to moral closure the relationship between the culture of slavery and individual character. Witness, for example, Douglass's strained attempt to identify the meaning of his life's story in 1855 and beyond. In *My Bondage and My Freedom*, for example, Douglass presents what might be termed a false ending to his narrative, an ending presented not at the conclusion of the narrative but rather at the beginning of the second part of the book, "Life as a Freeman." Noting the "joy and gladness" he felt after his successful escape from the South—feelings that, "like the rainbow of promise, defy alike the pen and pencil" (*My Bondage* 350)—Douglass attempts to make concrete this rainbow of promise by devoting his pen to the narrative of moral victory:

> All efforts, before, to separate myself from the hateful encumbrance, had only seemed to rivet me the more firmly to it. Baffled and discouraged at times, I had asked myself the question, May not this, after all, be God's work? May He not, for wise ends, have doomed me to this lot? A contest had been going on in my mind for years, between the clear consciousness of right and the plausible errors of superstition; between the wisdom of manly courage, and the foolish weakness of timidity. The contest was now ended; the chain was severed; God and right stood vindicated. I was a FREEMAN, and the voice of peace and joy thrilled my heart. (*My Bondage* 350)

Thus ends the paragraph, but not, of course, the book. Indeed, in the next paragraph, Douglass notes, "I was soon taught that I was still in an enemy's land" (350), forced now to recognize that slavery is indeed a national system. Of course, the victory Douglass describes here is not a communal victory but rather a material victory (escape) that supports a philosophical one: the resolution of the contest in his mind, the vindication of Christianity as a guide for individual character and struggle. But the application of this religious framework remains problematic, as becomes clear when Douglass's symmetrical syntax enters again in the narrative's actual ending to identify another binary opposition, this time to describe his relationship not to slaveholders but to former allies. Describing his opposition to the Garrisonians, Douglass notes, "To those with whom I had been in agreement and in sympathy, I was now in opposition. What they held to be a great and important truth, I now looked upon as a dangerous error" (392). There are new contests, beyond the clear divisions of right and wrong and into the more complex realms of interpretation, and Douglass most frequently rediscovers his former symmetrical eloquence when describing those new contests.

The contests continue past 1855 and become ever more complex. Arguably, the story of his life that Douglass presents in *Life and Times* is the story of his ongoing recognition that, as before, all efforts to separate himself from the hateful encumbrance only served to rivet him the more firmly to it. Consider, for example, Douglass's slightly revised presentation of his elation at escaping the South:

> All efforts I had previously made to secure my freedom, had not only failed, but had seemed only to rivet my fetters the more firmly and to render my escape more difficult. Baffled, entangled and discouraged, I had at times asked myself the question, May not my condition after all be God's work and ordered for a wise purpose, and if so, was not submission my duty? A contest had in fact been going on in my mind for a long time, between the clear consciousness of right and the plausible makeshifts of theology and superstition. The one held me an abject slave—a prisoner for life, punished for some transgressions in which I had no lot or part; the other counseled me to manly endeavor to secure my freedom. This contest was now ended; my chains were broken, and the victory brought me unspeakable joy. But my gladness was short-lived, for I was not yet out of the reach and power of the slaveholders. (*L&T* 648)

More modest in its claims, this version of his escape offers a more sophisticated explanatory framework for this significant transition in Douglass's life, and for the larger narrative that hinges on that transition. The question Douglass now asks of God is one that emphasizes the logic of theology—"and if so, was not submission my duty?"—a theology that now joins superstition as one of the "plausible makeshifts" that guide and control one's actions. And in this version, action is the point: the victory Douglass describes is less a victory of understanding than a victory over competing conceptions of identity that lead, in turn, to competing conceptions of behavior. God and right are not now vindicated; rather, the consciousness of right has won a victory over the false consciousness engendered by Douglass's cultural training. Douglass's ongoing entanglement in the slave system, an entanglement that requires an ongoing struggle for liberty and a search beyond makeshift understandings to just and enabling frameworks, provides the significant conclusion to this paragraph. Thus Douglass prepares for his opposition to the Garrisonians in *Life and Times*, now far from the ultimate chapter of his story. While that opposition is still neatly symmetrical, its force is checked not only by the changed focus of the chapter in which it appears but also by the fact that it now follows Douglass's representation of an earlier opposition when he was on the side of the Garrisonians, in a chapter he adds when he returns to this period of his life in *Life and Times*. Summarizing briefly the differences between the Garrisonians and those of the "Gerrit Smith, Myron Holly, and William Goodell school," Douglass notes, "It is surprising how small the difference appears as I look back on it, over the space of forty years; yet at the time of it this difference was immense" (*L&T* 673–74).

Naturally, the changes in the narratives reflect Douglass's changing concerns as his life proceeds; his changing conception of the story he lives changes the narrative of that life, the meaning he draws from it, and the implicit philosophical and moral framework he hopes the narrative will support. The changes reflect also the changing demands Douglass faced as he attempted to assert control over his life and his story. Douglass is, in effect, the historian of a changing subject, and he must adjust his explanatory framework as the subject itself changes. But if the framework must change with the subject, so the subject changes with the application of each new explanatory framework. Hayden White argues that "interpretation in history consists of the provisions of a plot structure for a sequence of events so that their nature as a comprehensible process is revealed by their figuration as a *story of a particular kind*" (58); and one might say that Douglass's different autobiographical narratives are different historical interpretations that result in different kinds of stories. In 1845, he devotes himself to a clear moral distinction between belief and action, placing his readers inside the circle of slavery (and outside the circle of morality). In *My Bondage and My Freedom*, control over public identity and representation becomes itself a central concern, and there is no clear circle to either transgress or maintain. As Andrews has argued, "What Douglass wanted to probe in 1855 was the dynamics of authority and power in each of the major relationships of his life. His unspoken but implicit purpose was to revise the myth of his life so as to make his rebellion against Garrison a climactic moment, both understandable and justifiable according to Douglass's new sense of his past and his mission in the North" (*To Tell a Free Story* 219). In *Life and Times* Douglass tries to identify his own clear moral at the end, finding finally the victory he wished to claim in 1855, asserting that "[i]t will be seen in these pages that I have lived several lives in one: first, the life of slavery; secondly, the life of a fugitive from slavery; thirdly, the life of comparative freedom; fourthly, the life of conflict and battle; and fifthly, the life of victory, if not complete, at least assured" (*L&T* 913). The victory, though, seems less clear than Douglass claims. And however assured, it seems disturbingly incomplete, as is emphasized when this proves another false ending as Douglass adds a "Third Part" to his narrative in 1892. What is clear is that Douglass did indeed live "several lives in one," but while he presents those lives sequentially, I would suggest that they are best read together.

By 1881 and beyond, possible "climactic moments" of Douglass's life were at once more plentiful, more difficult to choose among, and more unmanageable. Douglass's generally less unified narrative reflects not only a man struggling to find a plot capable of doing justice to the implicit meaning of his life but also a man struggling to find and control the life and its meaning. The problem Douglass faced in dealing with this multiplicity of selfhood is underscored in his attempt to emphasize his role, in 1881, both as subject for historical study and as historian presenting that subject in its proper light, presenting both the times and the life *behind* and (Douglass clearly hopes) *beyond* those times. In the "Conclusion" to the 1881 narrative, he justifies this telling of his story by presenting himself as a representative historical figure through whom one might learn much about his times, presenting his narrative as "a small individual contribution to the sum of knowledge of this special period, to be handed down to after-coming generations which may want to know what things were allowed and what prohibited, what moral, social, and political relations subsisted between the different varieties of the American people down to the last quarter of the nineteenth century and by what means they were modified and changed" (*L&T* 912). But he emphasizes that this contribution is not merely raw material for future historians; it has been studied and treated appropriately by the subject himself. "My part," he notes, "has been to tell the story of the slave. The story of the master never wanted for narrators" (*L&T* 912). Beyond material for study, he provides the perspective appropriate to that material. Again, Hayden White's understanding of historiography is instructive here. "A historical narrative," White argues, "is . . . necessarily a mixture of adequately and inadequately explained events, a congeries of established and inferred facts, at once a representation that is an interpretation and an interpretation that passes for an explanation of the whole process mirrored in the narrative" (51). In 1845, Douglass presented a unified historical narrative in these terms, a representation of his life that was indeed an interpretation, an interpretation that explained clearly and well the nature and moral instability of the slavery system. By 1881 and beyond, the interpretation necessary to representation is more confused because its components are more multiple and mutually contradictory. Beyond the simple constructionist model Douglass finds no clear framework for emplotment, no clear moral to work towards, no clear heroes, no sharply defined cultural borders to either maintain or transgress. And he finds no clear method of interpretation capable of leading to a stable and unified representation, beyond the issue of representation itself. Indeed, the meaning of the story told in *Life and Times* involves the tension between emplotment and framework, between interpretation and representation. By 1881, Douglass becomes a historian overwhelmed by his own subject; not the *emplotter* but the *emplotted*.

## The Roots of Identity

The simple constructionist model leads Douglass, in 1845, to a relatively straightforward model of education and of what might be called conceptual-cultural literacy; that is, once one has identified the conceptual boundaries of the cultural circle, one need only transgress those boundaries or stand in opposition to the world within the circle to reach new and potentially liberating perspectives.[12] In 1845, beyond the systemic shell of identity are the more significant moral roots, roots that ground one in a divine realm and that make the struggle against slavery a struggle between humanity and God. But as Douglass constructs a more complex model of individuation and struggle, he emphasizes the specifically human struggle in which he is engaged. And as the struggle becomes more human, more political, its moral grounds become more complex and even relative. In all versions of his life, Douglass holds to a Christian conception of essential identity; but by 1855 he works to emphasize not the divine roots of but rather the cultural battles over identity, making explicit the implicit moral logic of his 1845 version of his struggle with Covey while also claiming for himself the agency by which he wins that struggle.

In the *Narrative* Douglass's breakthrough begins with the combination of a lifelong but vague recognition that something was wrong about his condition (as he contrasted his situation to that of white children, or as he witnessed the physical abuse of his elders) and his acquisition of the tools of a partial literacy (Mrs. Auld's initial instruction of "the A, B, C"). Like Hurston's Janie, who begins with the nickname "Alphabet" at the beginning of *Their Eyes Were Watching God* and learns continually that her search for identity would require "new thoughts" and "new words" (77 & 109), Douglass begins as an alphabet but lacks the cultural literacy he needs to fashion for himself a stable identity. But his imminent identity finds its conceptual framework when Mr. Auld warns his wife that " 'Learning would *spoil* the best nigger in the world. . . . It would forever unfit him to be a slave' " (*Narrative* 37). These words provide Douglass with the conceptual framework that previously he lacked: "These words sank deep into my heart, stirred up sentiments within that lay slumbering, and called into existence an entirely new train of thought. It was a new and special revelation, explaining dark and mysterious things, with which my youthful understanding had struggled, but struggled in vain. I now understood what had been to me a most perplexing difficulty—to wit, the white man's power to enslave the black man" (*Narrative* 37). Now equipped to view his world through the cultural fissures created by the hypocrisy fundamental to the U.S. slavery system, Douglass boards this "new train of thought" and rides it down its interpretive track, redefining his relation to the slaveholder's world, so that "what he most dreaded, that I most desired[;] [w]hat he most loved, that I most hated," and so on, working the oppositions down "the pathway from slavery to freedom" (*Narrative* 38). And Douglass completes the spiritual overtones of this episode by finding in it the directives of personal endeavor, setting out now "with a high hope, and a fixed purpose, at whatever cost of trouble, to learn how to read" (*Narrative* 38).

The new train of thought becomes, in fact, an interpretive method, a mode of reading and of negotiating the relation between himself and his world. That is, like any good convert, he applies the lessons of his revelation to the task of reading his world with new eyes and fundamental assurance: "It gave me the best assurance that I might rely with the utmost confidence on the results which, he said, would flow from teaching me to read. What he most dreaded, that I most desired. What he most loved, that I most hated. That which to him was a great evil, to be carefully shunned, was to me a great good, to be diligently sought; and the argument which he so warmly urged, against my learning to read,

only served to inspire me with a desire and determination to learn"
(*Narrative* 38). This interpretive method provides Douglass with the key
to understanding the U.S. cultural system, the key that he presents in his
Appendix when he distinguishes between "the Christianity of this land,
and the Christianity of Christ" (*Narrative* 97), a distinction that relies not
on some abstract theoretical distinction fundamental to all religious
doctrine but rather on the mode of interpretation that Douglass's life
story both represents and provides. "I mean, by the religion of this land,"
he explains, "that which is revealed in the words, deeds, and actions, of
those bodies, north and south, calling themselves Christian churches, and
yet in union with slaveholders" (*Narrative* 100). To see accurately these
words, deeds, and actions, of course, one needs to view U.S. culture from
the perspective provided by Douglass's experience.[13]

Indeed, the striking power of the 1845 *Narrative* is its success in joining
representation and interpretation in a mutually illuminating relationship—
perhaps a version of what Baker, discussing David Walker's *Appeal*, has
termed a "superliteracy that writes, not in the terms of the other, but in
lines that adumbrate the suppressed story of *an-other*" (*Workings* 43).
Working towards his concept of "black theoretical negotiations," Baker
argues that "the African American's negotiation of metalevels, in combination with his or her propensity for autobiography as a form of African
survival, has always enabled him or her to control a variety of levels of
discourse in the United States" (42). Such control extends from a negotiation capable of reconfiguring the dominant discourse, turning its very
terms against itself, exposing its own failure to join word and deed, and
substituting in turn, as Baker claims for Walker's *Appeal*, "a new covenant,
a new constitution" (43). As Baker explains, "The most forceful, expressive cultural spokespersons of Afro-America have traditionally been those
who have first mastered a master discourse—at its most rarefied metalevels
as well as at its quotidian performative levels—and then, autobiographi-
cally, written themselves and their *own* metalevels palimpsestically on the
scroll of such mastery" (42). This is what Douglass achieves in the 1845
*Narrative*. The mode of understanding Douglass gains from his experiences enables him to record those experiences and becomes the lesson to
be learned from his narrative of those experiences, and he traces this mode
of understanding to the "master discourse" of U.S. Christian religion, the
framework that explains his life and that his life, in turn, explains. To
move from his initial revelation gained from Mr. Auld to the application

of this lesson in subsequent experience and finally to his distinction between the Christianity of this land and the Christianity of Christ is to make the historian's progress from the philosophy that guides one's perception of history to the examination of events in history to the establishment of an explanatory framework that justifies one's philosophy and accounts for events. All of the *Narrative* can be read through this framework—its meanings become clear thereby—and all of the (personal) history presented in the *Narrative* leads to the seemingly inevitable conclusion and justice of this framework.

The power of the 1845 *Narrative* extends not only from this conceptual framework and interpretive method but also and more significantly from Douglass's willingness to undermine his own achievements for the sake of establishing the foundational authority of his framework. There are two turning points in the *Narrative*: learning to read, and the fight with Covey. Both would seem to support an interpretation of the *Narrative* that presents Douglass as a heroic individual fighting against incredible odds. I would argue, though, that the second of the turning points qualifies the heroic credit Douglass might gain from the first, and that together they qualify Douglass's achievement in order to emphasize the governing authority of his moral/conceptual framework. Ultimately, the hero of this narrative is the Christian God, and if there are incredible odds, they are against not the slave but the slaveholding nation.

Douglass's education, one might say, comes in two forms, cultural and spiritual. Joining the two educations into a moral perspective is the great task of the *Narrative*, and one that is more complex than it might at first seem. The first education includes his experience and the tools of literacy by which he learns to inscribe his identity and by which he is himself inscribed. Indeed, his approach to acquiring literacy reminds one of the justice of Bakhtin's assertion that language must be appropriated and that "[p]rior to this moment of appropriation, the word does not exist in a neutral and impersonal language (it is not, after all, out of a dictionary that the speaker gets his words!)" (294). Douglass, who becomes a "ready listener," hears the word *abolition*, and finds indeed that "[t]he dictionary afforded me little or no help"; he learns the word's meaning by reading a newspaper, and thereby learns to draw "near when that word was spoken," looking for new lessons, new opportunities for moments of appropriation (*Narrative* 43). Literacy requires the ongoing discovery and analysis of the cultural text, using the intuition and strategies gained from experience.

But while charting the course of this increasingly literate discovery, Douglass refers throughout the *Narrative* also to his other education—his acquisition of spiritual literacy—as when he notes that he considers his removal to Baltimore "a special interposition of divine Providence in my favor" (*Narrative* 36). Recognizing that others might view this belief as "superstitious, and even egotistical," Douglass makes a point of holding true to "the earliest sentiments of [his] soul" by emphasizing that "in the darkest hours of my career in slavery, this living word of faith and spirit of hope departed not from me, but remained like ministering angels to cheer me through the gloom" (*Narrative* 36). "This good spirit," he asserts, "was from God, and to him I offer thanksgiving and praise" (*Narrative* 36). Here and elsewhere, Douglass works to give voice to this spirit, as when he represents in a single "apostrophe" those times when his "thoughts would compel utterance" in his oft-cited "soul's complaint," one of the few examples of the "high style" of rhetoric in the book, and a passage that he reprints in *My Bondage and My Freedom* and in *Life and Times*:[14] " 'You are loosed from your moorings, and are free; I am fast in my chains, and am a slave! You move merrily before the gentle gale, and I sadly before the bloody whip! You are freedom's swift-winged angels, that fly round the world; I am confined in bands of iron! O that I were free! O, that I were on one of your gallant decks, and under your protecting wing! Alas! betwixt me and you, the turbid waters roll. Go on, go on. O that I could also go!' " (*Narrative* 59). As his direct presentation of this speech suggests, Douglass works to join his cultural and spiritual educations in what I have termed his interpretive method and his moral/conceptual framework, articulating now the frustration that comes from recognizing the difference between life within and beyond the circle of enslavement. And if by giving voice to this difference he finds hope for himself (the "complaint" ends with his expression of faith that "There is a better day coming" [*Narrative* 60]), he suggests different conclusions for those who do not share his frustration. His "train of thought," after all, leads to conclusions that echo rather directly the injunction in Isaiah 5:20: "Woe unto them that call evil good, and good evil; that put darkness for light, and light for darkness." But in a narrative that begins by refuting a biblical argument for slavery (*Narrative* 17), and in a culture that had long generated moral arguments on all sides of the slavery issue, Douglass could hardly have expected all to accept his view that Providence was in his favor.

It is important, therefore, to notice the complex relation between his cultural and spiritual growth that prepares Douglass for his other major turning point, his fight with Covey. His representation of his soul's complaint at the sight of the sails on the Chesapeake—a quotation that serves as an amalgam of various such complaints—signals his developing ability to articulate what before was intuitive and only partially understood. This complaint hearkens back to his discussion of the slave songs, which in "tones loud, long, and deep . . . breathed the prayer and complaint of souls boiling over with the bitterest anguish" (*Narrative* 24). Douglass notes that he did not at the time "understand the deep meaning of those rude and apparently incoherent songs," by which thoughts "came out—if not in the word, in the sound, . . . words which to many would seem unmeaning jargon" (*Narrative* 24). By the time he reaches the sight of the sails in his chapter on Covey, the meaning of words that give voice to Douglass's soul's complaint are clear. Articulated, the complaint heightens Douglass's awareness of himself and his position, and this is, of course, crucial to his successful struggle with Covey and then to his escape.

But literacy itself doesn't get him through the turning point with Covey, at least by the logic of the narrative; Douglass is unambiguous in his assertion that "Mr. Covey succeeded in breaking me." And as he continues to describe this success, he makes clear that his eventual resistance to Covey is something of a wonder: "I was broken in body, soul, and spirit. My natural elasticity was crushed, my intellect languished, the disposition to read departed, the cheerful spark that lingered about my eye died; the dark night of slavery closed in upon me; and behold a man transformed into a brute!" (*Narrative* 58). This is success indeed, and it forces one to break any direct connection between Douglass's acquisition of literacy and his transformation. Having "seen how a man was made a slave," the reader must wonder how it is possible that that slave, in turn, "was made a man"—though Douglass's use of the passive voice for both transformations seems particularly significant in light of Covey's success.

The answer, I would suggest, is suitably ambiguous, and directs the reader less to Douglass's masculine heroism than to those spiritual foundations of identity—"the earliest sentiments of [his] soul"—that had been a part of his story from the beginning. Presenting his sudden resolution to fight back when Covey prepares to beat him yet again, Douglass does not claim the credit for this resolution: "from whence came the spirit," he adds significantly, "I don't know" (*Narrative* 64). But if one follows the moral logic of the *Narrative*, one might well argue that the spirit issues from a transcendent source. Covey's success, then, takes on new significance, for one can see that this success was necessary to Douglass's own success. For in reducing Douglass to a brute, Covey has successfully beaten the cultural training (its directives for behavior, its ethical confusions, its definition of role and place) out of Douglass. But Douglass's foundational point in the *Narrative* is that the fundamental humanity of the enslaved cannot be denied; in removing from Douglass his own heightened awareness of his condition and confusion as one of the enslaved, Covey reduces Douglass to his fundamental humanity. This is where Covey's "disposition" to deceive all, including the Almighty, seems significant indeed. Of course, the central point of the *Narrative* is that the "Almighty" cannot be deceived. When Covey reduces Douglass to a brute, he changes the nature of his ongoing struggle to dominate. No longer struggling against merely a man, having reduced that man to his essence, Covey finds himself struggling with the Almighty. Thus it is that Douglass presents his transformation by this struggle in Christic terms: "I felt as I never felt before. It was a glorious resurrection, from the tomb of slavery, to the heaven of freedom. My long-crushed spirit rose, cowardice departed, bold defiance took its place" (*Narrative* 65). Enabled and inspired by the spirit this time, Douglass finds both the spirit and a new sense of responsibility for the future. Trapped within the circle, he acquires help from beyond.[15]

Douglass's ability to use what I have called the simple constructionist model to emphasize the restrictive boundaries and clear failures of the slavery system provides the 1845 *Narrative* with a neat moral economy; and in 1855 and beyond, Douglass works to hold to that clear moral logic by emphasizing the mutually supporting relation between his spiritual and cultural enlightenment. Whereas in 1845 Mr. Auld's admonition to his wife "stirred up sentiments" in Douglass and "called into existence an entirely new train of thought," in 1855 this admonition does less to introduce something entirely new than to inspire "a sort of rebellion," and awakens "a slumbering train of vital thought" (*My Bondage* 218). And in place of the series of symmetrical oppositions that represent an interpretive method in 1845, Douglass presents a shorter version of those oppositions and emphasizes his long-standing but now newly armed political opposition to slavery: "*He* wanted me to be *a slave*; I had already voted against that on the home plantation of Col. Lloyd. That which he most loved I most hated; and the very determination which he expressed to keep me in ignorance, only rendered me the more resolute in seeking intelligence" (*My Bondage* 147).

In a chapter entitled "Religious Nature Awakened," Douglass presents a more extended discussion than that he presented in 1845 of the process by which he learned the meaning of the word *abolitionist*. Interestingly, whereas in 1845 Douglass emphasizes the word *abolition*, in 1855 he emphasizes human agency in the word *abolitionist*;[16] more interesting still, though, is Douglass's careful interpretation of these words, for he reads beyond the words themselves into the cultural politics that inform their significance. Noting that "[t]here was HOPE in those words," Douglass offers his reading of the grounds for hope:

> I had a deep satisfaction in the thought, that the rascality of slaveholders was not concealed from the eyes of the world, and that I was not alone in abhorring the cruelty and brutality of slavery. A still deeper train of thought was stirred. I saw that there was *fear*, as well as *rage*, in the manner of speaking of the abolitionists. The latter, therefore, I was compelled to regard as having some power in the country; and I felt that they might, possibly, succeed in their designs. When I met with a slave to whom I deemed it safe to talk on the subject, I would impart to him so much of the mystery as I had been able to penetrate. Thus, the light of this grand movement broke in upon my mind, by degrees. (*My Bondage* 230)

In 1845, Douglass had noted that "[t]he light broke in upon me by degrees" (*Narrative* 43), but now he explains how his own interpretive skills enabled that process of enlightenment, and he emphasizes his ability to read human nature to construct an understanding of the systemic struggle suggested by the words. Speaking of the Columbian Orator, Douglass speaks confidently of his readiness to engage in religious debate: "With a book of this kind in my hand, my own human nature, and the facts of my experience, to help me, I was equal to a contest with the religious advocates of slavery" (*My Bondage* 226).

Moreover, Douglass himself becomes an agent in the volatile flow of literacy struggles, passing on to others the "mystery" he has himself penetrated. Douglass here rides not a new but a "deeper train of thought" (*My Bondage* 230), one that leads, by the end of the same paragraph, to an allusion to Nat Turner and a reading of sacred history: "The cholera was on its way, and the thought was present, that God was angry with the white people because of their slaveholding wickedness, and, therefore, his judgments were abroad in the land. It was impossible for me not to hope much from the abolition movement, when I saw it supported by the Almighty, and armed with DEATH!" (*My Bondage* 231). Douglass here joins the hope gained by literacy to hope in God; that is, he reads through words, human nature, and U.S. culture to the grounds for hope, thus suggesting the moral framework by which signifier and signified find their proper relationship. This relationship is strengthened as he moves, in the next paragraph, to an account of his religious conversion, and then, later in the same paragraph, to an accounting of the process by which he learned to write. In his more complex portrayal of the moral struggle against slavery in 1855 and beyond, Douglass replaces the clear moral oppositions of the Garrisonians with the more militant moral agency necessary for political and physical battle. His emphasis shifts from abstract morality to human agency—to his struggle against human nature uncontained and unleashed, and against a culture that provides human nature with the threatening authority.

This shift is revealed, for example, in Douglass's changing presentations of Sandy Jenkins's attempt to protect him with a magic root. In 1845, Douglass rather carefully distances himself from any belief in the power of the root. He takes the root to please Sandy, and although Covey's subsequent "singular conduct" "really made me begin to think that there was something in the *root*," he quickly notes that Covey's conduct is better explained by the fact that it is Sunday (*Narrative* 63). The power of religion over Covey's conduct leads Douglass to a refiguration of the word *root*, applying it now, I would suggest, to the spiritual essence that joins all in a common humanity: "[H]ad it been on any other day than Sunday," he notes with tongue in cheek, "I could have attributed the conduct to no other cause than the influence of that root; and as it was, I was half inclined to think the *root* to be something more than I at first had taken it to be" (*Narrative* 63). From "that root" to the italicized "*root*," Douglass here prepares for his description of the day *after* the Sabbath, when "the virtue of the *root* was fully tested" (*Narrative* 64). Of course, Covey's behavior that day shows that his habits of deception have separated him from his own roots; Douglass, more firmly planted, prevails.

In 1855, Douglass's initial response to Sandy's advice is at once more explicit and more ambiguous. Noting that he is putting Sandy's "thoughts in my own language," Douglass presents Sandy as "a genuine African" and representative of a "system for which I have no name" (*My Bondage* 280). He notes that "all this talk about the root, was, to me, very absurd and ridiculous, if not positively sinful"; and, as before, he takes the root "to please [Sandy], rather than from any conviction of its excellence" (*My Bondage* 281). But he presents Sandy also as "the good Samaritan" who had, "almost providentially, found me, and helped me when I could not help myself." "[H]ow did I know," Douglass wonders, "but that the hand of the Lord was in it?" (*My Bondage* 281). The root here almost begins to embody a transcultural spiritual power; and he ends these reflections by noting, "I saw in Sandy too deep an insight into human nature, with all his superstition, not to have respect for his advice; and perhaps, too, a slight gleam or shadow of his superstition had fallen upon me" (*My Bondage* 281). Ultimately, Douglass is still careful to distance himself from any "ignorance" or "superstition" (*My Bondage* 298); but he is careful also to distance himself from his own religious training at the time.[17] The two false faiths blend together, offering Douglass a courage the source of which remains somewhat ambiguous.[18] Douglass presents a similar blending when he explains, again with tongue in cheek, the change in Covey's behavior from Sunday to Monday: "All went well with me till Monday morning; and then, whether the root had lost its virtue, or whether my tormentor had gone deeper into the black art than myself, (as was sometimes said of him,) or whether he had obtained a special indulgence, for his faithful Sabbath day's worship, it is not necessary for me to know, or to inform the reader; but, this much I *may* say,—the pious and benignant smile which graced Covey's face on *Sunday*, wholly disappeared on *Monday*" (*My Bondage* 282). Douglass here deconstructs all theology, applying it freely to explain behavior that needs no explanation, showing both how much and how little theology, in whatever form, can come to.[19]

But the transcultural blend signals the impetus for Douglass's own self-transformation; for the recognition of falsely grounded conceptual frameworks that a comparative view enables prepares the reader to understand how exactly Douglass finds the spirit and the will to resist Covey. For, in *My Bondage and My Freedom*, the spirit and will are unambiguously Douglass's, and he finds them by willfully transcending his cultural training. Douglass now notes that he had resolved on Sunday to resist should Covey decide to beat him on Monday, and he explains as well how this Sunday decision was possible: "My religious views on the subject of resisting my master, had suffered a serious shock, by the savage persecution to which I had been subjected, and my hands were no longer tied by my religion. Master Thomas's indifference had severed the last link. I had now to this extent 'backslidden' from this point in the slave's religious creed; and I soon had occasion to make my fallen state known to my Sunday-pious brother, Covey" (*My Bondage* 282). Douglass here indicates that he must lose his religion to regain his faith; more broadly, he must forget his cultural roots to regain his spiritual roots, which, as with Delany, involves assuming responsibility for his fate in the physical realm. "I now forgot my *roots*," he exclaims in a new twist on the word, "and remembered my pledge to *stand up in my own defense*" (*My Bondage* 283). The contest, now presented in greater detail, still leads to "a resurrection from the dark and pestiferous tomb of slavery," though now the resurrection concludes in a "heaven" of only "comparative freedom" (*My Bondage* 286). The spirit responsible for this resurrection is his own "long-cowed spirit" which has been "roused to an attitude of manly independence" (*My Bondage* 286). And with the resurrection comes moral responsibility to continue the struggle, for "[a] man, without force, is without the essential dignity of humanity. Human nature is so constituted, that it cannot *honor* a helpless man, although it can *pity* him; and even this it cannot do long, if the signs of power do not arise" (*My Bondage* 286). The chapter ends by noting subsequent struggles against "always unsuccessful" attempts to whip Douglass (*My Bondage* 287). More significantly, the chapter ends with that increasingly prominent African-American motto borrowed from Byron's *Childe Harold's Pilgrimage*: "Hereditary bondmen, know ye not / Who would be free, themselves must strike the blow?" (*My Bondage* 287).[20] Cultural training stripped away, one discovers now that the divine spirit awaits rather than creates its revolutionary embodiment. Those who see the 1845 *Narrative* as a masculinist paradigm of struggle, in other words, might better look to *My Bondage and My Freedom* and *Life and Times*, as Douglass emphasizes his own agency in his struggles, and consequently faces more directly the terms of his identity.

## The Performance of Identity

Embodying that spirit became more difficult as times changed and as Douglass's own public role and attendant responsibilities became more complex. Douglass found himself in positions no black American had occupied. Morevover, he found himself in battles that could not be identified in specifically moral terms (though Douglass and others sometimes tried to do so); that could not be wholly lost or won; and in which one could not readily identify, anticipate, or respond to one's allies and enemies. Increasingly, Douglass seems uncertain about the terms of his identity within this world and unable to define any other terms. He can only play his role nobly and well, hoping to bring to the part something of himself, something beyond the script. Indeed, in *Life and Times* Douglass presents his public role as a kind of ongoing performance upon the cultural stage, a performance by which he hopes to negotiate a celebrated identity above and beyond the cultural scripts available to him, as a celebrated actor might transcend his or her individual roles. In *Life and Times*, that is, the antislavery-advocate-turned-historian takes history to the theater, where social tensions and historical transitions can be scripted in the performance of this public actor.

Moreover, Douglass found it difficult to emphasize the universal spirit, for his world insisted on focusing not on the spirit in black Americans but rather on the black embodiment of that spirit, the body that was under increasing scrutiny by racialized science and social politics. In *Life and Times*, discussing the "vast changes" in his world and in his own public role at the end of the Civil War, Douglass notes that "[t]hough slavery was abolished, the wrongs of my people were not ended. Though they were not slaves, they were not yet quite free. No man can be truly free whose liberty is dependent upon the thought, feeling, and action of others, and who has himself no means in his own hands for guarding, protecting, defending, and maintaining that liberty" (*L&T* 815). As he moves from the narrative of his life to the more complex story of his bondage and his freedom and finally to the much more encompassing story of his life and times, Douglass's experience takes him far "beyond the boundaries of binary thinking that govern his 1845 *Narrative*," as Andrews has noted (*To Tell a Free Story* 231). Like Henry Adams, Douglass finds himself in a world of multiplicity, and his struggle to define his life and his public world within that multiple world is more challenging than Adams's own struggle. The most famous black representative of his time, and a public figure constantly subjected to the cultural gaze,[21] Douglass can no longer rely on a simple constructionist model of culture and identity, one capable of providing him with the relative moral comfort of an outsider or even of a man who is securely and unjustly constructed. Time and time again, he rediscovers that he remains at least partially "dependent upon the thought, feeling, and action of others," and that the task of "guarding, protecting, defending, and maintaining" not only his liberty but also his public identity requires increasingly complex tools (*L&T* 815). As he faces controversy in his relation to Harriet Beecher Stowe, to John Brown, to the Freedmen's Bank, to the subject of postwar black migration northward, to presidents and politicians, and generally to both white and black opinions and expectations, Douglass finds himself in a world in which there are few clear moral choices, and no clear insiders and outsiders.[22]

As Douglass continues the ongoing narration of his life, his central task is to recreate a unified identity—a secure public role, representative but still independent—from the world of multiplicity he faces. The task involves, of course, making sense of the world that produced him. As Adams writes in *The Education of Henry Adams*, "Every man with self-respect enough to become effective, if only as a machine, has had to account to himself for himself somehow, and to invent a formula of his own for his universe, if the standard formulas failed" (472). But for Douglass, the standard formulas for defining racial identity did not fail to linger, develop, or otherwise maintain their practical power over experience. His own "education" had been a lesson in multiplicity and complexity. At one time presented by a white antislavery colleague as a " 'graduate from the peculiar institution, with my diploma written on my back' " (*L&T* 661),[23] Douglass then passes through "the hard school of adversity" in his initial three-year experience as a northern laborer (*L&T* 661); he proceeds to the school of Garrisonianism, which he could call by 1852 "a school which has many good qualities, but a school *too* narrow in its philosophy and too bigoted in spirit to do justice to any who venture to differ from it" (qtd. in Andrews, *To Tell a Free Story* 216); and he graduates from that school by entering a new one, "the best school possible for me," his experience with the *North Star* (*L&T* 708). But there was always another school and new but familiar lessons. As his narrative proceeds, each liberation from some cultural form of bondage and racial inscription is displaced by another sphere of construction, and the spheres by which he finds himself contained are not concentric or even distinct circles but overlapping circles. There is always another discourse to appropriate, to account for, and to be appropriated by. In *The Education*, Adams views himself as "a manikin on which the toilet of education is to be draped in order to show the fit or figure"; "[t]he object of study," Adams asserts, "is the garment, not the figure" (xxx). Douglass often seems uncomfortable with the garments of education he is forced to wear, and he follows the story of his life to a discomforting conclusion, as if completing his narrative of transformation begun in the 1845 *Narrative* by showing his readers how he was transformed from slave to man to manikin. Whereas Adams argues that the "young man" who is "the subject of education" is "a certain form of energy," and that "the object to be gained is economy of his force" (xxx), Douglass—always engaged in the task of transforming once again object into subject—seems to suffer from a dispersal of force that requires an ever-expanding economy.

Indeed, in the opening pages of his 1892 supplement to *Life and Times*, Douglass explains that he has returned to the task of telling his story reluctantly, having left it behind with a "sense of relief as might be felt by a weary and over-burdened traveler when arrived at the desired end of a long journey." The journey is not over, for he finds himself "summoned again by the popular voice, and by what is called the Negro problem, to come a second time upon the witness stand and give evidence upon disputed points concerning myself and my emancipated brothers and sisters who, though free, are yet oppressed and are in as much need of an advocate as before they were set free" (*L&T* 939). But such advocacy is complicated by the fact that the evidence he has given before—which itself should have been unnecessary—has been ignored, and Douglass now faces increasingly explicit charges against the race, and must confront the kind of evidence now considered admissible. For "[t]hough this is not altogether as agreeable to me as was my first mission, it is one that comes with such commanding authority as to compel me to accept it as a present duty" (*L&T* 939). But this new duty challenges even the variously schooled Douglass with its educational requirements. In his conclusion to the 1881 *Life and Times*, as I have noted, Douglass asserts that the slave's version of history is needed, since the master's version has already been told, and he notes that the masters have had the decided advantage in shaping that story; "They have had their day in court," he asserts, and "[l]iterature, theology, philosophy, law, and learning have come willingly to their service" (*L&T* 912–13). In 1892, Douglass amplifies his awareness of this cultural control, for in his attempt to answer to "the Negro problem," he notes,

> I am pelted with all sorts of knotty questions, some of which might be difficult even for Humboldt, Cuvier, or Darwin, were they alive, to answer. They are questions which range over the whole field of science, learning, and philosophy, and some descend to the depths of impertinent, unmannerly, and vulgar curiosity. To be able to answer the higher range of these questions I should be profoundly versed in psychology, anthropology, ethnology, sociology, theology, biology, and all the other ologies, philosophies and sciences. (*L&T* 939)

In these "ologies," of course, Douglass faced not only the increasing specialization and professionalization of what counted as knowledge and scientific investigation but also the authority invested in these modes of disciplinary understanding—behind which, Douglass recognized, is the fact that "[t]he law on the side of freedom is of great advantage only where there is power to make that law respected" (*L&T* 815). He faces the task directly but with some uneasiness. On the one hand, for example, he claims for his trip to Egypt "an ethnological purpose" by which he could combat "American prejudice against the darker colored races of mankind, and at the same time . . . raise colored people somewhat in their own estimation and thus stimulate them to higher endeavors" (*L&T* 1006).[24] On the other hand, on the page that follows this statement of purpose Douglass falls into a rather bland generalization of black identity, asserting that "the negro works best and hardest when it is no longer work, but becomes play with joyous singing" (*L&T* 1007). One wonders what happened to the subtlety of Douglass's 1845 reading of apparently joyous singing, and one is led to notice that Douglass draws no direct or necessary connection between battling prejudice and raising black Americans in their own estimation.[25] The two prongs of this double task extend back to Douglass's other task, to "account to himself for himself somehow," for if Douglass was summoned to respond to this "power to make" the law "respected," he was summoned also to fashion an identity capable of standing securely in its field.

Somewhat strangely, the initial voice for this refashioned self, of which one can hear echoes later in the narrative, is borrowed in part from *Othello*. When describing the conclusion of the Civil War—and the apparent success of the cause, the "great labor of [his] life," with which he had been identified and which had provided him with a clearly defined public role—Douglass notes his "strange and, perhaps, perverse" reaction, a "great and exceeding joy . . . slightly tinged with a feeling of sadness"

(*L&T* 811): "I felt I had reached the end of the noblest and best part of my life; my school was broken up, my church disbanded, and the beloved congregation dispersed, never to come together again. The anti-slavery platform had performed its work, and my voice was no longer needed. 'Othello's occupation was gone' " (*L&T* 811). No doubt there is a certain cultural inevitability in Douglass's identification with Othello. Douglass's marriage to a white woman, for example, the story of which he presents briefly in the exhausted and defensive pages of the 1892 "Third Part" that supplemented the 1881 autobiography, could only have supported his self-assigned role as a U.S. Othello.[26] Discussing this "shocking offence" to "popular prejudice," Douglass deals briefly and bitterly with this time when "False friends of both colors were loading me with reproaches" (*L&T* 961), and during which President Cleveland stood firm "in the face of all vulgar criticism" by paying Douglass "all the social consideration due to the office of Recorder of Deeds for the District of Columbia" (*L&T* 961).[27] But although Othello remains a somewhat strange choice for his public role (certainly, Douglass does not want or mean to associate himself with the whole of Othello's character or with his tragic end) Shakespeare's tragedy still provides a sadly appropriate script for Douglass to follow, speaking as it does of greatness that stands on tenuous cultural grounds. As Othello relies on war for his occupation (and the respect that he gains thereby that would not otherwise be freely offered to a Moor in Shakespeare's Venetian world), so Douglass has relied on the war against slavery for his own occupation, and has gained respect and a public role thereby. If he has been criticized and accused, he also has been able to respond as Othello responds to the accusations against him early in the play: "My parts, my title, and my perfect soul / Shall manifest me rightly" (1.2.31–32). The confidence in these lines extends from the sure correspondence of public and private identity, the secure union of ability, social position, and character.

Othello is also an oddly appropriate role for Douglass in other ways. For if Douglass could recognize that this historical transition from slavery to "freedom" would inevitably affect the position of one of the most public of black Americans, so could others. Some twenty years before Douglass lamented his lost occupation, Warren Chase, a former state senator in Wisconsin and advocate of socialism and spiritualism, published in 1862 his generally socialist and rather quirky tract entitled *The American Crisis; or, Trial and Triumph of Democracy*. Chase nowhere mentions

Douglass, but in a brief chapter on the Underground Railroad asserts simply that due to the Civil War "[t]here will be no further occasion for the road, and hereafter 'Othello's occupation is gone' " (76). Significant when they come from Douglass, these words are ominous from one such as Chase, signaling as they do the conclusion of a social narrative in which black characters could play a public and celebrated role. Indeed, Chase follows these words with a striking conclusion to that narrative: "Slaves ran North till a President ran South, and then slaves could walk North by daylight" (76). The characters have changed, and the task of bringing closure to the narrative's plot has been taken from black and white abolitionists and antislavery soldiers and reassigned to a central and national white character. The new visibility of the northward-bound black body marks its invisibility in the national narrative.[28]

The second time Douglass's role as Othello enters the narrative explicitly is in his narration of his association with the Freedmen's Bank, an association that cost him much in reputation—bringing upon his head, by his estimation, "an amount of abuse and detraction greater than any encountered in any other part of my life" (*L&T* 842). Douglass's application of Othello here is a strange mix of defensiveness and intriguing metaphorical transformations. Andrews has argued that in *My Bondage and My Freedom*, Douglass appropriates the Prometheus metaphor to achieve a double identity by which he could alternately play devil and savior (*To Tell a Free Story* 231); and one might be justified in imagining an allusion to Prometheus in the same sentence from *Life and Times* in which Douglass quotes from *Othello*. Prometheus appears in the famous scene in Shakespeare's play where Othello prepares to take Desdemona's life, and confronts the finality of his action: ". . . but once put out thy light, / Thou cunning'st pattern of excelling nature, / I know not where is that Promethean heat / That can thy light relume" (5.2.10–13). Douglass, discussing his gradual realization that the Freedmen's Bank was a lost cause even before he was recruited to serve as its president, states that though the institutional edifice of the bank remained, "the life, which was the money, was gone, and I found that I had been placed there with the hope that by 'some drugs, some charms, some conjuration, or some mighty magic,' I would bring it back" (*L&T* 842). The quoted lines, of course, come from Othello's statement to the senators (1.3.93–94) when accused by Brabantio of enchanting Desdemona. And as Othello promises the senators a "round unvarnished tale" of his courtship, so Douglass offers his readers "a fair and unvarnished narration of my connection with The Freedmen's Savings and Trust Company" (*L&T* 841).[29] What makes Douglass's application of *Othello* here particularly strange is that he is defending himself against charges that his service was the death of the Freedmen's Bank, that he in fact failed to relume the light. Shakespeare's tragic story of one who has been deceived to the point of killing his own wife seems a strange explanatory framework for Douglass's own tale of discovering that upon accepting the presidency of the bank "I was married to a corpse" (*L&T* 842).[30]

These vague echoes of *Othello* do not by any means dominate *Life and Times*, but they are significant as signs of Douglass's general search for a paradigm of selfhood capable of defining his role on the postbellum stage. Iago succeeds with Othello largely by playing to the Moor's singular cultural isolation; and increasingly, Othello voices his self-consciousness about his color and the cultural assumptions associated with it. Douglass, who necessarily struggled throughout his career to respond to racial theory and social practice in whatever form they took, could not avoid a similar self-consciousness, for if he was able to echo the sentiment he never seems capable of the zeal with which Delany thanked God for making him a specifically black man. Speaking of his initial experiences with the anti-slavery forces, for example, Douglass notes that "[f]or a time I was made to forget that my skin was dark and my hair crisped," and then observes in the following sentences that he was, in fact, soon made to remember the burdens of cultural identity (*My Bondage* 366; *L&T* 661). Speaking of Rhode Island abolitionists Douglass acknowledges gratefully, "They took me with earnest hand to their homes and hearths, and made me feel that though I wore the burnished livery of the sun I was still a countryman and kinsman of whom they were never ashamed" (*L&T* 667). And in a chapter entitled "Elevation of the Free People of Color," speaking of one of many episodes of prejudice on a train, one that led to the rare conclusion of an apology from a white man (though "one of the lamest ever offered"), Douglass notes somewhat hopefully, "With such facts as these before me—and I have many of them—I am inclined to think that pride and fashion have much to do with the treatment commonly extended to colored people in the United States" (*My Bondage* 397–98). The disturbing irony of what he intends to be a humorous anecdote that follows suggests the extent to which Douglass understood that his color placed him at the far extremes of fashion: "I once heard a very plain man say, (and he was cross-eyed, and awkwardly flung together in other respects,) that he should be a handsome man when public opinion shall be changed" (*My Bondage* 398). Like Othello, Douglass knew both how much and how little to expect from "opinion, a sovereign mistress of effects" and "the tyrant custom" (*Othello* 1.3.227–28, 232), and like Othello, Douglass reveals that the discourse of race has its own logic that leads from black skin to black sins. The Prometheus metaphor of *My Bondage and My Freedom* is brilliant, but its grounds and its implications are beyond Douglass's control; and in *Life and Times* we see Douglass struggle for something more encompassing while often arriving at something less so. Ultimately, the presence of Othello and the other identifiable cultural roles that dominate Douglass's autobiography of 1881 and 1892— race leader, Recorder of Deeds, Minister to Haiti—are examples of Douglass's attempt to transcend a cultural script beyond his control in his performance of a variety of cultural roles, and of his increasingly vexed awareness of his audience.[31]

One thinks of an episode William Wells Brown describes in *The Black Man, His Antecedents, His Genius, and His Achievements* (1865) when he attends a theater in London to see the black actor Ira Aldridge's performance of Othello. The story is somewhat long, but I think relevant, both for its demonstration of Brown's proud attention to Aldridge's performance and for the form that racial pride here assumes:

> On looking over the columns of *The Times*, one morning, I saw it announced under the head of "Amusements," that "Ira Aldridge, the African Roscius," was to appear in the character of Othello, in Shakspeare's [*sic*] celebrated tragedy of that name, and, having long wished to see my sable countryman, I resolved at once to attend. Though the doors had been open but a short time when I reached the Royal Haymarket, the theatre where the performance was to take place, the house was well filled, and among the audience I recognized the faces of several distinguished persons of the nobility, the most noted of whom was Sir Edward Bulwer Lytton, the renowned novelist. . . .
> . . . At the end of the third act, Othello was called before the curtain, and received the applause of the delighted multitude. I watched the countenance and every motion of Bulwer Lytton with almost as much interest as I did that of the Moor of Venice, and saw that none appeared to be better pleased than he. (*The Black Man* 118–19)

We witness here the triangulation of cultural identity: as the audience celebrates Aldridge, Brown celebrates Bulwer Lytton's celebration of

Aldridge; the black spectator watches the white representative affirming the value of the black representative.[32]

Perhaps we are not altogether far from this scene when we witness Douglass's narration of an interview with President Lincoln, which he presents while acknowledging his concern that "the mention of it may savor a little of vanity on my part." Twice the interview is interrupted with the announcement that the governor of Connecticut is waiting to see Lincoln, and Douglass reports Lincoln's response:

> "Tell Governor Buckingham to wait, for I want to have a long talk with my friend Frederick Douglass." I interposed, and begged him to see the Governor at once, as I could wait, but no, he persisted that he wanted to talk with me and that Governor Buckingham could wait. This was probably the first time in the history of this Republic when its chief magistrate had found an occasion or shown a disposition to exercise such an act of impartiality between persons so widely different in their positions and supposed claims upon his attention. From the manner of the Governor, when he was finally admitted, I inferred that he was as well satisfied with what Mr. Lincoln had done, or had omitted to do, as I was. (*L&T* 797)

Here and elsewhere Douglass reports an understandable pride in achievements he could not have predicted or even hoped for as a young boy, but he signals as well his position in a culture in which his own public role could not escape the racial politics of social attitudes and practice. He sees the evidence of his achievement in Lincoln's behavior and in Buckingham's reaction; at this cultural level there were few other cultural mirrors available. Noting his plan to attend Lincoln's second inaugural reception, Douglass remarks, "I had for some time looked upon myself as a man, but now in this multitude of the *elite* of the land, I felt myself a man among men"; but the inevitable sentence follows: "I regret to be obliged to say, however, that this comfortable assurance was not of long duration, for on reaching the door, two policemen stationed there took me rudely by the arm and ordered me to stand back, for their directions were to admit no persons of my color" (*L&T* 803). Standing between the mirror the policemen provide and that which Lincoln provides, Douglass necessarily looks to Lincoln's opinion for a public identity capable of marking the transition from the culturally delimited "persons of my color" to "a man among men." Almost fulfilling Douglass's earlier hope that "a very plain man . . . should be a handsome man when public opinion shall be changed" (*My Bondage* 398), Lincoln stands, "[l]ike a mountain pine high above all others," in "grand simplicity, and *home-like beauty*," telling Douglass, " 'there is no man in the country whose opinion I value more than yours' " (*L&T* 804), and representing the hope that public opinion might well change.

This hope for a possible revolution of perspectives and attitudes becomes something of a staged affair in *Life and Times*, a drama that Douglass performs in a chapter entitled " 'Time Makes All Things Even.' " Douglass presents the story of his visit in later life with Captain Thomas Auld, suggesting that "the leading incidents" of this chapter "will . . . address the imagination of the reader with peculiar and poetic force, and might well enough be dramatized for the stage" (*L&T* 874). Following two long sentences in which Douglass summarizes Auld's enslavement and treatment of Douglass and Douglass's subsequent treatment of Auld in his lectures and writings, Douglass draws the scene to the eschatological framework upon which he had based his lectures and writings, the end of life when "all distinctions are at an end, and where the great and the small, the slave and his master, are reduced to the same level" (*L&T* 875). Beyond the now dated roles of master and slave Douglass presents for this stage production their new roles: Auld is "on his bed, aged and tremulous, drawing near the sunset of life," and Douglass, "holding his hand and in friendly conversation with him in a sort of final settlement of past differences," is "his former slave, United States Marshal of the District of Columbia" (*L&T* 875). As if speaking from the script Douglass has been writing over the course of his life, Auld says to Douglass, " 'Frederick, I always knew you were too smart to be a slave, and had I been in your place, I should have done as you did.' " Douglass, too, replies according to script, " 'Capt. Auld, I am glad to hear you say this. I did not run away from *you*, but from *slavery*; it was not that I loved Caesar less, but Rome more' " (*L&T* 877). The pathos of the scene is completed when we learn that Auld had "rescued" Douglass's grandmother "from her destitution" after reading Douglass's *Narrative* (*L&T* 877)—and perhaps also by Douglass's notice that when Auld's death is reported in the paper "the fact that he had once owned me as a slave was cited as rendering that event noteworthy" (*L&T* 878).

What is most significant, though, is the lesson to be learned from these mutually supportive performances, as Douglass's cultural constructionist model becomes the stuff of a grand theatrical production. Douglass notes that this episode of his life had, like so many others, been a matter of some controversy, "made the subject of mirth by heartless triflers, and by serious-minded men regretted as a weakening of my lifelong testimony against slavery"; and the published reports of the meeting were, accordingly, "in some respects defective and colored" (*L&T* 876). This, Douglass argues implicitly, is not only bad form but also bad interpretation. The meaning of this sentimental play is quite clear. Douglass notes that he told Auld that "I regarded both of us as victims of a system," and he presents the same message yet more emphatically to his readers: "Our courses had been determined for us, not by us. We had both been flung, by powers that did not ask our consent, upon a mighty current of life, which we could neither resist nor control. By this current he was a master, and I a slave, but now our lives were verging towards a point where differences disappear, where even the constancy of hate breaks down and where the clouds of pride, passion, and selfishness vanish before the brightness of infinite light" (*L&T* 876). Following the logic of his life's work, Douglass here places, as he has before, the cultural constructionist model of individual identity and social roles within the ultimate framework of divine government.[33]

And here as elsewhere, Douglass resembles Henry Adams in his struggle to find a law of science capable of explaining inexplicable human behavior without abandoning the moral framework that makes such laws attractive. In other words, given the evidence of experience and history, how can one avoid concluding that human nature is inherently evil without also sacrificing one's sense of a moral universe? One is reminded of Adams's frustration over the attempt to write the history of the Jefferson and Madison administrations. While working on his *History of the United States during the Administrations of Jefferson and Madison* in the 1880s, Adams complained in a letter to Samuel J. Tilden,

> In regard to them [Jefferson, Madison, and Monroe] I am incessantly forced to devise excuses and apologies or to admit that no excuse will avail. I am at times almost sorry that I ever undertook to write their history, for they appear like mere grass-hoppers, kicking and gesticulating, on the middle of the Mississippi river. There is no possibility of reconciling their theories with their acts, or their extraordinary foreign policy with dignity. They were carried along on a stream which floated them after a fashion without much regard to themselves. (491)

Adams's stream and Douglass's current seem equally compelling, and if Douglass's current leads one ultimately upward to clouds and beyond to infinite light, while Adams's is as constant, heavy, and imposing as the Mississippi River, one is tempted to say that it is largely because Adams could afford the luxury of a cynical relation to the moral views that science could not quite compel him to abandon.[34] Douglass could not afford to consider, with Adams, "individuality" as "the free-will dogma of the science" of history; nor could he conclude, with Adams, that "history is simply social development along the lines of weakest resistance, and that in most cases the line of weakest resistance is found as unconsciously by society as by water" (491). Douglass's role required him to see himself first as a victim of the system and then as a victor over the system, and finally as an individual within the system. And in this staged production of his meeting with Auld, Douglass struggles to script the double roles of victims before the system and individuals before God. Aware that time takes its time to make all things even, Douglass looks for a role that will suggest both cultural and moral closure.

Ultimately, Douglass looks to his narrative to present a unified identity capable of drawing the meaning of his life to a sure conclusion; as actors earn a reputation that transcends any individual role or performance, so Douglass looked to be the significant actor behind the various limiting roles he played. But as he struggles to negotiate the lifelong transition from a representative to a represented self, as he makes the gradual turn from an ideologically unified identity towards a self-consciously artistic performance of identity in the tenuously scripted pages of *Life and Times*, Douglass seems increasingly like a man struggling against the current. Still five chapters away from the end of the 1881 *Life and Times*, Douglass looks hopefully to this lifelong task of constructing a public identity by which he could live comfortably and securely: "The most of my story is now before the reader. Whatever of good or ill the future may have in store for me, the past at least is secure. As I review the last decade up to the present writing, I am impressed with a sense of completeness—a sort of rounding up of the arch to the point where the keystone may be inserted, the scaffolding removed, and the work, with all its perfections or faults, left to speak for itself" (*L&T* 844). Of course, and as Douglass's return to this structure of selfhood in 1892 indicates, the past cannot be protected from the future any more than the future can be isolated from the past. The past is never secure, and the structure never complete.

Throughout his career as autobiographer, Douglass had struggled with the tensions between fact and art; increasingly, his life called for the touch of an artist, and increasingly Douglass seems to have lost his touch. Far from the ideological perspective and certainty of purpose that provided Douglass with the terms for a unified narrative in 1845 and for a mutually modifying relation between experience and narration in 1855, Douglass in 1881 and beyond to 1892 struggles to find an art capable of encompassing the facts of his life. One thinks of Douglass's figurative return to the Chesapeake Bay, where once he gave to his soul's complaint a voice capable of representing a communal condition. He reports returning to this scene in his thoughts while on his European tour: "A few years back my Sundays were spent on the banks of the Chesapeake Bay, bemoaning my condition and looking out from the farm of Edward Covey, and, with a heart aching to be on their decks, watching the white sails of the ships passing off to sea. Now I was enjoying what the wisest and best of the world have bestowed for the wisest and best to enjoy" (*L&T* 1014). While one cannot help but note with Douglass the significant contrast between his early and late conditions, this seems still an example of clumsy artistry and disappointing closure. The white sails of freedom have been appropriated by the tourist, who discovers himself with evident pride in the closed circle of the European "wisest and best," far from the community for which he spoke in 1845.

More expressive of his situation are the words that close his final version of his life: "I have been the recipient of many honors, among which my unsought appointment by President Benjamin Harrison to the office of Minister Resident and Consul General to represent the United States at the capital of Haiti, and my equally unsought appointment by President Florvil Hippolite to represent Haiti among all the civilized nations of the globe at the World's Columbian Exposition, are crowning honors to my long career and a fitting and happy close to my whole public life" (*L&T* 1045). This "happy close" offered, at best, a dubious closure to his narrative, for in this final chapter of his life Douglass once again responds to controversy regarding his performance of his public role. Indeed, his published response to charges that he was responsible for the failure of the attempt to establish a naval station in Haiti (a response originally published in the *North American Review* in 1891) dominates the last two chapters of the 1892 *Life and Times*. The moral battle has become both more complex and less compelling than in early years, as Douglass reports his refusal to carry out a duplicitous diplomatic proposition that sounded to him "like the words of Satan on the mountain" (*L&T* 1041), a characterization as appropriate in its way as those moral assignations he made earlier in his literary career, but one far less likely to find a broad audience or to serve as a foundation for individual or communal identity. Douglass finds himself victim to a new twist on a familiar cultural narrative, characterized as "more a Haitian than an American" (*L&T* 1042).[35] And if the tensions of this double role that linger in Douglass's closing sentences indicate his determination to continue fighting the good fight in whatever form it takes, the conflicted role of his double appointments speaks of an art undiscovered and an old cultural story uncontained by Douglass's narrative of his life.

# 6

## *Unsolved Mysteries and Emerging Histories*
### Frances E. W. Harper's *Iola Leroy*

In her introduction to the Schomburg Library edition of Frances E. W. Harper's *Iola Leroy*, Frances Smith Foster notes the grave risks to her hard-won career as poet, orator, and activist that Harper faced in writing the novel. Many white Americans in the last decade or so of the nineteenth century not only saw but celebrated, and were deeply influenced by, some of the most strategically racist literature the nation had yet produced. Accordingly, as Foster argues, Harper faced a heightened challenge not only to her own reputation but also to her inevitable role as a representative of her race: "Were she to fail to produce a novel that would refute the myths created by writers such as Thomas Nelson Page, were she to fail to arouse sympathies equal to those stirred by writers such as Helen Hunt Jackson, Harper knew her failure would be cited as evidence not only of her own declining abilities [she wrote the novel at age sixty-seven], but also of the artistic inferiority of Afro-Americans in general" (xxxiv).[1] In a culture long accustomed to viewing condescendingly or to otherwise defining the limited terms by which African-American writers would be recognized and valued, the stakes had been raised.[2] Professor H. T. Johnson epitomized the dominant cultural view when he wrote in 1890 that African-American literature had been thus far " 'more commendable in point of matter than in meritorious manner,' " arguing that no longer would it be enough to simply enlighten (qtd. in Foster, Introduction to *IL* xxxii). As Foster notes, W. E. B. Du Bois in 1911 applied this general critical distinction specifically to Harper, in a eulogy for *The Crisis* "in which he declared that Harper should be remembered more for her good intentions than for the success of their execution" (xxxv).

I begin with this view of the cultural and literary politics Harper faced not only because I wish to argue that she succeeded in both her self-assigned and "other-defined" tasks, but also because questions about the "manner" of her response to her historical situation still keep many from appreciating her success. In his 1988 essay "Is Frances Ellen Watkins Harper Good Enough to Teach?" Paul Lauter (whose answer is yes) summarizes the problem well when he speculates that "in the face of such wide scholarly inattention to Harper, one might easily call into question not the defects of that scholarship but the standards of value that have led one to find Harper important" (28). The "standards of value" applied to *Iola Leroy* by literary scholars are both revealing and representative; indeed, one could say that the history of critical responses to this novel is a narrative of the variable course of African-American critical self-defini-tion.[3] While many critics have acknowledged that *Iola Leroy* is an admira-ble novel when considered on Harper's terms, they have found reason to question the nature and political validity of those terms and have criticized this novel not only for what it is but also for what it is not. Some, like Sterling Brown, Arthur P. Davis, and Ulysses Lee, have viewed this novel of "ennobling sentiments" as having an emphasis on "dull" piety over focused politics (qtd. in Carby, Introduction xii). Later critics, with broader conceptions of political discourse, have seen in Harper's use of sentimental conventions the politics of either assimilation or compla-cency.[4] Still others have seen in *Iola Leroy* an idealization of the nineteenth-century cult of true womanhood that amounts to an acquiescence to standards of identity established by the dominant culture.[5]

When her work is not attacked by those who see in it no literary value, it is sometimes hit by critical friendly fire. That is, even among those who value this novel, *Iola Leroy* is often praised less as a literary work than as a historical document; barely distinguishable from such evaluations are those that praise the novel for the "major themes" (more precisely, the historical, cultural, and political issues) it addresses, often regardless of Harper's manner of address. I suspect that the problem will only be amplified by Foster's recent edition of the "three rediscovered novels" that Harper published serially in the *Christian Recorder*: *Minnie's Sacrifice* (1869), *Sowing and Reaping* (1876–1877), and *Trial and Triumph* (1888–1889). In each of these novels, Harper presents a clear moral lesson, an emphatically Christian warning about the dangers of intemperance, greed, and disunion within the African-American community. In her Introduction to her edition of Harper's three rediscovered novels, Foster distinguishes Harper's work from other nineteenth-century African-American literature; but in doing so, Foster practices the politics of criticism that she seems to resist. These novels, Foster argues, "are a welcome relief from the black-as-victim-of-racism-and-discrimination depictions that permeate some other nineteenth-century stories. Yet they are not 'raceless' melodramas of life in middle-class resorts or heroic tales of impoverished isolates making their ways through moral and material minefields to worldwide acclaim and material or psychic riches" (Introduction to *MST* xxviii). One suspects that what is good for Foster's critical goose will serve as well for someone else's critical gander: these novels might well be viewed condescendingly as middle-class melodramas or heroic tales of impoverished isolates or even black-as-victim-of-racism-and-discrimination depictions. While I agree that Harper's work is distinctive, I do not think that this means that we must form evaluative judgments that distinguish it from other work in the field—changing Lauter's question, in effect, from "Is Harper good enough to teach?" to "Is Harper better to read than others?"

I will suggest here that Harper directs her attention to more complex questions, questions that require from her a correspondingly complex literary response. In her Introduction, Foster argues cogently that we have reason to question our assumptions about Harper and her audience, for these are works published in the *Christian Recorder*, directed specifically to an African-American audience. "These novels," Foster argues, "are clearly not protest stories or guided tours of black folk culture designed primarily to convert and convict readers outside of the African American culture. These books speak about and to African Americans themselves" (Introduction to *MST* xxvii). In this, Foster echoes Joyce Ann Joyce's attempt to reenvision the role of critic and of literature itself, arguing that the fundamental standard of value to apply to African-American literature is "the Black artist's position as outsider, his or her ability to step outside the Western contrivance of a duality between art and life" ("Black Woman

Scholar" 551), bringing readers to a liberating awareness of and involvement in creative art as "an act of love" ("The Black Canon" 343).[6] But
beyond Joyce's "outside" and Foster's "inside" is a community that cannot
be so easily separated from the maze of U.S. culture. For even to speak to
a black audience in the late nineteenth century was to speak to an audience
that could not avoid the politics of cultural identity that make Douglass
such a discomforting representative. For Harper as for many others, there
was no "outside" to step towards except for that which existed in a
complex and threatening relation to the inside.[7]

As a consequence, and as a fundamental condition of literary identity,
any conception of a union between art and life would necessarily involve
the recognition that a failure in art by one would be viewed as a failure in
life for many. Foster has noted the similarity between Harper and her
character Annette in *Trial and Triumph*, and one must note as well the
lesson Annette is taught in her own literary struggles by Mr. Thomas,
who "has encouraged her efforts, and taught her to believe that not only
is her own honor at stake as a student, but that as a representative of her
branch of the human race, she is on the eve of winning, or losing, not
only for herself, but for others" (*MST* 227). I do not see how we can
avoid the recognition that even when writing to a black community—a
community inevitably shaped in large part by the cultural politics of the
time—Harper was responding in part to a white presence; as Raymond
Hedin puts it, within nineteenth-century African-American texts "are
encoded the very cultural relationships which, outside the texts, serve to
shape them. In the intratextual relationship of black character and story to
these white presences, black texts reveal both their sense of restriction and
their strategies for coping with it" (182).[8] I agree, then, with William J.
Spurlin, who has highlighted the dangers of "reducing the multiplicities"
both of black texts and of African-American culture generally to "a
homogenized essence that excludes the similarities to Western forms of
discourse which African American texts both inscribe and in which they
are always already inscribed" (735). The question is, how can one account
for these multiplicities and these mutual inscriptions without simply
assimilating African-American literary culture within yet another Eurocen-
tric homogenized essence?

This is, I believe, the question that *Iola Leroy* is designed to address, for
this novel is primarily a study of discursive systems, one that recognizes
the ability of one discursive system to inscribe its impression on another.

Certainly, this is a novel intended to teach, a novel in which meaning is important, but its meaning cannot be separated from its manner. Harper, who began her career as a teacher, identified education not only with what she called the "power of knowledge" but also with civic responsibility and moral character, a "feeling heart" joined with a "devising brain" in a mutually modifying relationship ("Factor" 276). To fulfill this ideal, Harper uses what Bernard W. Bell has called a combination of "the sentimentality and rhetoric of romance with the psychological and socio-logical truth of mimesis" (58)[9] to locate a specifically African-American mode of understanding, one that resists cultural imperialism by claiming authority over white culture's central ideological icons. This novel about the breakup of African-American families and the search for mothers after the war embodies a "signifyin(g)" strategy for re-turning American cultural discourse to a stable conception of justice.

I do not use this term casually, for the modes of (re)figuration that inform Gates's use of the term *signifyin(g)* have both particular and broad applications to Harper's literary and discursive strategies: particular in her use of such words as *shadow* and *mystery*, and broad in her transformation (her "motivated repetition" [*Signifying* 66]) of sentimental literary conven-tions, of images of African-American identity (both historical and liter-ary), and of the terms, process, and goals of education itself. As I will argue, one's understanding of this novel is influenced profoundly by the body of knowledge one claims as cultural literacy. The more one knows about nineteenth-century African-American culture, the more one is drawn to read this novel along what Gates calls "the y axis of blackness" (*Signifying* 47). Focusing the novel on African Americans capable of "passing" for whites, Harper situates the novel at the point where one axis intersects the other, and thereby appropriates the discourse of racial difference, universalizing a mode of understanding that draws its authority from African-American experience.

## The Mysteries of (Mis)understanding

In saying that Harper "appropriates the discourse of racial difference," I refer to Mikhail Bakhtin's assertion that "language . . . lies on the borderline between oneself and the other," and that it "becomes 'one's own' only when the speaker . . . appropriates the word, adapting it to his [or her] own semantic and expressive intention" (293). Harper understood keenly the need to "appropriate the word," for, as I've noted in the Introduction, the narrator in *Trial and Triumph* worries about the black community, echoing Delany in complaining that the white race serves as translators and commentators:

> The literature they read was mostly from the hands of white men who would paint them in any colors which suited their prejudices or predilections. The religious ideas they had embraced came at first thought from the same sources, though they may have undergone modifications in passing through their channels of thought, and it must be a remarkable man or woman who thinks an age ahead of the generation in which his or her lot is cast, and who plans and works for the future on the basis of that clearer vision. (*MST* 240)

Indeed, those who were thinking ahead would find the same white men waiting for them; Harper, looking ahead, was well versed in the ethnological theories of her age, the increasingly deliberate and influential attempts to dress racism in the authoritarian garb of science.

Throughout the century, the biblical version of genesis had been variously displaced and reinterpreted to account for the developing scientific theory of polygenesis, which in turn enabled disciples of this theory, both northern and southern, to reinterpret the culturally troublesome declaration that "all men are created equal." Later in the century, Darwinism gave racist thought a new discursive vehicle, and advocates rode it for all it was worth.[10] In one of the strangest attempts to "prove" scientifically that the black and white races are different species, Peter A. Browne argued in the 1840s that the hair of the African race is, as Thomas F. Gossett summarizes, "more like wool than like the hair of a white man. Thus, he noted that 'the hair of the white man *will not felt*, but the wool of the Negro *will felt*.' There was no difference between Negro hair and that of sheep except in 'degree of felting power'" (*Race* 80). Gossett notes also the account of an African-American pastor responding to this "proof," assuring his congregation "that they were under the special protection of God, since they were the lambs of the world with wool instead of hair" (81). We cannot know whether the pastor's tongue was in his cheek as he spoke; we can only note the power of the figurative discourse of religion to both encompass and diffuse the increasingly obvious figurative usage of scientific discourse. Still, the blurred distinctions between science and pseudoscience were a threatening cultural tool, for truth was not the issue; all that mattered was an explanatory system capable of discursive (en)closure, for which many whites were prepared to sacrifice religion.

The ideal of education, that most central of models for cultural self-definition, was of course corrupted by the new thought.[11] As George M. Fredrickson has observed, "racial Darwinism" enabled some to argue, after the war, that education of African Americans amounted to "the artificial preservation of the unfit" (251), and that therefore the nation should not waste its time on such unscientific efforts. At the same time, racial Darwinism enabled other whites to reassure themselves that humanitarian efforts could be rather strictly defined, and that the nation was required to help blacks *only* by way of education. If blacks, thus aided, should fail, then the question of racial equality would be settled scientifically. In either case, education was safely either held or withheld by the dominant culture, and was used to define the "emancipated" community either by implication or by design. Harper's task, accordingly, was not only to "appropriate the word" but also to appropriate the communal voice of the word, the concept of education itself.

She begins this task in the subtitle of her novel: "Shadows Uplifted." One can see in this subtitle the familiar theme of uplift, as in the motto of nineteenth-century black club women, "Lifting as We Climb";[12] more generally, uplift would correspond to the cautious program of African-American education associated with Booker T. Washington. "Shadows," of course, was a culturally prominent metaphor for incomprehension or for otherwise incomplete understanding. Throughout the nineteenth century, shadows were often lifted from previously limited minds, as veils were lifted from figurative eyes. Shadow also can be paired with light to suggest troubled times and good times, as in Harper's story "The Two Offers," when the narrator notes that Laura Lagrange's husband "had desolated her young life, by turning its sunshine to shadows, its smiles to tears" (*BCD* 113). Shadow can refer to a kind of projected double, a philosophical and cultural mirror, as for example that which we encounter in Melville's "Benito Cereno." Shadow can also refer to relational ethics, as when Harper writes about the shadow of the home (thereby relating the event or person in question to the sacred domestic sphere) or when Harper and others write of the "shadow of slavery."[13] Douglass, for example, writes in his address "Did John Brown Fail?" (presented at Harpers Ferry in 1881), "Slavery is indeed gone; but its long, black shadow yet falls broad and large over the face of the whole country" (13). But one can see in this subtitle something else as well, for *shadows* was also, at least by the late nineteenth century, a derogatory slang term used by whites in reference to African Americans.[14] In her subtitle, then, Harper appropriates this word, and combines in it interracial politics, *intra*racial aims, and educational ideals. The subtitle announces the novel's central argument: the shadows of cultural confusion, miscomprehension, and racial tension that threatened the nation's future would be lifted only when those other "shadows"—those whom Harper calls in her address on "Enlightened Motherhood" a "homeless race" (*BCD* 285)—were lifted to their rightful place in the communal home.

Harper establishes the terms of this argument, and begins the novel, by confronting her white readers with their inability to interpret culturally familiar discourse. In the first pages of the first chapter, Harper draws readers into a "shadow" culture—that of the slaves—and introduces her readers to the discursive network of that culture, the "mystery of market speech." Her depiction of slaves talking enthusiastically about "splendid" fish, and about butter "just as fresh, as fresh can be" (7–8) invokes images of the happy "darkies" who inhabited the pages of white supremacist fiction gaining popularity at the time. On the novel's second page, though, the narrator wonders at this "unusual interest manifested by these men in the state of the produce market," and raises the question that many readers might well have forgotten to ask: "What did it mean?" (*IL* 8). The answer is that, during the war, "when the bondman was turning his eyes to the American flag," "some of the shrewder slaves . . . invented a phraseology to convey in the most unsuspected manner news to each other from the battle-field" (*IL* 8–9).[15] The "mystery of market speech" is thus solved by learning this phraseology, this cultural discourse that appropriates authorized (and in that sense, *legal*) language for illegal but moral ends. As Mary V. Dearborn argues, this opening episode reminds us that "Implicit in the notion that communication is subversive is the fact that language itself can be a means to power" (45); the language we encounter here, argues Karla F. C. Holloway, is "a shape-changing dialect" that indicates the novel's larger project, "its revision of the traditional use and interpretation of words" (133–34).

The primary point here is not that this particular mystery is now clear, nor is it merely that the slaves had to formulate their own language to circumvent the will of the dominant race; rather, the point lies in the discursive nature of the mystery itself, the extent to which one's ability to understand is controlled by one's cultural training. As one reads, one encounters other such mysteries, each of which reveals the cognitive and moral limitations inherent in and enforced by the dominant cultural system. Consider, for example, Dr. Gresham, whom the reader first meets in a field hospital, and who is clearly attracted to Iola Leroy, whom he believes to be a white lady generously lowering herself to serve the needs of the northern soldiers. Initially, Dr. Gresham cannot understand how Iola can bring herself to kiss a black patient; and as he explains this to Colonel Robinson, the reader discovers the terms of his confusion: "I cannot understand how a Southern lady, whose education and manners stamp her as a woman of fine culture and good breeding, could consent to occupy the position she so faithfully holds. It is a mystery I cannot solve" (*IL* 57). This description is essentially a circular equation of cultural identity. If one is a southern lady, then one must have the advantages of education and good breeding that provide the manners and fine culture that are, by definition, the qualities of a southern lady. The perfect circle of definition represents the cognitive closure that is the raison d'etre of any cultural system. When this closure leads to culturally exotic behavior, those within the cultural circle are faced with a mystery they cannot solve. When Colonel Robinson provides the essential information, that "Miss Leroy was a slave," Dr. Gresham can relocate her in the cultural formula, and he says revealingly, "What you tell me changes the whole complexion of affairs" (*IL* 58).

This use of the word *mystery* was by no means unique to Harper's works. Intriguingly, the phrase also appears rather prominently in popular "histories" of the Underground Railroad, at the point at which the author tells a story of the origin of the term *Underground Railroad*. Eber Pettit constructs from memory a newspaper article on a successful escape with the headline "A Mystery Not Yet Solved!" (35); H. U. Johnson reprints that title and Pettit's reconstruction of the article, presenting it now not as a performance of memory but as a document of history (11). One encounters yet another application of the word *mystery*—in this case used to both blur and emphasize the distinctions marked by "the color line"—in the fascinating novel *Cousin Franck's Household, or Scenes in the Old Dominion* (1853), authored anonymously under the name "Pocahontas," and clearly designed to capitalize on the success of *Uncle Tom's Cabin*. Late in the novel, we meet the "stranger guest" Mr. Oglethorpe, "a gentleman of polished manners, bland and intelligent, with a delightful fund of general information" (231). A "Southerner by birth" and a graduate of the University of Virginia, Oglethorpe is marked by "something a little reserved and mysterious in his bearing." When he endorses the plan of the slaves to escape, "the mystery of Mr. Oglethorpe's character [is] deepened," and "[d]uring the short, rapid ride to the river, not a word escaped him that served to solve it; and we had no courage to invade the sad reserve, in which he has always moved, as if in an enchanted circle. But it was plainly seen in his manner, and especially in his countenance, that powerful emotions were contending within" (245). The mystery is solved when Oglethorpe tells his story, that he was once a slave, and that he is the brother of the slave Selma, of whom her mistress once exclaimed (and not with pride), "Selma is my shadow!" (230).

Mysteries of various kinds occur throughout *Iola Leroy*, one of which requires the service of a spy to determine Iola's racial origins. And as the narrator guides the reader through these mysteries, the terms of cultural closure become increasingly clear, and are perhaps best summarized by Alfred Lorraine, arguing with his cousin Eugene Leroy about Eugene's decision to marry his former slave. Having asserted that Eugene's decision is an act of madness, and that a culture has the right to protect its racial integrity, Lorraine finally ends the argument with the most fundamental defense of cultural attitudes: "I wasn't reasoned into it, and I do not expect to be reasoned out of it" (*IL* 72). When the terms of cultural self-identification are most directly challenged—terms that are necessarily both inclusive and exclusive—the individuals whose identities are thus threatened inevitably retreat to an affective allegiance to what Clifford Geertz calls the culture's "conceptual world" (24), an allegiance that is not only irrational but also defiantly extrarational.[16] Harper would no doubt prefer a moral reading of this conceptual world, like the one she offers in an 1859 public letter, "Miss Watkins and the Constitution," in which she anticipates the reader's puzzlement over the continuance of slavery, asking the reader, "Is it a great mystery to you why these things are permitted?" And she answers:

> Wait, my brother, awhile; the end is not yet. The Psalmist was rather puzzled when he saw the wicked in power and spreading like a Bay tree; but how soon their end! Rest assured that, as nations and individuals, God will do right by us, and we should not ask of either God or man to do less than that. In the freedom of man's will I read the

> philosophy of his crimes, and the impossibility of his actions having a
> responsible moral character without it; and hence the continuance of
> slavery does not strike me as being so very mysterious. (*BCD* 48)

Human culture is clear enough, as are the limitations of the understanding
enabled by culture. Equally clear are human crimes, if not to those within
the cultural circle then at least, Harper argues, to God—who has, as
Harper puts it in her 1856 poem "The Burial of Moses," "mysteries of
grace, / Ways that we cannot tell" (*BCD* 79).[17] The more tightly one clings
to the confines of one's culture, the more tightly one feels the pressure of
the restrictively exclusive understanding of that culture.

The central demystifying confrontation in the novel is, of course, Iola's
own self-confrontation in chapter 12, "School-Girl Notions." Raised to
believe that she is white, Iola, "being a southern girl and a slave-holder's
daughter, always defended slavery when it was under discussion" (*IL* 97).
After confronting "[t]he intense horror and agony" of her story, Iola
discovers a new sense of self: "I feel that my mind has matured beyond
my years. I am a wonder to myself" (*IL* 114).[18] Similarly, when Minnie of
*Minnie's Sacrifice* encounters a black woman who claims to be her mother,
she wonders of herself, "Was this the solution of the mystery which
enshrouded her young life? Did she indeed belong to that doomed and
hated race, and must she share the cruel treatment which bitter, relentless
prejudice had assigned them?" (*MST* 50–51). In both cases, the discovery
leads to a larger discovery of the world's terms, and the complete
interpretive shift that comes with a change of complexion. In *Iola Leroy*,
the protagonist's self-revelation foreshadows further a yet more pointed
demystification, that between the white Dr. Latrobe and the African-
American Dr. Latimer, whom Latrobe believes to be white. Latrobe
boasts, "The Negro . . . is perfectly comprehensible to me" (*IL* 227), and
claims that he can always identify a "nigger," no matter how white he or
she may appear, for "there are tricks of blood which always betray them"
(*IL* 229). Latrobe reminds one of Minnie's companion Carrie, who asserts
"I know white people from colored, I've seen enough of them" (*MST* 54),
and she is right. But in *Iola Leroy* Harper pointedly challenges this kind of
confidence, for when Latimer reveals his racial origins, Latrobe is both
astounded and effectively silenced, leaving not only the room but the
novel itself. Harper's novels focus on those like Iola, Minnie, and Latimer
who are living evidence that the culture's categories of understanding are

incapable of accounting for the world that functions just beneath the cultural veneer.

In her identification of the conceptual boundaries of white culture, Harper identifies the contours of the cultural battlefield in which African Americans found themselves after the Civil War. When the novel progresses to the beginning of the Reconstruction era, the slave "shadow" culture is replaced by new shadow cultures: the contending forces of the Invisible Empire of southern oppression and the shadowy motives of northern protection—both of which, the novel makes clear, present life-threatening problems of interpretation to African Americans. The novel notes the most familiar dangers: the South's reliance on both violence and legal gymnastics; the North's manipulation of blacks for political gain and its application of what might be called the "conquest by alcohol" strategy that had been so effective in robbing native Americans of their land and culture. Harper emphasizes the difficulty of recognizing these dangers and of identifying motives beneath the surface of events, but she notes as well perhaps even graver dangers where many readers might expect them least: in the field of education itself.

In this field, we encounter what might be called "shadow politics" in all their threatening complexity. Consider, for example, one commentary on post-Reconstruction racial politics, travel writer Henry M. Field's *Bright Skies and Dark Shadows* (1890), a book that begins with a map of Florida and a dedication to the early Florida developer Henry M. Flagler. In his Preface, Field notes that he presents this narrative of a southern journey to "furnish a background, the more effective by contrast, for the dark subject of my story," for "It is under these 'bright skies' that the 'shadows' creep on the scene. Out of the palms and the orange groves starts up a spectre, the ghost of something gone, that, though dead and buried, sleeps in an unquiet grave, and comes forth at midnight to haunt us in our dreams. The Race Problem is the gravest that ever touched a nation's life" (i). Lest those who read this imagine that Field views black Americans as zombies, ghosts, or some other stereotypically monstrous Other, he assures his readers often and forcefully (though never persuasively) that he is a friend to the African race. He argues against various colonization schemes inspired by the "shadow of the African" that "still darkens the South," schemes geared towards "The Expatriation of a Whole Race," as one chapter title has it (154). He denounces the violence of the Ku Klux Klan. He praises the industriousness, the endurance, and the possibilities of "the black race." Ultimately, this geographical study of the "race problem," by which Africans become shadows over the landscape and creeping shadows within the landscape, leads to the conclusion that "education is the only remedy." Noting that "one who himself belongs to the white race, will not object to its retaining its supremacy if it be by fair means, by superior intelligence or character," Field notes also that many blacks are likely to be "suspicious of special instruction, as if you wanted to gain some advantage over them." But, he argues, "at least they cannot resist the uplifting force of general education." "The only remedy for ignorance," he argues, "is knowledge," and he envisions a day "[w]hen the schoolmaster is abroad in the land," and "there will be raised up . . . a labouring population, no matter how poor or how humble, not below the rank and file of the foreign contingent of our New York democracy, and quite intelligent enough to exercise the right of voting without danger to the State" (174–75). He concludes this argument by noting that "[n]o matter how the blacks may increase they can never be a match for the superior intelligence and power of organization of the whites," assuring his resistant white readers that the black race is in no danger of being fully uplifted for centuries to come, so that "our Southern friends may safely postpone the catastrophe of negro domination to the next generation!" (176, 178). This is organization indeed—including the mocking rejoinder to prevailing southern fears. Throughout this book, as he does here, Field demonstrates his firm belief in the power of knowledge, including the power to organize and contextualize the vehicles of knowledge—a system of education based on the assumption of white supremacy and constructed so as to sustain the cultural grounds for that assumption.

Operating within this cultural field, *Iola Leroy* takes as its fundamental assumption that in the new, postbellum battles, the enemies are no longer easy to identify, and allies offer, at best, a dubious hope. The only sure weapon is that of education, but the nature of education has already been called into question. Readers know from the early chapters of the novel (if they didn't know before) that racism was not limited to the South; it is of little comfort, then, to read of "a new army that had come with an invasion of ideas, that had come to supplant ignorance with knowledge" (*IL* 146). As the northern aristocrat Dr. Gresham puts it, arguing with clear racial-Darwinist logic (and sounding very like Henry M. Field), "[p]ower . . . naturally gravitates into the strongest hands. The class who have the best brain and most wealth can strike with the heaviest hand. I have too much faith in the inherent power of the white race to dread the competition of any other people under heaven" (*IL* 223). Of course, Dr. Gresham assumes that the field of competition lies beneath a specifically white heaven. The actual terms of this competition is best revealed by Mr. Cloten, the storeowner who provides Iola with secure employment, as he reflects on the tension between the northern and southern "civilizations." Recognizing that Northerners could counter southern prejudice "with better grace if we divested ourselves of our own," Cloten demonstrates a sound understanding of the inherently hegemonic impulse of cultural systems when he argues, "We should stamp ourselves on the South, and not let the South stamp itself on us" (*IL* 212).[19] Naturally, the impact of these mutual stampings will be felt most fully by African Americans—those who had already been defined by the racial theories of the day, "stamped with blackness," as Henry Field James asserts in his 1856 antiabolitionist novel *Abolitionism Unveiled* (124). By the forces of socialization and education, African Americans would be further stamped and thereby transformed from unsolvable cultural mysteries to components in the ruling cultural formula.

## Enlightened Shadows

Essentially, Harper demonstrates that the combined lights of the northern and southern cultures produce only ominous shadows and argues that such shadows can be lifted only by those who stand beyond the cognitive limitations of these cultural systems. The nation as a whole needs to learn what Iola Leroy has herself discovered: "Thoughts and purposes have come to me in the shadow I should never have learned in the sunshine" (*IL* 114).[20] The "thoughts and purposes" that come to one in the shadows are, of course, the products of experience, the benefits of the "ministry of suffering"; but while they are facilitated by experience, they are not simply defined by it. Indeed, the real value of experience in the shadows is the very fact that one is excluded from the "sunshine"—the conceptual frameworks, with all their attending limitations—of a rigid civilization. It is, after all, significant that Aunt Linda and Uncle Daniel, the two most prominent representatives of black "folk" culture in the novel, completely uneducated by any dominant cultural standard of measurement, are capable of seeing "visions" of events in both this world and beyond, visions that speak of a universal law that encompasses those "fiction[s] of law" (as Stowe puts it in *Uncle Tom's Cabin* [308]) that rule individual cultures.

This view of the essential spirituality of African-American character was by no means new; Harper simply puts her own spin on what George M. Fredrickson has called "romantic racialism," the idealization of the black race as more spiritual, more emotional, and even more feminine (in accordance with gender stereotypes of the nineteenth century) than the Anglo-Saxon race. Romantic racialism is what we see in Lydia Maria Child's comparison "between women and the colored race." "Both," asserts Child, "are characterized by affection more than by intellect, both have a strong development of the religious sentiment; both are exceedingly adhesive in their attachments" (qtd. in Norton 162). This flexible stereotype not only supported paternalist arguments for slavery (a danger that Child recognized) but also lent cultural force to Methodist bishop Gilbert Haven's assertion that the black race was in fact the superior race, "the choice blood of America" (qtd. in Fredrickson 102).[21] Harper draws from this stereotype and turns it back against the dominant culture, suggesting that the black race has these qualities because it has not been corrupted by the dominant culture's mode of education. Returning to the conception of education that I mentioned earlier, Harper's call for a marriage of "the devising brain and the feeling heart," we can see now that this conception of education is the province of women generally and of African-American women specifically. If local laws are to align with universal laws, then those who hold the tools of education must learn how to use them by looking, with "feeling hearts," to African-American culture.

They must do so not because African Americans have any inherent racial claim to spiritual insight, but rather because African Americans have come to understand and embody most fully those moral and philosophical ideals to which the nation claimed devotion. Like *Uncle Tom's Cabin*, one of Harper's most noticeable literary models, *Iola Leroy* operates within an eschatological paradigm, viewing temporal events and individual cognitive processes according to an unchanging order. As Reverend Carmicle says late in the novel, "Justice is always uncompromising in its claims and inexorable in its demands. The laws of the universe are never repealed to accommodate our follies" (*IL* 259). This view of American cultural stability, relying on an alignment of historical practice and providential design, was a central feature of American self-idealization, institutionalized in (to offer only one of many prominent examples) George Bancroft's *History of the United States*. It was a central feature of nineteenth-century African-American literary strategies as well.[22] Indeed, Martin Delany advocates this view for the development of Africa in his *Official Report of the Niger Valley Exploring Party* (1861), arguing that "Christianity certainly is the most advanced civilization that man ever attained to, and wherever propagated in its purity, to be effective, law and government must be brought in harmony with it—otherwise it becomes corrupted, and a corresponding degeneracy ensues, placing its votaries even in a worse condition than the primitive" (108–9). Presenting slavery in the familiar image of "a fearful cancer eating into the nation's heart, sapping its vitality, and undermining its life," Harper presents Christianity as the only possible means of national recovery. As Iola expresses it, "there is but one remedy by which our nation can recover from the evil entailed upon her by slavery," and that remedy is "A fuller comprehension of the claims of the Gospel of Jesus Christ, and their application to our national life" (*IL* 216).

Harper argues that only those beyond the boundaries of local conceptions of justice—only those who stand, as Anne Norton puts it, "outside the circle of civil society" (163)—can see universal laws. In fact, she argues that they can see them specifically because their instincts have not been distorted by corrupted modes of perception. As Aunt Linda, Uncle Daniel, Marie Leroy, and many others in the novel realize, there is a vast difference between institutional Christianity, which has been corrupted by the institution of slavery, and experiential Christianity. This, too, was part of the battle African Americans faced after the Civil War, for, as Eric Foner has noted, "[m]ost Northern missionaries believed the old-time slave preachers must be replaced by new men trained in theology" (91).[23]

Again, it is useful to consider Martin Delany's prewar application of American issues to the problem of African self-development. Addressing the influence of missionaries in the Niger Valley, Delany represents the inevitable African response: "He at once comes to a stand. 'Of what use is the white man's religion and "book knowledge" to me, since it does not give me the knowledge and wisdom nor the wealth and power of the white man, as all these things belong only to him? Our young men and women learn their book, and talk on paper (write), and talk to God like white man (worship), but God no hear 'em like He hear white man! Dis religion no use to black man' " (*Official Report* 108). As I have noted,

Delany, in this document especially, argues not against Christianity but rather for the recognition that "[r]eligion . . . requires temporal and secular aid" (108), a position that Harper carefully promotes in her work and emphasizes in *Trial and Triumph*. Bernard W. Bell has noted the similarity between *Iola Leroy*'s Robert Johnson and the title character of Delany's novel *Blake* in their rejection of white Christianity, and one might add Mr. Thomas from *Trial and Triumph*, who exclaims against the "great deal of bosh in the estimate some of us have formed of white people," and argues soundly, "Talk of the heathenism of Africa, of hostile tribes warring upon each other and selling the conquered foes into the hands of white men, but how much higher in the scale of moral progression was the white man who doomed his own child, bone of his bone, and flesh of his flesh, to a life of slavery?" (*MST* 235). Certainly, Harper's characters, like Delany's, reject white Christianity; more to the point, however, is the affirmation of Christianity that fills the cultural and spiritual space cleared by this rejection. The same Mr. Thomas, after all, later warns a friend against "making the mistake that better educated men than you have done," namely, "putting Christianity and its abuses together"; and Mr. Thomas echoes Delany in considering Christianity "the world's best religion" (*MST* 212–13). As Uncle Daniel argues when Robert Johnson suggests that Daniel should study theology, "I'se been a preachin' dese thirty years, an' you come yere a tellin' me 'bout studying yore ologies. I larn'd my 'ology at de foot ob de cross. You bin dar?" (*IL* 168). Or as Janie puts it in *Their Eyes Were Watching God*, "you got tuh *go* there tuh *know* there" (183). Obstructed by its own cultural formations, blinded by its own "ologies," the dominant culture can no longer go there; and without the aid of this marginalized culture, it cannot hope to know there.

Like other nineteenth-century African-American writers, Harper equates literacy and freedom; but her conception of literacy as presented in *Iola Leroy* involves not only the awareness that her own rhetorical skills will be used as a gauge of her (and her race's) inherent ability, but also the awareness that the dominant culture's conception of literacy offers only a dubious freedom at best. *Iola Leroy* is an example of what Robert B. Stepto has termed "the Afro-American discourse of distrust," a response to sympathetic readers who are "confused about whether access to literacy for that individual [the author] was to be for their purposes or those which the individual might construe" ("Distrust" 304, 302). The difference between experiential Christianity and institutional Christianity, between understanding gained at the foot of the Cross and "ologies," is, at base, a difference of literacy. In its own subservience to the institution of slavery, the dominant culture has forgotten how to read: "But slavery had cast such a glamour over the Nation, and so warped the consciences of men, that they failed to read aright the legible transcript of Divine retribution which was written upon the shuddering earth, where the blood of God's poor children had been as water freely spilled" (*IL* 14).[24] Harper here echoes Douglass, who noted in an 1881 address at Harpers Ferry, "Slavery had so benumbed the moral sense of the nation, that it never suspected the possibility of an explosion like this, and it was difficult for Captain Brown to get himself taken for what he really was" ("Did John Brown Fail?" 17). In stark contrast to this kind of illiteracy is the story in *Iola Leroy* of a slave who, realizing that literacy is "the key to the forbidden knowledge," teaches himself by inscribing his developing understanding on the earth itself: "He got the sounds of the letters by heart, then cut off the bark of a tree, carved the letters on the smooth inside, and learned them. . . . He made the beach of the river his copybook, and thus he learned to write" (*IL* 45). If "[t]he Union had snapped asunder because it lacked the cohesion of justice" (*IL* 24), its only hope for such cohesion, and therefore for the kind of transcendent Union that is so prominent a part of the national mythology, would be to learn how to read the divine transcript, to acquire the moral literacy that it had sacrificed to slavery. Indeed, Harper is quite clear on this point in *Minnie's Sacrifice*, in which the narrator, discussing the Civil War, considers transcripts, readers, and modes of education: "Was it not the hope of freedom which they were binding as amulets around their hearts? They as a race had lived in a measure upon an idea; it was the hope of a deliverance yet to come. Faith in God had underlain the life of the race, and was it strange if when even some of our politicians did not or could not read the signs of the times aright these people with deeper intuitions understood the war better than they did?" (*MST* 65). The narrator offers these reflections as Louis takes an Underground Railroad journey northward, with all black conductors risking time and blood to help him. Another of Harper's anomalous contradictions, Louis had formerly thought he was white, and had taken a kind of Underground Railroad backwards, in effect, to join the Confederacy. Informed of his parentage, he learns to read himself, and to trust those more skilled readers who had lived with that kind of self-knowledge all their lives, and who had lived on an idea now in the process of being translated into action.

The novel offers hope in this regard, the hope of mutual uplift, a hope dependent on the dominant culture's willingness "to clasp hands with the negro and march abreast with him to freedom and victory" (*IL* 24). The answer to the nation's problems is not for the North to "stamp its impression" on the South, but rather for white culture generally to receive the impression of African-American culture. In Delany's *Blake*, as I have noted earlier, Henry Blake's plan is referred to as an "organization," the beauty of which is that "punishment and misery are made the instruments for its propagation" (40). The plan of rebellion is both structured and encouraged by the principles and methods of oppression, so that "[e]very blow you receive from the oppressor impresses the organization upon your mind" (40). Confronting the more complex cultural situation after the war, Harper extends this antithetical perspective beyond the realm of politics and rebellion, applying it to a mode of understanding, even a mode of being. Although Dr. Gresham has yet a long way to go, by the end of the novel he has come a long way from the man who could not imagine kissing an African American. Once again, his comments indicate the "complexion of affairs": "Iola, I learned to love you in the hospital. I have tried to forget you, but it has been all in vain. Your image is just as deeply engraven on my heart as it was the day we parted" (*IL* 230). While Gresham still considers most African Americans inferior, he recognizes as well, however particular that recognition may be in its origin and focus, that "the true reconstruction of the country" depends on those like Iola who are capable of replacing the nation's corrupted institutions with "more stately temples of thought and action" (*IL* 236). As in Douglass's "The Heroic Slave" the white Mr. Listwell is converted to the antislavery movement once Madison Washington's face is "daguerreotyped on [his] memory," so the change in Gresham is a change effected by the inscription of Iola's image upon his heart.

### Histories of (Mis)understanding

Like *Uncle Tom's Cabin*, *Iola Leroy* is a novel designed to inspire readers "to feel right" by engraving upon readers' hearts images representative of a transcendent standard of thought and of action, a union of meaning and of mode, of matter and of manner. Harper, however, locates the vehicle of that transcendent standard specifically in African-American thought and literary culture. Critics have noted that Harper includes in *Iola Leroy* portions of her essays and lectures, and in fact Harper includes much from many of her works. Readers of Harper's fiction, poetry, essays, and speeches encounter again and again key words and phrases and recurring plots that together serve as a kind of conceptual framework for reimagining identity by *reimaging* cultural politics as moral struggles. One encounters again and again, for example, the story of Moses, various stories of sacrifice, tales of trials and triumphs; and one encounters words like *mystery, blood, sowing and reaping, sunshine and shadow*, and various examples of words written or impressions inscribed. Many of the plots and much of the language Harper uses have dual meanings, read one way in the world's terms, and another when read as if written by a divine author. Woven together—which would be my image for describing Harper's most prominent literary approach—Harper's narrative and discursive patterns form a strong and consistent fabric. As readers become a part of this fabric, they can use these narrative and discursive threads to mend the fabric of their own lives. Certainly, *Iola Leroy*, in so many ways the culmination of Harper's literary career, is her most carefully woven textual performance.

But Harper goes yet further, and I would suggest that African-American self-expression constitutes the subtext of this novel, a subtext that accounts for the world from which that expression rises, and to which it must respond. Harper's writings are in fact rich in historical and literary allusions, to the extent that she, like Brown, might well be termed a cultural editor. Like Brown in *Clotel*, Harper in *Iola Leroy* repeats significant phrases and plots from other sources, placing familiar lessons in new settings, and reworking cultural plots and recasting cultural identities in new literary scripts. In *Iola Leroy*, for example, Tom Anderson heroically gives his life for the sake of Union soldiers when he leaps from a beached boat under heavy fire to push it into the water, reasoning that "Some one must die to get us out of this. I mought's well be him as any. You are soldiers and can fight. If they kill me, it is nuthin' " (*IL* 53). Harper had told this story before, in *Minnie's Sacrifice* (*MST* 67), and again in her speech "A Factor in Human Progress" (*BCD* 279–80); and so, too, had Brown, in *The Negro in the American Revolution* (1867), in which his hero, "Big Bob," announces, "Somebody's got to die to get us out of this, and it may as well be me!" (215). Brown follows his narration of this episode with a poem; but the episode was captured in a different poem in 1865. This one, entitled "Black Tom," purportedly was written "By a Yankee Soldier" and is included in *The Freedmen's Book*, which Lydia Maria Child edited and published as a textbook for the freedmen's schools, and which includes poems by Harper as well. Although in the Yankee soldier's poem "Black Tom" is struck by a bullet while marching through the forest, the poem is followed by a narrative of the episode at the water, in which Tom is quoted as saying, "If they kill me, it is nothing; but you are soldiers, and are needed to fight for the country."[25] Here and elsewhere Harper draws from others to maintain and develop legendary narratives capable of serving the African-American community by preserving and transforming its past.

That community is represented even in the names Harper chooses for her characters. For example, I have noted the significance of Harper's use of the word *mystery*, and I have noted as well (as have others) congruencies between Harper's work and that of Martin Delany. In this light, it is worth noting that Delany founded a newspaper called *The Mystery* (1843), which he edited before his brief stint as co-editor, with Frederick Douglass, of the *North Star*. In 1848, Victor Ullman reports, *The Mystery's* "subscription list was taken over" by the African Methodist Episcopal Church to enable the publication of the *Christian Herald*, which in 1852 became the *Christian Recorder*, in which some of Harper's poems were published along with her novels. It is worth noting as well that the eventual bride of Iola's brother Harry is Lucille Delany, whose name recalls not only that of Martin Delany but also that of Lucy A. Delaney (also spelled Delany), author of the narrative *From the Darkness Cometh the Light, or Struggles for Freedom* (c. 1891). Iola herself marries Dr. Frank Latimer, whose name recalls that of George Latimer, the fugitive slave seized in Boston in 1842, and the subject of Douglass's first appearance in print (in *The Liberator*, Nov. 18, 1842). The name of the title character recalls the pen-name "Iola" used by the educator and journalist Ida B. Wells, with whom Harper had both personal and professional ties, in her "weekly letters" to the *Living Way* in the late 1880s.[26]

The name of Dr. Frank Latimer's astounded colleague, Dr. Latrobe, recalls that of the Latrobe family, one of the most prominent families of Baltimore, where Harper was born. Included in this family are, among others, Benjamin Henry Latrobe, who is credited with the professionalization of architecture in America, and whose elder brother, Christian

Ignatius, wrote *Journal of a Visit to South Africa in 1815 and 1816* (1818).
Among his many accomplishments, Benjamin Henry Latrobe was an
occasional student of African-American culture, and Eileen Southern
reports that "[t]he most detailed contemporary description of dancing in
the Place Congo is found" in Latrobe's journal, observations written
during an extended visit to New Orleans in 1818–1820 (135). Latrobe's son,
Benjamin Henry Latrobe, Jr., was like his father an architect and engineer,
and builder of the marvelously durable stone-arch bridge called by doubt-
ers of the 1830s and beyond "Latrobe's Folly." Charles Hazlehurst Latrobe,
grandson of the patriarch, was during the war a lieutenant of engineers in
the Confederate army. Finally, John Hazlehurst Boneval Latrobe, lawyer
and inventor of the popular Latrobe stove, helped found the Maryland
State Colonization Society and succeeded Henry Clay as the president of
the national society in 1853, a post Latrobe held for thirty-seven years.[27]
Collectively, this fascinating family reflects the complex cultural field that
African Americans faced before and after the war, including the white
appropriation of the issue of African-American liberty by way of the
American Colonization Society.[28]

Perhaps most interesting, though, is the patriarch himself, Benjamin
Henry Latrobe, for in this single figure one can see the symbolic architect
of the exclusionary dominant cultural system. Latrobe had won great
fame for his work on the south wing of the Capitol during Jefferson's
administration and was put in charge of rebuilding the Capitol after the
war of 1812. In Baltimore, Latrobe designed the imposing Baltimore
Cathedral. In Philadelphia, he designed the Bank of Pennsylvania, still
standing when Harper moved there by 1854, and the imposing Bank of
Philadelphia. The Capitol, a cathedral, and a bank: government, religion,
and finance—these achievements make Latrobe (whose fame was extensive
in America generally, and, one would assume, in Baltimore particularly) a
perfect representative of the standing order.[29] Indeed, in the novel, Dr.
Latrobe argues against African-American rights and equality by appealing
to government ("we are numerically stronger in Congress"), to economics
("we own nineteen-twentieths of the land"), and to religion (we have
"introduced [Africans] to the world's best religion") (*IL* 224–25). In the
name *Latrobe*, then, Harper finds not only a symbol of the Baltimore
society that pressured her family to leave the area after the Compromise
of 1850 but also the paradigm of the dominant culture itself.

And, finally, we might introduce into this symbolic community Iola's white suitor, Dr. Gresham, whose name recalls the economic term "Gresham's law."[30] Gresham's law states, as Simon Newcomb puts it in his 1886 *Principles of Political Economy*, that "*A cheaper or depreciated currency always tends to displace a more valuable one*" (415); or, as it was more familiarly phrased, "bad money drives out good." According to this law in its simplest form, people will hoard gold, for example, when its intrinsic value exceeds the value of paper money, sometimes called "the shadow" of the metallic currency, or they will hoard the currency of the better metal. Gresham's law was mentioned often in the heated public debates over the gold standard and the free silver movement in the last decades of the nineteenth century, and was used by "monometalists" in arguments against the "bimetalists" arguing for a return to the "double standard," using both gold and silver. Summarizing the debates in his 1888 *Principles of the Economic Philosophy of Society, Government and Industry*, Van Buren Denslow notes first that "[t]he rock on which Bimetallism, as a theory, rests, is that the perturbations in value of a currency depending on the production of two metals will be less than in a currency depending on the production of either singly"; "The quicksand which has done most to undermine this rock," Denslow continues, "has been the frequent and fallacious citation of what certain partially informed weather-prophets have supposed to be the operation of 'Gresham's law' " (368).

Harper's Dr. Gresham, of course, begins by finding it inconceivable to kiss an African American and ends by wanting to marry Iola, asking her "to be mine as nothing else on earth is mine" (*IL* 112), a phrase he repeats when he proposes to her a second time later in the novel (*IL* 230). As I have said, Gresham still considers most African Americans inferior to most whites—and in asking Iola to marry him, he is asking her to pass for white. As he says of Robert, "he would possess advantages as a white man which he could not if he were known to be colored" (*IL* 218); and as he ventures during a discussion of "open questions," "I sometimes think that the final solution to this question will be the absorption of the negro into our race" (*IL* 228). When Iola resists his proposal by talking about social barriers, he argues in turn, "Iola, I see no use in your persisting that you are colored when your eyes are as blue and complexion as white as mine" (*IL* 232). He is, in other words, looking to take out of circulation she whom he considers the most valuable of the race; she avoids identifying herself with the Anglo-Saxon race—which, she argues, uses its position to "minister to a selfish greed of gold and a love of domination" (*IL*

116)—and decides to devote herself to the African-American community.[31] This choice is, indeed, at the center of this novel; many of the central characters in *Iola Leroy*—Iola and Harry, their mother, Robert—face such a choice. And among those who decide to circulate among those with whom they have been cast, and not with those among whom they could pass, is Iola's eventual choice, Dr. Latimer, "a man of too much sterling worth of character to be willing to forsake his mother's race for the richest advantages his grandmother could bestow" (*IL* 240). Those considered more valuable by prevailing cultural standards choose to stay within the black community and to labor towards uplifting the race and promoting the recognition of its value. In effect, they resist Dr. Gresham's temptation and thus Gresham's law.

I wish here only to indicate the shadowy presence of an African-American community, with its attendant history of a developing public voice struggling against the forces of the dominant culture, inscribed upon the text of *Iola Leroy*.[32] As George Latimer inaugurated Douglass's appearance in print, so Frank Latimer encourages Iola, who expresses to him the desire "to do something of lasting service for the race," to "write a good, strong book" (*IL* 262), the subject of which, Latimer suggests, should be Iola herself. We end, then, with a novel about authorship, about writing (authorizing) the self—and, beyond that, about writing the race. As Latimer argues, " 'out of the race must come its own thinkers and writers. Authors belonging to the white race have written good racial books, for which I am deeply grateful, but it seems to be almost impossible for a white man to put himself completely in our place. No man can feel the iron which enters another man's soul' " (*IL* 263). Harper argues, though, throughout the novel, that although the white race cannot put itself in the "place" of African Americans, yet it needs the benefits of the African-American perspective if it is to re-place its moral center. As much as African Americans themselves, those confined within the perspectival boundaries of the dominant culture need "the hand of an artist to weave it [African-American experience] into the literature of the country" (*IL* 262).

In this subtle and intricate novel, Harper effectively reverses the terms of education, arguing that it must be a mutual effort, and not just the socialization of one culture according to the terms of another. As Elizabeth Ammons argues, Harper "draws on and intermixes a conglomeration of inherited forms—melodrama, journalism, adventure fiction, slave narrative, abolitionist fiction, the realistic novel, oral tradition, the romance—to reach toward a new form" (*Conflicting Stories* 27); and while I would suggest that William Wells Brown reached in similar ways by drawing from a variety of inherited forms, I agree with Ammons's estimate of the significance of Harper's artistry in creating a novel capable of "speaking in code" (32). Like Robert Johnson when he learns to read, Harper herself uses the "machinery" of the dominant culture to overthrow that culture's own formative, prescriptive "institution," education (*IL* 16). In yet another episode drawn from history, when a white gentleman comes to the school where Iola teaches, Iola suspends "the regular order of the school" so that the gentleman can talk to the children about "the achievements of the white race." Eventually, he asks the children how the white race did it. The children respond, "they've got money"; and when the gentleman asks how the white race got the money, the children respond, "They took it from us." The gentleman is left to reflect that "one of the powers of knowledge is the power of the strong to oppress the weak" (*IL* 147).[33] In this novel, Harper challenges the dynamics of oppression by redefining the nature of knowledge, a redefinition negotiated by way of the power of literature, not realistic but sentimental literature, capable of speaking beyond that world "that we can see with our eyes or grasp with our hands" (*IL* 219). In her closing "Note," Harper calls for her African-American readers to "grasp the pen and wield it as a power for good, and to erect above the ruined auction-block and slave-pen institutions of learning" (*IL* 282). *Iola Leroy* guides us through the spiritual and discursive terrain that takes us from the slave pen to the literary pen, and from the shadows of marginalized identity to a newly centralized national ideal, waiting in the shadows to be realized.

As we observe this transition from slave pen to literary pen, from the physical constructions of a restrictive culture to the spiritual constructions of moral culture, we see what I have called Harper's architectural vision of the post-Reconstruction United States.[34] The Latrobe patriarch again offers a useful model for understanding, this time not in his material constructions but in his moral understanding of human life and culture. In an 1819 entry in his journal, Latrobe writes, "We are all Slaves, nationally and individually[,] of habit: our minds and our bodies are equally fashioned by education; and altho' the original dispositions of individuals give specific variety to character, the general sentiment, like the general manners, modes of living and cooking, of sitting and standing and walking can only be slowly changed, by the gradual substitution of a new habit for the Old" (244). Harper recognized both the possibilities and dangers of cultural constructions of order, of identity, of race; in all of her writings she works to help her readers work their way through the slow change out of the minds and bodies fashioned by U.S. education into new moral habits. And, throughout, she recognizes that education is both institutional and experiential. The protagonist of *Minnie's Sacrifice* represents well Harper's cause, for Minnie looks forward with genuine enthusiasm to the "privilege to be the pioneer of a new civilization." Harper asserts the importance of this constructive project next to the more material advances of science, arguing that "If he who makes two blades of grass grow where only one flourished before is a benefactor of the human race, how much higher and holier must his or her work be who dispenses light, instead of darkness, knowledge, instead of ignorance, and over the ruins of the slave-pen and auction-block erects institutions of learning" (*MST* 68). If we are all slaves, Harper might answer Latrobe, then we are also all guards of the slave pen, and we might as well use both our authority and our helplessness wisely by putting the materials of the pen to better purposes.

And as the narrator summarizes Minnie's thoughts and her sense of duty, she makes it clear that this new civilization will require a new conception of union, a union won not by the armies of the North—be they armed with swords or with ideas—but rather by armies yet unseen: "She would say in her letters to Louis that the South will never be rightly conquered until another army should take the field, and that must be an army of civilizers; the army of the pen, and not of the sword. Not the destroyers of towns and cities, but the builders of machines and factories; the organizers of peaceful industry and honorable labor; and as soon as she possibly could she intended to join that great army" (*MST* 68). This army, whose ranks remain open to all, is the army left out of the storeowner Mr. Cloten's imagined battle—the mutual stampings of a monolithic and implicitly exclusionary North and South. More to the point, this is the army of engineers unimagined by Latrobe and his world. In *Sowing and Reaping*, Paul Clifford, an antitemperance business man, is chastised for refusing to invest in a saloon. "You have always got some moon struck theories," his proposed partner John Anderson complains, "some wild, visionary and impracticable ideas" (*MST* 96). Anderson, on the other hand, is interested in investing "in a few acres, or town lots of solid *terra firma*" (*MST* 96). Like Clifford, Harper holds to "wild, visionary and impracticable ideas," all the while arguing that she is standing on *terra firma*. Her novels are her attempts, in effect, to build on that land.

I will not insist that Harper's literary structures are unique; nor would I argue that Harper's strategies for identifying the nature of the journey from slave pen to literary pen, and for identifying her diverse readers' roles in this shared cultural quest, are themselves unique. The theme of mutual uplift, for example, goes back at least as far as Phillis Wheatley. Harper, one of the most widely known and informed African-American activists of her time, certainly knew her literary contemporaries and predecessors; and she was intimately involved as well in the subtle complexities of racial awareness, prejudice, and politics in the abolitionist, feminist, and temperance movements. Certainly, one can see in her work her own refigurations of and borrowings from the strategies of the writers I have mentioned and of many others besides. As Mae Gwendolyn Henderson has argued, "[t]he self-inscription of black women requires disruption, rereading and rewriting the conventional and canonical stories, as well as revising the conventional generic forms that convey these stories" (30). In this regard, what makes Harper significant is simply the fact that she has been so often overlooked and undervalued, and her work reduced to the level of statement, theme, and critical categories that place her securely within conventional modes of (literary) understanding.

At the beginning of her important book *Specifying: Black Women Writing the American Experience*, Susan Willis observes that "[h]istory gives topic and substance to black women's writing" (3). That this is true in regard to *Iola Leroy* has long been recognized, but what is important in *Iola Leroy* is not the history Harper received, but rather the history she returns. Harper reminds us that history is not a static or monolithic concept, a definitive structure containing clear conceptual oppositions, but rather a dynamic and diverse process filtered through the variably conditioned minds of individuals who cannot escape their roles as historical agents. The history in *Iola Leroy* is not the events Harper includes, nor the political and cultural postbellum situation she addresses; history is not that to which she responds but rather the action of her response itself, not the vision the novel presents but rather the mode of (re)envisioning it embodies—process and not result. In this conception of history, each individual stands as a particular configuration of various cultural influences, including not only those influences one would claim, but also those that threaten one's most fundamental sense of identity. One can hear this history best by listening to individual voices giving particular form to the complex cultural relations not only of the world around but also and especially of that within.

# *Epilogue*

Early in Charles W. Chesnutt's *The Marrow of Tradition*, two doctors—the northern white Dr. Burns and the southern black Dr. Miller—travel south together on the train. Looking at these two "very different and yet similar types of manhood," the narrator notes that "a celebrated traveler, after many years spent in barbarous or savage lands, has said that among all varieties of mankind the similarities are vastly more important and fundamental than the differences." But as his narrative train speeds on its "journey southward," the narrator adds immediately that if we should find ourselves "looking at these two men with the American eye, the differences would perhaps be the more striking, or at least the more immediately apparent, for the first was white and the second black, or, more correctly speaking, brown; . . . even a light brown." Having presented the view from the American eye, the narrator then offers the perspective of yet another eye, by which Dr. Burns represents "a fine type of Anglo-Saxon, as the term is used in speaking of our composite white population," while Dr. Miller's "erect form, broad shoulders, clear eyes, fine teeth, and pleasingly moulded features showed nowhere any sign of that degeneration which the pessimist so sadly maintains is the inevitable heritage of mixed races" (49).

These three perspectives on the two men indicate the terms and necessity of Chesnutt's attempt throughout the novel to deconstruct the discourse of race, exposing the binary oppositions of racialist thought that veil a world of unnamed variety. But a variety unnamed is a variety available to discursive appropriation, and it is worth noticing that here the perspective of the "American eye" is bracketed by, on the one hand, a perspective informed by trips to "barbarous and savage lands," and, on the other, a perspective that finds in one man Anglo-Saxon features and finds in the other a victory over the argument that miscegenation breeds degeneration. One wonders which of these three perspectives is the best representation of the American eye: the first, that finds its evidence of similarities within an evolutionary framework that itself promotes a hierarchy of differences; the second, that classifies by the labels *white* and *black* people whose skin color is neither white nor black; or the third, in which the individual subject becomes an embodiment of the mastering discourse of scientific racialism and can hope to be, at best, a living argument against the informing authority of that discourse. Chesnutt here draws attention to the ways in which one's eye can be disciplined by culture—shaped by a history of social prejudices and racial domination—to see differences where others would see similarities. Culture thus becomes a closed perceptual field, training people to see a world that seems unchangeable when viewed from within that field.

*The Marrow of Tradition* examines the consequences of a social and historical reality enclosed within the perceptual field of the American eye, and Chesnutt himself often struggles uncomfortably with his own training in that field. Frustrated over the social boundaries in which he was forced to live, Chesnutt complained about his life in the South, "I occupy here a position similar to that of the Mahomet's Coffin. I am neither fish[,] flesh, nor fowl—neither 'nigger,' poor white, nor 'buckrah.' Too 'stuck-up' for the colored folks, and, of course, not recognized by the whites" (*Journals* 157–58). He imagined life would be better in the North; for although he knew that his Mahomet's Coffin of selfhood would not "reach *terra firma*" in his relation to either to the black or the white population, he still imagined it would be a relief to "be in sight of land on either side" (158). In his fiction, Chesnutt responds to this cultural reality not by looking for new materials for the construction of identity but rather by reworking the available materials. In his effort to envision new worlds of understanding, he tries to bring the present world, in all its strange familiarity, to consciousness, and thereby bring it to bear upon itself.

Race, one might say, both enters and exits U.S. literature through what Chesnutt terms the American eye—transcribing perceptions shaped by social prejudices and assumptions, and particularizing those prejudices and assumptions for the reader. This, of course, is hardly news, for if white readers and writers have been slow to acknowledge and confront the construction of race in literature, black readers and writers certainly have not. Such confrontations are at the center, for example, of Harper's work. Harper's career as a writer was necessarily devoted not only to constructing a reconfigured black community but also to deconstructing white images (literary and otherwise) of black identity and potential. One character in Harper's intricate novel *Trial and Triumph* complains to a white merchant with whom he shares "kindred intellectual and literary tastes" that books by black authors go unread by white readers (222); and of the "unaspiring" inhabitants of one depressed neighborhood the narrator explains, "The literature they read was mostly from the hands of white men who would paint them in any colors which suited their prejudices or predilections" (*MST* 240). Similarly, in her essay "The Negro as Presented in American Literature," included in *A Voice from the South*, Anna Julia Cooper discusses the role literature plays in the promotion of distorted and essentialized images of races and cultures. Noting the tendency of white writers to base their black characters on the writers' perceptions of whatever black people they happened to encounter, Cooper complains that "a few with really kind intentions and a sincere desire for information have approached the subject as a clumsy microscopist, not quite at home with his instrument, might study a new order of beetle or bug. Not having focused closely enough to obtain a clear-cut view, they begin by telling you that all colored people look exactly alike and end by noting down every chance contortion or idiosyncrasy as a race characteristic" (186–87). Considered as a mode of envisioning, the American eye sees incorrectly but with increasing particularity, focusing on "chance contortions" as evidence of degeneration and using idiosyncratic materials to construct what will count as representative images.

I want to offer here a rather extreme example of what Cooper calls a "clumsy microscopist," Thomas Dixon, Jr.—for in his novel *The Clansman* (1905), arguably the most influential racist work the United States has yet produced,[1] Dixon brings his own microscope to bear on the American eye. The novel builds to that all-but-inevitable moment in turn-of-the-century white supremacist literature when a black man rapes a white woman, presented as the flower of southern culture and Aryan civilization. In this novel, two women are raped, a mother and a daughter, both of whom immediately commit suicide. Looking to discover the identity of the rapist, Doctor Cameron acts on his belief that "a microscope of sufficient power will reveal on the retina of these dead eyes the image of this devil as if etched there by fire," for, the doctor notes, just as "Impressions remain in the brain like words written on paper in invisible ink," so, too, "images in the eye" (312–13). Nothing can be found in the daughter's eye, for she is too young, so the doctor turns to the mother who, at thirty-seven, "was the full-blown perfection of womanhood with every vital force at its highest tension" (313). When his young assistant can see nothing, the doctor explains, "Your powers of vision are not as trained as mine" (313). But when the doctor trains his own trained vision on the dead mother's eye, unsurprisingly (in this novel) he finds "the bestial figure of a negro—his huge black hand plainly defined—the upper part of his face is dim, as if obscured by a gray mist of dawn—but the massive jaws and lips are clear—merciful God!—yes!—it's Gus" (314). Although his assistant suggests, "I'm afraid the image is in your own eye, sir, not the mother's," circumstantial evidence is taken as confirmation of the doctor's impressions, and they immediately take their findings to the head clansman of the township, the Grand Cyclops of the Den (314, 318).

The eye projects the image; the microscope reflects the eye; and the Grand Cyclops envisions justice: this novel performs a trick done with pseudoscientific mirrors, projecting the violation of a racialized maternal eye to reconfirm the privileged vision of the paternal eye of justice.[2] Although Dixon himself asserts otherwise, clearly the image is, indeed, in the doctor's own eye, and Dixon supports that image in his handling of its fictive environment, the world of *The Clansman*. It is as Toni Morrison has said in her own exploration of such images on the American eye, "the subject of the dream is the dreamer. The fabrication of an Africanist persona is reflexive; an extraordinary meditation on the self; a powerful exploration of the fears and desires that reside in the writerly conscious. It is an astonishing revelation of longing, of terror, of perplexity, of shame, of magnanimity" (17). *The Clansman* is only an obvious example of such fabrications, in which we can observe what Morrison has called the transformation of the "old pseudo-scientific and class-informed racisms whose dynamics we are more used to deciphering" to a metaphor used to refer to and disguise "forces, events, classes, and expressions of social decay and economic division far more threatening to the body politic than biological 'race' ever was" (47, 63). And it is threatening precisely because, as Dixon realized, the image of projected fears can be inscribed with invisible ink upon the reader's eye.

In their attempts not only to tell stories but also to give their readers the means by which to understand those stories, the authors I have discussed in this book necessarily confront the stories that exist, the images that have been inscribed, and try to undermine the conventions of understanding that we bring to such stories. Returning to the scene with which I began, Chesnutt's vision of the two doctors on a train headed south, I would note again the significance of the triangulated perspective the narrator offers: two doctors who look much the same; two doctors who look much different; and two doctors who stand as race representatives in Chesnutt's commentary on culturally determined modes of understanding and categories of identity. One might say that Chesnutt here both anticipates and complicates Ricoeur's observation that "From the point of view of progress, mankind is one; from the point of view of the history of civilization, mankind is multiple" (86). As Chesnutt might have it, from the point of view created when the American eye looks at progress, humankind is multiple, and some are excluded from the dominant race's construction of progress; but from the point of view of civilization, represented by Chesnutt's "celebrated traveler," humankind is one, and its vision of progress is obscured by the insistence of the American eye. The third perspective, of course, suggests Chesnutt's own struggle with the increasingly dominating authority of racial science, defending Dr. Miller on the grounds of his "erect form, broad shoulders, clear eyes, fine teeth, and pleasingly moulded features [which] showed nowhere any sign of that degeneration which the pessimist so sadly maintains is the inevitable heritage of mixed races." But however much Chesnutt's own struggle with racial thought is visible here, the necessity of this response to a ruling discourse of racial identity does not rule the narrative perspective of this scene, for the narrator's triangulated perspective places all three points of view within a larger framework that demonstrates the limitations of available modes of understanding to identify and describe the two men on the train. As we see the two men, we see also the inadequate lenses available for this viewing.

In this book, I have presented six of the most prominent African-American writers whose careers began in the ten or fifteen years preceding the Civil War, each of whom worked both to expose the inadequate lenses available for viewing cultural realities and to construct an adequate lens for envisioning a possible future. I have focused on texts in which familiar cultural materials—those conceptual and institutional "tools" that Ricoeur places within "the abstract level of progress"—are brought together in revealing incongruity, guiding readers to consider the incoherence of their worlds. U.S. progress, by Ricoeur's definition, had led to the development of what Chesnutt calls the American eye and a social system susceptible to the surveillance of Dixon's Grand Cyclops. I have focused on texts informed by a sophisticated understanding of the interpretive strategies by which one can enter into what Ricoeur calls "the existential level of ambiguity," a questioning of national destiny and divine judgment. And I have focused on texts devoted to a renewed apprehension of "the mysterious level of hope," careful delineations of the boundaries of human understanding joined by a reverent regard for a mystery beyond those boundaries. These texts represent that mystery by addressing directly the contradictions and incoherence of cultural modes of understanding. They point to cultural mysteries—inexplicable events, inadequate and self-contradictory discourse, incomprehensible lives—and argue that these mysteries, joined with a renewed assertion of an all-encompassing divine mystery, point to the need to explore other histories, those experiences unaccounted for in the official texts of U.S. cultural practice and self-definition.

But the incoherent dominating text grew ever more complex with the failure of Reconstruction and with the development of institutional modes of group identification (for example, the emergence of eugenics as an influential explanatory model that presented itself as a social program). It became more difficult to encompass that text in literature, to use the existing cultural materials to expose a fundamental and threatening communal incoherence, to use the materials of "progress" to reconfigure the vision of the American eye. In my discussion of Douglass and Harper I have explored the ways in which two of the most skillful antebellum activists responded to this growing challenge after the war, and one might follow similar developments in the careers of Brown, Delany, and Jacobs. Douglass's own prominence complicated this task, and I have argued that he is finally overwhelmed by the materials he must use for his construction of selfhood. Harper, similarly aware of the newly subtle and multifarious threats to black identity following the war, builds upon the strategies of Brown and Delany before her to create a world in which history can be both represented and challenged, and in which cultural materials can be encompassed in a fictive unity to promote an imagined community.

As I suggested at the end of my Introduction, Harper worked toward a vision of literature as analogue of the black church. Such a literature would be, of necessity, a structure with many rooms capable of serving many needs. It is appropriate, then, to conclude with the words of one who followed Harper, and one who learned from Brown: Pauline E. Hopkins, who includes so much in the gorgeous architecture of her novel

*Contending Forces*. In her Preface to the novel, Hopkins offers a simple but important reminder of the cultural work of fiction: "The colored race has historians, lecturers, ministers, poets, judges and lawyers,—men of brilliant intellects who have arrested the favorable attention of this busy, energetic nation. But, after all, it is the simple, homely tale, unassumingly told, which cements the bond of brotherhood among all classes and all complexions" (13). Hopkins's own tale is hardly simple, for she includes in her house of fiction the offices of the historian, the lecturer, the minister, the poet, the judge, and the lawyer. The contending forces negotiated by each of these public servants are encompassed in a novel that argues ultimately for renewed citizenship in a moral government, the dictates of which can be discerned when one arrives where the protagonists Sappho and Will arrive at the novel's conclusion, as they stand on a ship bound for Europe and watch "the receding shores with hearts filled with emotion too deep for words" (402). From wordless understanding to verbal art, Hopkins works to return her readers to U.S. shores with reconfigured vision. In this study of seemingly simple stories and faithful narratives, I have tried to be attentive to the demands of a literature that works to cement "the bond of brotherhood among all classes and all complexions," a sentimental ideal that should remind us that sentimental literature finds its authority in its ability to inspire and guide the reader's response. To respond to this literature is to enter into history, to explore old fields with new eyes, and to recognize anew both the burden and the promise of history.

# Notes

## 1. *The Profession of Authorship and the Cultural Text:* William Wells Brown's *Clotel*

1. Brown had begun including an M.D. after his name by 1864 or 1865, and advertised himself as a "Dermapathic and Practical Physician" in three printings of a "Medical Notice—the New Cure" that appeared in the *Liberator* (Farrison, *William Wells Brown* 400). In those years, of course, Brown was not alone in presenting himself as a medical practitioner on the authority only of his readings on medicine. On Brown's "brief capitalist career as a banker" that extends from his career as barber, see Peterson, 569–70.

2. On Brown as trickster, see also Yellin, *The Intricate Knot*, 159–60.

3. David Brion Davis echoes this observation in his discussion of the "paranoid style" of antebellum politics and culture. "[M]en who moved to booming cities or newly-created communities," Davis notes, "encountered a shifting melange of teams and alliances. Individual success depended, in large measure, on effective presentations of self and on convincing definitions of new situations. . . . New statuses and relationships, whether economic, religious, or political, demanded innovations in staging" (26). The inevitable frustrations and problems arising from these newly staged performances of selfhood were reflected in "both the popular and literary levels of culture," where "we find a virtual obsession with hoaxes, imposters, frauds, confidence men, and double identities" (*The Slave Power Conspiracy* 27).

4. On the condition of the northern "free" blacks, see Litwack, *North of Slavery*; Horton; and Takaki, ch. 6.

5. On Brown's approach to textual authority late in his career, see Andrews, "Mark Twain."

6. The full title of Lewis's work is *Light and Truth; Collected from the Bible and Ancient and Modern History, Containing the Universal History of the Colored and the Indian Race, from the Creation of the World to the Present Time.* For a recent discussion of this work and of nineteenth-century black historians in general, see Walker, ch. 5.

7. It is important to note also Brown's significant influence on others. One

can see traces of at least one of the versions of *Clotelle*, for example, in Frances
E. W. Harper's *Iola Leroy* and Pauline Hopkins's *Contending Forces*. And, as
Eric J. Sundquist notes, Hopkins drew much of the historical background in
her novel from Brown's *The Rising Son* (*To Wake the Nations* 570). In a later
chapter, I will note other significant ties between Brown and Harper; on
Harper's and Hopkins's borrowings from *Clotelle*, see Carby, *Reconstructing*,
71–72 and 146–47. Moreover, in an ironic twist, one can see Brown's story of
George and Mary Green, most of it reproduced verbatim, in Johnson's *From
Dixie to Canada*. In his Preface, Johnson claims to be presenting "some
realistic record" of the Underground Railroad for "posterity," the result of "a
systematic research into the matter" (v–vi). The story of George Green first
appears in Brown's *Three Years in Europe* under the title "A Narrative of
American Slavery" (Johnson's title is "George Green, or Constancy Re-
warded"). Farrison refers to this story as "Brown's first attempt to write an
antislavery romance," though he notes as well that Brown ends the first
printing by claiming that the story had been told to him in 1852 by George
Green himself (*William Wells Brown* 204, 206). Finding one's way through
this maze of influences and borrowings can be difficult. For example, Bentley
speculates that "George Green was probably modeled after Stowe's George
Harris, a Mulatto hero who had similarly blurred the boundary between
violent rebellion and liberation" (507), and this is possible, since *Uncle Tom's
Cabin* was published serially before *Three Years in Europe* appeared in 1852.
DuCille, noting that Brown seems to echo Stowe in his allusions to Hungar-
ian refugees, notes also that Joan Hendrick has traced "Stowe's source to a
commentary that appeared in the New York *Independent* in January 1851"
(156n). My point is that one must handle questions of influence with great
care, for much of the antislavery literature we read did not *create* images,
narratives, and arguments so much as resituate, reconfigure, and reinvigorate
them.

8. Similarly, Farrison notes that Brown's claim that *The American Fugitive
in Europe* (the U.S. edition of *Three Years in Europe*) contained "a dozen or
more additional chapters" "was not altogether accurate" (253).

9. Similarly, another poem included in *The Anti-Slavery Harp*—"The Blind
Slave Boy," by "Mrs. Dr. Bailey"—provided Brown with a story he tells in
*Clotel*, including the poem but omitting the author's name.

10. On Brown's autobiographies and their changing emphases, facts, and
claims, see Andrews, *To Tell a Free Story*; Yellin, *The Intricate Knot*; Gara,
Introduction, ix–xvii; Castronovo, 527–28; and Farrison.

11. Jefferson reports that the British journalist William Farmer is the author
not only of the "Memoir of William Wells Brown" in *Three Years* but also of
the "Narrative of the Life and Escape of William Wells Brown" that appears

in *Clotel* and then again (with minor changes) as "Memoir of the Author" in *The American Fugitive in Europe* (Introduction 11). Farrison, however, notes Farmer's authorship of the *Three Years* memoir, but refers to the memoir in *American Fugitive* as "a reproduction of the first forty-six pages of the autobiographical sketch in *Clotel*" (*William Wells Brown* 252). When discussing the narrative that opens *Clotel*, Andrews follows Farrison in suggesting that "[a]lthough written in the third person as though by a biographer, this installment of Brown's life, which included a good deal of information on his experiences in the North and in England, was more than likely his own creation" (*From Fugitive Slave to Free Man* 4). For an excellent discussion of the relation between the memoir—itself a collection of texts—and *Clotel*, see Stepto, *From Behind the Veil*, 26–31; for the ways in which his more directly autobiographical texts shaped his other works, see Foster, *Witnessing Slavery*.

Farrison reports that Alonzo Moore was a native of Aurora, New York, and was the son of Brown's host during an 1844 visit in which Brown dealt effectively with an antagonistic crowd. Moore wrote his account of the event thirty years later; for Farrison's discussion of this matter, see *William Wells Brown*, 82–83.

12. For brief but useful commentary on Josephine Brown's *Biography of an American Bondman*, see Andrews, Introduction to *Two Biographies*, xxxiii–xliii.

13. Farrison summarizes Brown's borrowings from Beard as follows: "Having adapted passages from the Reverend John R. Beard's *Life of Toussaint L'Ouverture* in his *Clotel*, Brown used that biography much more extensively in his *St. Domingo*. In many instances he quoted or adapted Beard's sentences, changing them only to facilitate his own sentence structure, or shortening them by eliminating words not needed in his context. He changed words in some places apparently for the sake of simplicity, but without necessarily achieving that to any greater extent than Beard had already achieved it" (*William Wells Brown* 256).

14. For excellent discussions of Brown's revisions of *Clotel* through the years as they pertain to representations of gendered identity see Fabi; Yarborough; and Bentley, 515–16.

15. Brown tells here the story of Clotel's death that in one form or another and in different genres he told throughout his career. Douglass also tells this story (and before Brown's version appears) in an 1846 speech included in the Appendix of *My Bondage and My Freedom*, 403–4.

16. Farrison notes also that "Captain Frederick Marryat had previously synopsized a similar story in his 1839 *A Diary in America, with Remarks on Its Institutions*" (*Clotel* 250n).

17. On responses to *Uncle Tom's Cabin* and on both pro-and anti-Uncle Tom literature, see Gossett, *Uncle Tom's Cabin and American Culture*.

18. For a general discussion of Brown's adaptation of literary conventions throughout his career, and of his use of documentation, see Lewis.

19. The presentation of a divine order upholding all the rest is a commonplace of nineteenth-century U.S. history generally and of black American writing specifically, from the cautious warnings that issue from Phillis Wheatley's poems to the visionary militancy of Nat Turner and David Walker to the consistent lessons of Frances Harper.

Much has been written on the secular religion of America; see, for example, Hatch; Tuveson; and Wood, ch. 3. For valuable interrogations of this vision of the U.S., see especially Bercovitch, *The American Jeremiad* and *The Office of The Scarlet Letter*; and Berlant. For a discussion of this vision of the nation as it was represented by nineteenth-century U.S. historians, see Levin; and Callcott. On the influence of this vision in works written by black historians, see Walker, ch. 5.

20. Oakes also discusses marriage to set up a larger cultural/historical analysis and echoes Brown when he explains, "The legal conundrum of slave marriages is an example of a more general problem that I am concerned with throughout this book: the degree to which relationships we take for granted are in fact deeply political, are in fact grounded in carefully developed laws regulating the power of the persons involved" (xvii). For excellent discussions of the presence of marriage in African-American literature, see duCille; and Tate.

21. For an overview of such musical and social forums, see Southern, ch. 5.

22. In Child's story, the sentence is as follows: "The tenderness of Rosalie's conscience required an outward form of marriage; though she well knew that a union with her proscribed race was unrecognized by law, and therefore the ceremony gave her no legal hold on Edward's constancy" ("The Quadroons," 62). By including the role of Clotel's mother in this act of conscience, Brown of course emphasizes the social, moral, and educational role of marriage.

23. For a different perspective on Georgiana Peck and the economy operating in *Clotel*, see Peterson, 570.

24. Interestingly, Brown reports this bargain three times in roughly the same language, once for each laboring group: the field slaves, the house servants, and the bricklayers (165–66).

25. *Clotel* was published in London. In his Preface, Brown notes that "[t]he fact that slavery was introduced into the American colonies, while they were under the control of the British Crown, is a sufficient reason why Englishmen should feel a lively interest in its abolition." He appeals to his readers for "aid in bringing British influence to bear upon American slavery" (16). In the final sentences of his Conclusion, Brown calls for "the voice of the whole British nation" to "be heard across the Atlantic, and throughout the length and breadth of the land of the Pilgrim Fathers" (246).

26. I am grateful to Joe Poulin, graduate student at the University of New Hampshire, for introducing me to Whelpley's book.

27. On the complex racial and cultural dynamics of blackface minstrelsy, see Lott.

## 2. *God's Economy and Frado's Story:* Harriet E. Wilson's *Our Nig*

1. On the critical and cultural implications of the publication and format of the recent second edition of *Our Nig*, see Dearborn, 31–33; Gardner; and B. White, 20, 46n.

2. On Wilson's health, and on her presentation of health and pain in the narrative, see C. Davis.

3. The final tragedy of this book is that Wilson's experiment apparently failed, for her young son died shortly after the book was published.

4. For backgrounds on Wilson, see B. White, whose essay is a model of careful research. Among White's numerous and valuable findings is the resounding evidence that the Hayward family (the model for *Our Nig*'s Bellmonts) had "strong abolitionist connections" (34). See also Gardner, who speculates that "abolitionists knew about the book but . . . may have consciously chosen *not* to publicize it" (227).

5. On this question, see Dearborn, 31–33.

6. See Gates, Introduction, xlvi, lii, lv; and *Figures*, 143.

7. Similarly, Blyden Jackson is compelled to argue not only that *Our Nig* is a good novel—"*elementary*" rather than "*simple*"—but that "it is a better novel than the first novel written by a black American male. Of Frado and Clotel, Frado is the superior artifact" (363).

8. White's documentary evidence supports her speculation that Wilson was "bound out" to the Haywards under the "vendue system" or "New England method" of disposing of the poor, "in which the poor were auctioned off or bound out" (" 'Our Nig' and the She-Devil," 46n).

9. On the text as product, see Holloway; see also Peterson's economic reading of *Our Nig*.

10. On Wilson's intended audience, see also Doriani; and Fox-Genovese. We should remember, as well, that Frederick Douglass, addressing himself to a racially mixed audience, had been sharply critical of northern prejudice and of abolitionists themselves since the late 1840s and pointedly in his revisionist 1855 autobiography *My Bondage and My Freedom*. See also Mitchell.

11. I am thinking in particular of the "scientific" racialism one encounters in Nott and Gliddon and in Cartwright. For background on racialist thought and science, see Fredrickson; Gossett; and Stanton.

12. It is worth noting that Frances E. W. Harper tells this same story about

black women (what she calls simply "the old story") in *Minnie's Sacrifice* and *Trial and Triumph* (11). Harper, though, argues forcefully against assumptions about the different natures and responsibilities of the sexes—assumptions that make possible a society "which closed its doors against" one seduced woman "and left her to struggle as best she might out of the depth into which she had fallen" without also pouring "any righteous wrath upon" the seducer's "guilty head" (191–92). Here and elsewhere Harper argues forcefully against a double standard that calmly watches the sowing of wild oats and harshly judges fallen women.

13. On the complex deceptions and legends accompanying the pro-and antislavery movements generally and the Underground Railroad specifically, see Gara, *The Liberty Line*.

14. On Mag's and Frado's similar situations and their different responses to their situations, see Tate, 37–38.

15. The economic arguments surrounding slavery are as complex as nineteenth-century religious, scientific, and legal justifications of slavery. For useful entrances into the economic issues and arguments, see Abbott; Bender; Kaufman; Shore; and Temperly. For additional background, see Fredrickson; Genovese; Takaki; and Tise.

16. To modern ears, and even to those nineteenth-century ears that have heard arguments comparing slavery to English labor, Brown's reference to the "point of law" might sound rather thin, but even the existence of a framework that could enable one to claim rights by pointing to existing laws was significant. See, for example, the list of American laws that Brown includes at the end of the second edition of his *Narrative of William W. Brown, A Fugitive Slave*—the Appendix of which leads ultimately to a comparison between northern American labor and slavery.

17. For useful background on sociology, see Lepenies. On the professionalization of knowledge in the United States, see Hall.

18. For a recent reconsideration of Fitzhugh, see Grammer.

19. G. Brown's discussion of abolition as "the reformation of labor" and of Stowe's views of Irish versus black domestic servants (54–59) seems relevant here. On the condition of "free blacks" in the North, see Litwack, *North of Slavery*. On issues concerning labor and gender, see Bennett; P. Foner; Lown; and Turbin.

20. For additional background on the cultural and political climate of the time, and on perceptions of black labor as a threat to white labor, see Anbinder.

21. On the complex position of race in the development of American political and industrial culture, see especially Saxton, chs. 6 and 11. In ch. 7, Saxton, like Roediger, emphasizes the cultural, political, and economic role of

blackface minstrelsy (on which see also Lott). For general background on the intersections of racially charged moral and political reform arguments, see Gerteis (in which, on the political climate in New Hampshire, see 98–99).

22. For a reading of the nature and significance of Wilson's economic enterprise that differs significantly from the one I present here, see Holloway.

23. Gates and others have argued that Frado's conversion to Christianity is not real, that "Frado never truly undergoes a religious transformation, merely the *appearance* of one" (Introduction xlix). However, I agree with Tate that Wilson offers her own version of the familiar African-American distinction between profession and practice—or, as Douglass puts it, "between the Christianity of this land, and the Christianity of Christ" (*Narrative* 97). As Tate argues, "Although the appendix clearly characterizes Wilson as a pious Christian . . . her faith is not without doubt and it mounts a sustained interrogation of the conventional practice of Christianity throughout the text" (47). The fact that Frado struggles to understand and accept Christianity should not be taken as evidence that she does not finally consider herself a Christian.

24. It should be noted, however, that while Jane certainly never confuses the two rivals, Wilson apparently does, referring in the final pages to Jane's happiness with "Henry."

25. See, for example, Bell, 49; for a more recent analysis, see Tate, 33. In their consideration of the significance of this play on color-coded standards, critics sometimes treat it as if it were innovative, but Maria W. Stewart uses this as her central figurative device for opening her 1835 *Productions of Mrs. Maria W. Stewart*: see 4–5; see also 52. In fact, this device emerges with some frequency in works by and about nineteenth-century African Americans. In an 1846 letter that he reprints in *My Bondage and My Freedom*, Frederick Douglass had sharply attacked standards that allowed the ridicule and oppression of African Americans "with impunity by any one, (no matter how black his heart,) so he has a white skin" (374). In 1853, William Wells Brown wrote in *Clotel* of one Thomas Corwin, "one of the blackest white men in the United States" (178); and in *Incidents in the Life of a Slave Girl*, Linda Brent identifies a Methodist class leader and town constable as a "white-faced, black-hearted brother" (70). One often encounters other versions of this figurative turn; for example, one character in Harper's *Trial and Triumph* praises Annette in conversation with a friend, noting that " 'I told her . . . that I had had a vision that some one who was fair, was coming to help us. She smiled and said she was not fair. I told her she was fair to me' " (*MST* 284). One hears echoes of this phrase everywhere, as in the anonymously authored novel *Uncle Daniel's Story of "Tom" Anderson and Twenty Great Battles*, about white Northerners during and following the Civil War, in which a white character says of black

"Aunt Martha," "God never made a better heart under any white skin than she had under her black one" (237).

26. On the charity of the rich and the transition from the "nineteenth-century concept of charity" prominent in Wilson's time to the "new paternalism" that followed the Civil War and Reconstruction, see Fredrickson, ch. 7.

### 3. *Reading the Fragments in the Fields of History:* Harriet Jacobs's *Incidents in the Life of a Slave Girl*

1. Dorothy Sterling has called the convention not only "the first public political meeting of U.S. women" but also "the first interracial gathering of any consequence" (*Turning* 3). *Incidents'* editor, Lydia Maria Child, attended the convention, as did many other prominent women. The convention passed resolutions denouncing prejudices against color, promoting the renewal and practice of Christian principles, and arguing against the practice of many churches. The convention delegates also "organized a campaign to collect a million signatures on petitions to Congress asking for the abolition of slavery in the District of Columbia and the Florida Territory," and "prepared six pamphlets and 'open letters' for publication" (Sterling, *Turning* 4). Significantly, agreements about the public efficacy of Christian virtue and sympathetic motherhood were more easily reached than agreements about attendant redefinitions of women's social role. On the 1837 convention in the context of women's reform activism generally, see Ginzberg, ch. 1; on the 1837 convention and the justification and political influence of petitions, see Ginzberg, ch. 3 and Lerner, ch. 8.

2. The phrase is from a letter from Jacobs to Amy Post; in *Incidents*, 232.

3. On Jacobs's/Brent's relation to her readers, see Yellin, *Women & Sisters*, 92; Carby, *Reconstructing*, 51; Andrews, *To Tell a Free Story*, 253–54; and Sidonie Smith.

4. Braxton presents "the archetype of the outraged mother" as "a counterpart to the articulate hero," noting of this archetype that "She is a mother because motherhood was virtually unavoidable under slavery; she is outraged because of the intimacy of her oppression" (19).

5. For backgrounds on reform movements and sensational literature, see Reynolds.

6. On the role of motherhood in *Incidents*, see also S. Sherman.

7. On the nineteenth-century eroticization of the vice of slavery—making the slave narrative, in Robin Winks's phrase, "the pious pornography of their day" (qtd. in Andrews, *To Tell a Free Story* 243)—see Andrews, 242–44.

8. See J. Sherman on Brent's position "between the brutal, exploitative bonds of slavery and the idealized, altruistic bonds of true womanhood" (167).

9. On black women and the cult of true womanhood, see Yee; Tate; and Carby, *Reconstructing*.

10. On the republican home, history, and women's writings, see Baym, "At Home with History," 278. On nineteenth-century American assumptions about the progress and perfection of history, see Levin. On women, theology, American historiography, and the "escape from history," see Ann Douglas, ch. 5. On American republican ideologies of womanhood, see Margolis, 33–39 and 115–24; and especially Kerber.

11. See Bloch on "the conflation of the virtuous with the feminine" in Revolutionary America—the process by which conceptions of republican civic virtue gave way to feminine virtue "in an increasingly competitive male political system" wherein "the distinction faded between virtuous men committed to public service and unvirtuous men pursuing narrow self-interest" (57). As Bloch argues, "the representation of public virtue as a feminine trait hinged on the exclusion of women from institutional public life. If virtue was regarded as outside politics, what better way to conceive of it than as feminine?" (57).

12. Drawing attention to the sequence of this list, Grimké notes that "I have not placed reading before praying because I regard it more important, but because, in order to pray aright, we must understand what we are praying for; it is only then we can 'pray with the understanding and the spirit also' " (17).

13. Perhaps it is worth noting that Grimké doesn't quote further from this chapter of Daniel; verse 10 reads: "Many shall be purified, and made white, and tried; but the wicked shall do wickedly: and none of the wicked shall understand; but the wise shall understand."

14. Similarly, J. Sherman refers to Brent's double bind of slavery and true womanhood, noting that "Both systems denied her a selfhood; neither had words to authorize her choices" (168). As I argue, to create choices, Jacobs (through Brent) had to reconfigure authorized modes of discourse and knowledge.

15. Mr. Sands (identified by Yellin as Samuel Tredwell Sawyer), runs for and is elected to Congress as the Whig candidate (*Incidents* 189).

16. On Jacobs's use of the "perspective of the homeless," see Sidonie Smith, 94–102; and Becker.

17. On Jacobs's experiences with and comments about Stowe, and on her situation after reaching the North, see the letters collected in the Appendix of Yellin's edition of *Incidents*; see also Yellin's Introduction; *Women & Sisters*, ch. 4; and "Texts and Contexts." See also Carby, *Reconstructing*, 47–61.

18. See Andrews on the differences between Thoreau's concept of autobiography and that of black autobiographers (*To Tell a Free Story* 2).

19. My example here is not as strange as it might seem. In her discussion of scientific ways of knowing, its "epistemological positions" (50), Code quotes from scientist Anna Brito's "accounts of her work with lymphocytes," in which Brito claims that " 'the nearest an ordinary person gets to the essence of the scientific process is when they fall in love. . . . You, the scientist, don't know you're falling in love, but suddenly you become attracted to that cell, or to that problem. Then you are going to have to go through an active process in relationship to it, and this leads to discovery' " (qtd. in Code, 152).

20. Many critics have noted Jacobs's use of sentimental conventions, though the implications of this feature of her narrative have not been fully explored. See especially Nudelman; Vermillion; Foster, *Written by Herself*, ch. 6; Tate, 26–32; and Andrews, "The Changing Moral Discourse."

21. For backgrounds on sentimental fiction, see Baym, *Woman's Fiction*; and Reynolds.

22. See, for example, Yellin, "Text and Contexts," 274; and *Women & Sisters*, 93; see also Carby, *Reconstructing*, 58.

23. I am referring, of course, to Jacobs's letter to Amy Post, in which she says that "Woman can whisper—her cruel wrongs into the ear of a very dear friend—much easier than she can record them for the world to read" (*Incidents* 242).

24. On Jacobs's attempt to "structure an alternate vantage of understanding, an alternative epistemology, that mirrors Linda's reconstituted Subjectivity," particularly as it relates to the relation between (black) author and (white) reader, see Nelson, ch. 7. As Nelson argues, "The text repeatedly appeals to the sympathy of its readers, but at the same time it warns them to be careful about the motives and critical of the results of that sympathetic identification" (144, 142).

## 4. *The White Gap and the Approaching Storm:* Martin R. Delany's *Blake*

1. Concerning mysterious events, as Nell Irvin Painter notes, Delany's "trip down the Mississippi River to New Orleans, Texas, Louisiana, Mississippi, and Arkansas in 1839, made under circumstances that are not known, constitutes a curious chapter in Delany's larger education" (151). Concerning apparent contradictions, as Painter notes about Delany's reconstruction plan for a "Triple Alliance" among labor, landowners, and capital, "Delany saw no contradiction between his belief in the need for black/white and labor/employer unity and his ability to represent his race, most of whom worked for others and at whose expense such unity would be achieved. Without realizing it he took a class position that soon put him at odds with large

numbers of blacks" (164); later Delany would campaign for southern Democrats, unaware that "being a Democrat meant even more than being pro-Confederate and pro-planter in the low country; it meant being a scab as well" (168). Delany met with angry crowds of blacks who "beat their drums and refused to listen to what they called a damned 'nigger Democrat,' " hardly the title Delany had worked for when he spoke years earlier of a nation within a nation. Painter's conclusions should be balanced by other, more celebratory biographies by Ullman and Sterling. All three biographical treatments end with comments on the ongoing search for materials relating to Delany's life and work. As Marsh-Lockett reports, "Scholarship on him was handicapped when his papers and artifacts from his travels were lost in a fire at Wilberforce University on 14 April 1865" (79). See also Herzog, ch. 5.

2. In addition to the standard biographies, see Sollors, Titcomb, and Underwood; and Takaki, 136–44.

3. Blake has gone to some trouble to find his wife, and suspects that she is now the slave known as Lotty, but when he tracks her down, "her appearance was that of a woman ten years the senior of his wife." Presumably, Blake has not changed as much. In any event, she does not at first recognize him, and when he asks her the name of her husband, and she begins to say his name, Henry responds "O! My God! Is this my wife!" (180).

4. Chapters 28 and 29 were included in the January issue, introducing the public to the work.

5. Delany echoes this logic on the last page of the Conclusion to this text, arguing that "[a] child born under oppression, has all the elements of servility in its constitution; who when born under favorable circumstances, has to the contrary, all the elements of freedom and independence of feeling" (*The Condition* 208).

6. Similarly, in his speech on West Indies Emancipation, included in the Appendix to the 1881 *Life and Times*, Douglass notes that "[w]ith money and property comes the means of knowledge and power" (*L&T* 935). Speaking of the ongoing "battle against popular prejudice" Douglass anticipates a "brighter and better day," but warns black Americans that "whether it shall come late or come soon will depend mainly upon ourselves," for "[t]he laws which determine the destinies of individuals and nations are impartial and eternal. We shall reap as we sow. There is no escape. The conditions of success are universal and unchangeable. The nations or people which shall comply with them will rise, and those which violate them will fall, and will perhaps, disappear altogether. No power beneath the sky can make an ignorant, wasteful, and idle people prosperous, or a licentious people happy" (936).

7. This book, Olcott offers, is designed to prepare "Anti-Slavery Lecturers and Debaters" for "the great moral combat now raging" (3). Olcott encour-

ages lecturers to crib liberally from this text or simply to read it in public. See also Olcott's argument on black labor and theories of inherent inferiority (54–56).

8. As Delany argues in a comparative study of black and white achievements in *The Condition*, "Until colored men, attain to a position above permitting their mothers, sisters, wives, and daughters, to do the drudgery and menial offices of other men's wives and daughters; it is useless, it is nonsense, it is pitiable mockery, to talk about equality and elevation in society. The world is looking upon us, with feelings of commiseration, sorrow, and contempt. We scarcely deserve sympathy, if we peremptorily refuse advice, bearing upon our elevation" (43). Years later, Douglass would echo this view, asserting that a "poverty-stricken class will be an ignorant and despised class, and no amount of sentiment can make it otherwise." On the differences between Delany's and Douglass's views on black labor, see Stuckey, 29–31.

9. See Ullman, 138.

10. On hypotheses and conclusions in Delany's "history-making literature," see Reilly.

11. I am presenting Placido as the speaker here, though the text is ambiguous on this point. Placido initiates this exchange in his poem/prayer (259–60), and he responds to Madame Cordora's question about his use of the word "Ethiopia" to refer to the mixed group. However, this paragraph is preceded by Madame Cordora's question, "And are there really hopes of Africa becoming a great country, Colonel Montego?"—so one might assume that Montego is speaking. But at the end of the paragraph, the speaker asks, "Do you now understand it, Madame Cordora?"; and she responds, "Indeed I do, Senor Placido" (262).

As Miller notes in his edition of *Blake*, Delany in *The Weekly Anglo-African* of February 1, 1862, "made many of these points in a letter in which he expressed his clear preference for African emigration as opposed to Haytian emigration" (*Blake* 320n). Strangely, Miller fails to direct the reader also to Delany's *Official Report of the Niger Valley Exploring Party*. In this 1861 text, one finds the beginning of Placido's explanation here either repeated or anticipated almost verbatim (for the *Official Report* appeared during the time when *Blake* was being published serially, from 1861–1862, with this speech appearing in a late chapter). In the *Official Report*, Delany's discussion of nationality and political economy begins as follows: "The basis of great nationality depends upon three elementary principles: first, territory; second, population; third, a great staple production either natural or artificial, or both, as a permanent source of wealth; and Africa comprises these to an almost unlimited extent" (112).

12. On this speech and on the novel's handling of gender, see Herzog.

13. Walker notes that many black Americans "discerned a different purpose in God's providential system: to elevate the race in America and Africa. They believed that the Negroes' achievement in the United States was part of a providential plan" (91). On this vision of history as it relates to slave narratives generally and Frederick Douglass's specifically, see Andrews, *To Tell a Free Story*, 124–27; and Baker, *Blues*, 20–21. Of course, the same historical logic could also be used to justify slavery by arguing that Africans were brought to the Americas for a reason—as, for example, in James. As one character puts it, "How came the Africans to be transported to this continent? Was it a *mere* accident, or was it not in conformity to the settled policy of heaven? I maintain the latter" (124).

14. Note that Delany here capitalizes "White Gap," which he presents in lower case on page 43. There are many signs in this book of Delany's gradual discovery of his themes and strategies.

15. See Douglass's extended justification of the slave's "right to steal" from his master and others, in *My Bondage*, 246–48.

16. On the songs of the antebellum watermen, see Southern, ch. 6; Southern quotes from *Blake*, 147–48. On music and dance in New Orleans, see Southern, ch. 5.

17. For excellent discussions of this secret, see Reilly, 94–100; and Sundquist, 191 ff.

18. On the American Colonization Society and views of it among some antislavery forces as a slaveholding conspiracy, see Olcott; Child, *An Appeal*, ch. 5; Stebbins; Jay; and Clarke. For backgrounds on the ACS, see Staudenraus; P. Campbell; and Fredrickson. Delany discusses colonization in almost all of his works; for commentary, see Ullman; Sundquist.

19. The importance of Freemasonry in Delany's life and thought will require careful study in the coming years. As Ullman notes, "To Delany, Freemasonry represented and documented all of his conclusions from ethnological study, that the first flowering of all wisdom was among the blacks of Africa. Besides, its principles matched exactly the high level of behavior and responsibility among his people for which he was pleading weekly in *The Mystery*. Its activities included a tight-knit and secret mutual aid of tremendous importance to members subject to all of the perils of free Negroes at home or abroad. And finally, Delany judged Freemasonry to be a holy bond because of the enemies it made, particularly among white politicians" (76). Attracted to Freemasonry's rituals, its secrecy, and its ideals of fraternity (Ullman 76), Delany was also a fervent critic of its segregationist policies in the United States, which is the main subject of his pamphlet. Delany's devotion to Freemasonry informed, I would suggest, the title of his weekly, *The Mystery*, and certainly its original motto: "And Moses Was Learned in All the Wisdom

of the Egyptians." On the importance of Moses in Delany's version of Freemasonry, see his pamphlet; on *The Mystery*, see Ullman, ch. 5. Most of what has been written on Delany and Freemasonry so far either quotes from Delany's pamphlet or from Ullman's valuable but brief commentary. See Austin, 43–44 and 54; and Sundquist, 211–12. For background on black Freemasonry (including a brief commentary on Delany), see Grimshaw; and L. Williams. On elements of *Blake* as "a fictionalized African-American adaptation of Freemasonry," see Peterson.

20.  On the use of the daring and important but still limited successes of regional organizations to create the Underground Railroad as myth and propaganda, see Gara, *The Liberty Line*. See also the individual narratives presented as part of one official version of the Underground Railroad operations in Still.

21.  This, I would suggest, is the significance of Delany's use of Stowe's biblical verses at the beginning of each part of *Blake*.

22.  Interestingly, Rollin reports a late appearance of this phrase in an 1866 public letter Delany addressed to the black delegation in Washington, in which Delany supports their response to the inadequate position of President Johnson. Though he offers his support to this position presented "before the saged president," he is somewhat tentative in that support, calling the delegates to "not misjudge the president, but believe, as I do, that he means to do right." At the end of the letter, Delany urges trust in God, advising that "[i]nstead of despair, 'Glory to God!' rather let us cry. In the cause of our country you and I have done, and are still doing, our part, and a great and just nation will not be unmindful of it. God is just. Stand still and see his salvation" (283). On Delany's postwar political career and views, and on the response of the great and just nation, see especially Painter. For an excellent history of Reconstruction, including informed commentary on Delany's role in that era, see E. Foner.

23.  Canada had by this time become the significant narrative destination for many narratives of the Underground Railroad, including Stowe's. In *Blake*, Canada turns out to be a disappointment, a place where "privileges were denied" black men and women "which are common to the slave in every Southern state," and when Canadian authorities consider complaints from those thus denied, "the construction given by authority to these grievances, when requested to remedy or remove them, was, that they were 'local contingencies to be reached alone by those who inflicted the injuries' " (153). Part One of *Blake*, in other words, ends by pointing to a conventional narrative closure and then disclosing the actual conditions that make such closure impossible. This, of course, is the foundation for the continuation of the narrative into Cuba and Africa in Part Two.

24. Of course, this rhetorical questioning of religion in different hands could be used for different ends. For example, in the antiabolitionist satire *Mr. Frank, the Underground Mail-Agent* by "Vidi," a northern woman reduced to poverty is rejected by the church when her wealth is gone. As she witnesses the imminent death of her daughter, she cries, "Religion! religion! . . . do not talk to me about *that*! I have seen enough of it!" (123).

25. The narrator is not alone in this rational approach to astronomy. Delany published essays entitled "Comets" and "The Attractions of Planets" in the first volume of *The Anglo-African Magazine*, where chapters from *Blake* first appeared. Comets, he argues, are the means by which "the Author of all things" supplies "electricity . . . health to mankind, and the indisputable evidence of the existence, mercy, goodness, justice and power of an omnipresent God" (60). Similarly, the attraction of planets offers evidence of the "mighty economy" that displays "the wisdom of Omnipotence" (18).

26. On the significance of the name *Mendi*, see Floyd J. Miller's note 33 in *Blake*, 320. Mendi is an interesting presence in this novel, though I would suggest that this African chief serves to dress Blake himself—who is called "Chief" throughout chapter 70—in African authority. Sterling reports that following his trip to Africa, Delany, who claimed ties to African royalty, toured the East and Midwest, lecturing mainly to white audiences on "The Moral and Social Relations of Africans in Africa" and "The Commercial Advantages of Africa." At those lectures, Delany wore clothing that he identified, according to the Chicago *Tribune*, as "the wedding dress of a Chief," noting that "the embroidery had a specific meaning well understood in African high circles" (qtd. in Sterling, *Making* 225).

There are, of course, obvious parallels between this episode and Douglass's account of Madison Washington in "The Heroic Slave." Indeed, Delany seems to have Blake gradually accumulate a gathering of symbolic figures to embody: Madison Washington, Delany himself, and John Brown among them. For further commentary on Blake's symbolic embodiment of revolutionary and visionary figures, see especially Sundquist; Herzog; and Yellin, *The Intricate Knot*, ch. 9.

27. Even the black sailors on the ship are viewed as ominous "black clouds," and when ordered to disperse, for " '[w]e're not ready for a rain,' " a boy responds, " 'But you may have a storm' " (221). Moral forecasting—black clouds and coming storms—was of course a frequent image in racial discourse. See, for example, Douglass, "Did John Brown Fail?"; as Douglass argues, "Viewed thus broadly our subject is worthy of thoughtful and dispassionate consideration. It invites the study of the poet, scholar, philosopher and statesman. What the masters in natural science have done for man in the physical world, the masters of social science may yet do for him in the moral

world. Science now tells us when storms are in the sky, and when and where their violence will be most felt. Why may we not yet know with equal certainty when storms are in the moral sky, and how to avoid their desolating force?" (11). One encounters something similar in Douglass's "The Douglass Institute":

> John Brown used to say he had looked over our people as over a dark sea, in the hope of seeing a head rise up with a mind to plan and a hand to deliver. Any movement of the water arrested his attention. In all directions, we desire to catch the first sign. The first sign of clear weather on the ocean after a season of darkness and storm; the first sign of returning health after long and weary months of wasting fever; the first sign of rain after famine, threatening drouth; the first indication of spring, silently releasing the knotty and congealed earth from the frosty fetters of winter; the first sign of peace after the ten thousand calamities, horrors, desolations and alarms of war, evermore bring joy and gladness to the human heart. (87)

28. Similarly, in the revised and expanded edition of *Life and Times* (1892), Douglass argues that the "principle of self-protection [is] taught in every department of nature, whether in men, beasts, or plants. It comes with the inherent right to exist. It is in every blade of grass as well as in every man and nation" (*L&T* 1021).

Delany was not alone in looking to the economy of nature for solutions to racial struggles, though some commentators saw a strikingly different message in the economy. Consider, for example, James, *Abolitionism Unveiled*. One of James's fictional Captains, during a discussion of Stowe's *The Key to "Uncle Tom's Cabin,"* argues that "God governs this world by certain immutable laws established at the time of Creation," and that God necessarily foresaw "the relative position the various races and colors of men would occupy upon the face of this earth." Nature will sustain all, the Captain argues, if nature and human resources are "judiciously managed"—that is, as long as all social groups are holding to their assigned places (black labor and white management) and are "reciprocally co-operating in the various branches of industry" (123–24).

29. Delany was not, of course, unique in his application of scripturally charged harvesting metaphors to the subject of slavery and racial domination. In Frances E. W. Harper's *Minnie's Sacrifice*, Camilla declares, "Oh slavery! what a curse. Our fathers sowed the wind, and we are reaping the whirlwind!" (61); and in *Trial and Triumph*, Mr. Thomas argues that "[m]en fettered the slave and cramped their own souls, denied him knowledge and then darkened their own spiritual insight, and the Negro, poor and despised as he was, laid his hands upon the American civilization and has helped to mould its

character. It is God's law. As ye sow, so shall ye reap, and men cannot sow avarice and oppression without reaping the harvest of retribution" (214–15).

30. In the postbellum United States, Douglass echoes this view of the American people in his *Life and Times*, finding in this love of law support for his public career: "Happily for me the American people possess in large measure a proneness to acquiescence. They readily submit to the 'powers that be' and to the rule of the majority. This sheet anchor of our national stability, prosperity, and peace, served me in good stead in the crisis in my career, as indeed it had done in many others" (528).

## 5. *The Education of Othello's Historian:* The Lives and Times of Frederick Douglass

1. On Douglass's attention to this system of signs and "the linguistic significance of bondage," see Kibbey; see also Butterfield's study of Douglass's use of "language as a weapon" (ch. 4); and Hord, ch. 3.

2. In addition to V. Smith, see Moses, 71–75; Fishkin and Peterson, 189–90. For an excellent examination of Douglass's construction of gender and of his grounding in gender, see Leverenz; Franchot; and Yarborough. For an excellent discussion on these arguments, see Stephanie Smith.

3. Hereinafter, *Life and Times* will be identified by the abbreviation *L&T*.

4. Involved in this move also is Douglass's increasing attempt to document the received and hidden facts of his life, an attempt that marks an intimate shift in Douglass's approach to self-authentication. See Gates, *Figures*, ch. 4. On Douglass's handling of his relation to and representation of his past, see Stephanie Smith; and Sundquist, ch. 1.

5. On Douglass's literary confinement, see also Baker, *Long Black Song*, 78–79.

6. James M'Cune Smith, for one, is quite explicit about Douglass's representative role in his Introduction to *My Bondage and My Freedom* (132). On Douglass as representative man, see Zafar; Olney, "The Founding Fathers"; Martin; and Olney, " 'I Was Born' " 153–54.

7. On the role of songs in nineteenth-century African-American culture, see Southern. On Douglass's understanding of slave songs, see Stuckey, 32–38; and Kibbey, 165–67.

8. In *Life and Times*, Douglass amplifies this conception of cultural influence by inserting the word "always," though he amplifies also the qualifier of the original "greatly" by asserting, "A man's character always takes its hue, more or less, from the form and color of things about him." Also, he inverts the order of the sequential sentences he presented in 1855, now following the "form and color" sentence with the sentence that, in 1855, preceded it: "The

slaveholder, as well as the slave, was the victim of the slave system" (*L&T* 493). In 1855, of course, this sentence was in the present tense.

9. He continues: "A man's troubles are always half disposed of, when he finds endurance his only remedy. I found myself here; there was no getting away; and what remained for me, but to make the best of it?" (*My Bondage* 161). In *Life and Times* he shifts this question to the assertion that "naught remained for me but to make the best of it" (*L&T* 487).

10. The pirates are absent in *Life and Times*, replaced by a comparison of Tuckahoe to "descriptions I have since read of the old baronial domains of Europe"—part of Douglass's general attempt in 1881 to emphasize the vision of continuous progress implicit in his 1855 depiction of a battle between civilization and barbarism. Whereas in 1855 he writes, "Civilization is shut out," in 1881 he writes, "civilization was, in many respects, shut out" (*L&T* 487).

11. In 1845, Auld was the pirate, taking Douglass's wages (*Narrative* 84). As Andrews argues, in the *Narrative* Douglass "analogizes Auld to a 'grim-visaged pirate' and a 'robber'—an outlaw, in other words—to banish him from a consubstantial relationship with the northern reader" (*To Tell a Free Story* 128). Gore, not banished in 1845, is banished in 1855.

12. On Douglass and literacy, see Sundquist, 103–8.

13. As this reading suggests, I cannot agree with those who see an uneasy relationship or distance between the narrative proper and its Appendix. For readings of the relation of the Appendix to the narrative see Gibson, "Faith"; Stepto, *From Behind the Veil*, 26; and Butterfield, 66–67.

14. Douglass presents a version of this "apostrophe" in "The Heroic Slave," a story that emphasizes conversations, monologues, and other sounds overheard by eavesdroppers, intentional and otherwise. Madison Washington's great friend Mr. Listwell (who time and again demonstrates the justice of his name) overhears this soul's complaint and is converted by it to the antislavery cause (39–42). On nineteenth-century styles of rhetoric, see Cmeil. For a speculative view on Douglass's views on the vernacular, see Gibson, "Response," 47–48.

15. This is, I would suggest, the point behind Douglass's placement of his "apostrophe" to the Chesapeake. Moses, for one, finds it strange that Douglass "illustrated [his] brutalization by recalling" these "high-spirited emotions," noting that this "does not . . . sound as if his 'elasticity was crushed' or as if his 'intellect languished,' and these are not the thoughts of a brute or an automaton' " (75). See also Van Leer, 120. I am suggesting that what Douglass represents here are less his own emotions or thoughts than that within him which was indeed "high-spirited." My reading differs from that of Martin, who asserts that the "brutalization Frederick endured at Covey's hands increased his skepticism toward religion" (12); and my reading differs notably

from that of Van Leer, who finds in this episode an inversion of the conventions of the conversion narrative, by which "Douglass implicitly denies the divine origin of his conversion, turning it from 'God's plot' into just one among many ways of structuring a narrative" (121). Van Leer notes that following his depiction of the struggle with Covey, Douglass spends the rest of the chapter on "a series of harangues: against the invidiousness of the Christmas holidays, the brutality of slaveholding ministers, and the prohibition of black Sunday schools," and suggests that these harangues "follow oddly on what had been cast as a religious conversion" (122). I would suggest, though, that these complaints against the misapplication of faith follow rather naturally an account of an intense and intimate experience of religious faith, especially in a narrative that ends by distinguishing between the ideal faith and the actual practice of religion. Indeed, one could argue that in this chapter Douglass has established his spiritual authority for critiquing the hypocrisy of American Christianity, and that he is only applying the lessons implicit in his struggle with Covey: that it was, in fact, a struggle between the Christianity of the land working through Covey and the Christianity of Christ working through Douglass.

Although all scholars generally agree that Douglass's fight with Covey is the central episode of the *Narrative*, there are various readings of the episode, usually relying on different emphases. See, for example, Gibson, "Faith," 93–94; Zafar, 113–14; Sundquist, 131–32; and O'Meally, 202–5.

16. I would not push this point too far, for both words are italicized later on the same page in 1845; and the eventual emphasis in 1855 is on "abolition" and "abolition movement," terms not italicized but rather enclosed within quotation marks.

17. On Douglass and superstition as it relates to his grandmother, see Stuckey, 24–26. On Douglass's complex and often conflicted religious views, see especially Andrews, *To Tell a Free Story*; and Gibson, "Faith."

18. Interestingly, Douglass notes his departure to Covey's twice, in sequential sentences—the first a departure on Sandy's advice, and the second a departure on the strength of his experience: "At any rate, I started off toward Covey's, as directed by Sandy. Having, the previous night, poured my griefs into Sandy's ears, and got him enlisted in my behalf, having made his wife a sharer in my sorrows, and having, also, become well refreshed by sleep and food, I moved off, quite courageously, toward the much dreaded Covey's" (*My Bondage* 281).

19. See Van Leer for a reading of Sandy's root that conflates Douglass's initial and later uses of the word, tying it to Douglass's "black heritage" (126). See also Baker, *Long Black Song*, 77–78; O'Meally, 204–10.

There is some disagreement among scholars concerning how to read

Douglass's attitudes about Sandy's root, and some suggest that cultural biases might influence one's reading. For a good overview of these issues, see Wesling; Awkward, "Race, Gender, and the Politics of Reading"; Awkward, "Negotiations of Power"; Warren, "From the Superscript"; and Awkward, "The Politics of Positionality."

20. Byron's words were a prominent presence in a great deal of African-American writing. In his consideration of this chapter of *My Bondage and My Freedom*, Sundquist discusses the appropriateness of Byron's presence here and notes that "[t]he Byron passage, which Douglass had already used in 'The Heroic Slave,' had also appeared in Henry Highland Garnet's famous 1843 'Address to the Slaves of the United States,' and it would later be quoted by Delany in *Blake* and Du Bois in *The Souls of Black Folk*" (*To Wake the Nations* 124). The passage also appeared as Delany's second motto for his paper *The Mystery*; Byron's presence supplanted that of Moses in the masthead sometime in 1845. See Ullman, 60–61. The passage also appears in James M'Cune Smith's Introduction to *My Bondage and My Freedom* (130)— interestingly, appearing when Smith is discussing Douglass's visit to England and his decision to begin the newspaper that would be co-edited by Delany.

In a remarkable transformation of the import of these words, Douglass draws from Byron once again in the conclusion of the 1881 *Life and Times*, now presenting it in his discussion of his attempts to uplift black Americans, "a class whose aspirations need the stimulus of success" (*L&T* 914). Noting that he has "endeavored to deliver them from the power of superstition, bigotry, and priestcraft," Douglass notes also that in "theology I have found them strutting about in the old clothes of the masters, just as the masters strut about in the old clothes of the past. The falling power remains among them long since it has ceased to be the religious fashion in our refined and elegant white churches. I have taught that the 'fault is not in our stars, but in ourselves, that we are underlings,' that 'who would be free, themselves must strike the blow.' " And as he continues, Douglass makes clear what kind of blow he has in mind: "I have urged upon them self-reliance, self-respect, industry, perseverance, and economy" (*L&T* 913–14). On Douglass's quotation of Byron, see also Gibson, "Faith," 93.

21. On Douglass's "displacement" of Phillis Wheatley as the most famous African American in the nineteenth century, see Gates, "From Wheatley to Douglass."

22. Consider, for example, Douglass's complaint about "the colored waiters" on board the *Tennessee*, who, "trained in the school of servility," seemed to Douglass troubled by the "incomprehensibility" of his "presence and position." Reflecting on their reaction to him moves Douglass to discuss a

general condition of his life as a very public black American: "I refer to the matter simply as an incident quite commonly met with in the lives of colored men who, by their own exertions or otherwise, have happened to occupy positions of respectability and honor. While the rank and file of our race quote, with much vehemence, the doctrine of human equality, they are often among the first to deny and denounce it in practice" (*L&T* 848). For a more optimistic version of Douglass's late career, see Warren, "Frederick Douglass's *Life and Times*." For background on Douglass's postbellum career, see E. Foner; McFeely; and Martin.

23. When Douglass mentions Mr. Collins's introduction in *My Bondage and My Freedom* and *Life and Times*, he mentions also his apparent lack of preparation for the role he was asked to play, but his self-description also indicates that he had not yet fully discovered the text before him, his own leather-bound selfhood: "My hands seemed to be furnished with something like a leather coating, and I had marked for myself a life of rough labor, suited to the hardness of my hands, as a means of supporting my family and rearing my children" (*My Bondage* 365; *L&T* 661).

24. For discussions of Douglass's Egyptian and ethnographic explorations, see Martin, Part Three; and Warren, "Frederick Douglass's *Life and Times*." For backgrounds on racial theory and their influence on black thought and scripted identity, see Fredrickson; Gossett, *Race*; and Stanton.

25. In 1855 also, Douglass seems a careful reader of the underlying significance of working songs. "In the most boisterous outbursts of rapturous sentiment," he writes, "there was ever a tinge of deep melancholy. I have never heard any songs like those anywhere since I left slavery, except when in Ireland. There I heard the same *wailing notes*, and was much affected by them" (*My Bondage* 184).

26. By this act, in fact, Douglass steps into at least one reading of Shakespeare's play. As Levine reports, "John Quincy Adams concluded, even as he was waging his heroic fight against the power of the slave South in the House of Representatives in 1836, that the moral of *Othello* was 'that the intermarriage of black and white blood is a violation of the law of nature. *That* is the lesson to be learned from the play' " (39). On Douglass's marriage, see Moses.

27. Douglass's self-assigned role as a U.S. Othello might well have been in his thoughts also as he discussed the power of unsubstantiated rumor, a "method of political warfare," he notes, that "has not escaped the vigilant eye of the Afro-American press or of the aspirant and office-seeker, who, when he has found a public man supposed to be in the way of his ambition, has resorted to this device" (*L&T* 955–56).

28. On the white and black appropriations of the story of the Underground Railroad, see Gara, *The Liberty Line*.

29. Other African-American writers similarly promised to tell unvarnished tales, and I would suggest no direct interpretive significance beyond the fact of Shakespeare's presence in the cultural discourse. At the end of chapter 23 of *Clotel*, for example, William Wells Brown concludes his tale of the tragic fate of Henry Morton's daughter Jane by assuring his readers that this "is an unvarnished narrative of one doomed by the laws of the Southern States to be a slave" (210). In a different application of the word, Zilpha Elaw in her *Memoirs* tells her "dear reader," "This . . . was the manner of my soul's conversion to God, told in language unvarnished by the graces of educated eloquence, nor transcending the capacity of a child to understand" (57). In *From Dixie to Canada*, Johnson (who borrowed heavily and often verbatim from other writers, sometimes recasting their stories) speaks of the fugitive slave Jo Norton's "unvarnished tale" to white abolitionist Eber Pettit. Later, Johnson reports, Pettit listened again to Jo's "story of escape and tale of plantation life, and offered such suggestions as he thought advisable," after which Jo "went to bed, 'to sleep; to dream'" (39, 41). The Shakespearean overtones are absent from Pettit's version of the story in his *Sketches in the History of the Underground Railroad*. On Shakespeare's presence in nineteenth-century U.S. culture, see Levine. For Douglass's quotations of Shakespeare in his autobiographies, see the notes to the Library of America edition. See also Gibson's reading of the role of *Hamlet* in the 1845 *Narrative*, in "Reconciling Public and Private."

30. On the same page, Douglass also quotes from the Bible, Luke 19:8.

31. Certainly, it is interesting that Douglass claimed great admiration for the phrenologist George Combe (*L&T* 685), and that Smith goes to such great length to establish Douglass's identity on scientific grounds (as they then were considered). One should note, though, that Delany, who was known for being proud of his heritage and dark color, also was fascinated by and lectured on phrenology, as did other prominent black Americans.

32. On the complex dynamics of cross-racial identification, see Lott.

33. On Douglass's nostalgic accounts of his communion with his past acquaintances in slavery and his former home, see Mixon.

34. One might say that Douglass deserved more than Adams the title Adams claimed for himself, "conservative Christian anarchist." For explorations of the meaning of this title, see Munford, 65; and Levenson, 296–98.

35. On Douglass's experience in Haiti, and the increasing dilemma he found himself in when selected by Haiti to represent that country at the Columbian Exposition of 1893 in Chicago, see Warren, "Frederick Douglass's *Life and Times*."

## 6. *Unsolved Mysteries and Emerging Histories:* Frances E. W. Harper's *Iola Leroy*

1. For background on the southern women writers' roles in these literary battles, see Moss. For general background on sectional struggles in literature, see Faust; and Lively.

2. Graham has challenged the conventional view that *Iola Leroy* was written for black Sunday school youth, noting also (as does Elizabeth Ammons) that this was "the first widely distributed novel by a black woman in America" (170). Dearborn assumes a dual audience, and argues that *Iola Leroy* "presents . . . an implicitly subversive message to black readers, while it attempts simultaneously to mediate black experience for white readers, and to perform all the other genteel functions . . . critics claim for it" (45). See also Ammons, "*Legacy* Profile," 63. In her introduction to *"Minnie's Sacrifice,"* Foster argues that Harper's publication of these works in the *Christian Recorder* as well as the novels' messages require critics "to revise our notions that early African American publications were directed to white readers or that the black readership was too small and too dependent to count for much" (xxv). Certainly this is true, though we should recognize as well that many publications were available for a dual audience, and that many writers had reason to expect a white as well as a black readership. One wonders, also, whether the cultural politics of the time made it possible to fully disengage oneself from the white reading eye. For general commentary on Harper's response to the literary constructions of racial stereotypes, see Elkins.

3. The best overview and discussion of the critical response to Harper's work is in Carby, Introduction; see also Carby, *Reconstructing*, 62–94; and Washington.

4. See Bone, 19, 31–32; Bruce, 51; and (on Harper's poetry) Jackson, 270.

5. See, for example, Christian, *Black Women Novelists*, 22, 27–30; and McDowell, 284–87. For an excellent reconsideration of African-American sentimental literature, see Tate. It is worth remembering that forced marriage had been a subject of antebellum antislavery novels—see, for example, Letter XI in *Cousin Franck's Household* by "Pocahontas"—and that marriage was the subject generally of Reconstruction novels, representing particular views of the balance of the union of North and South. See also Hite.

6. I focus here on Joyce not only because I think she brings a powerful voice to current critical debates, but also because her strong stance clarifies the conceptual opponents in the debate, though it seems to me that her theory/life dichotomy replays the art/life dichotomy she justly criticizes. See also Barbara Christian's balanced critique of theory in "The Highs and the Lows of Black Feminist Criticism"; and Sherley Anne Williams.

One should consider here Mae Gwendolyn Henderson's brilliant approach to the role of gender in literary modes of understanding. Approaching the subject by way of Hans-Georg Gadamer and Mikhail Bakhtin, Henderson argues black women writers speak "as much to the notion of commonality and universalism as . . . to the sense of difference and diversity" by "speaking from the vantage point of the insider/outsider," a vantage point that enables one to "see what the other cannot see, and to use this insight to enrich both [one's] own and the other's understanding" (36).

7. In "My Statue, My Self," Fox-Genovese argues that "the [female] self . . . develops in opposition to, rather than as an articulation of, condition. Yet the condition remains as that against which the self is forged. And the condition, as much as the representations of self, constitutes an inescapable aspect of the Afro-American female literary tradition, especially of Afro-American women's autobiographies" (177). Although Fox-Genovese places Harper unproblematically in the pre-Hurston genre of uplift and respectabil-ity literature, I would argue that this novel—the plot of which leads Iola to consider writing a novel about herself—is an example of the complex literary response to the situation of the conditional and conditioned self. On Harper's recognition of the treacherous literary and cultural battlefields in which she was placed, see Young. As Young concludes, "*Iola Leroy* offers a particularly salient exploration of the process whereby 'literary' and 'political' discourse continue to make and unmake one another, in an ongoing battle—at once internecine and uncivil—of warring fictions" (293). Although I encountered Boyd's excellent study of Harper's life and work too late to account for it here, scholars interested in Harper will want to begin with *Discarded Legacy*.

8. It is important to note also that the same restrictions apply to white texts, the less heroic strategies of which have been rendered invisible to criticism.

9. See also Jane Campbell on "Harper's mythmaking," involving her attempt "to fuse the refutation of deplorably stereotypic views of black women with the romance conventions of her day," and specifically to fuse "the motif of the tragic mulatto with that of the Sentimental Heroine" (25).

10. For useful discussions of nineteenth-century racial theories, and of Darwin's own implication in those theories, see Fredrickson; Gossett, *Race*; Jordan; and Takaki. Although I find his biases disturbing, Jenkins is still useful as a source for information.

11. On the history of African-American education, see Ashmore; Bullock; Meier; and Rabinowitz.

12. See McDowell, 284.

13. See, for example, her 1858 letter to the *Liberator*, in which she speaks of "the shadow of slavery" (*BCD*, 47).

14. This meaning was first pointed out to me by Ms. Malvina Engelberg,

at that time an undergraduate at Florida International University. In her paper "The Password is Shadow," Engelberg argues that Harper "conjure[s] a parallel code by her appropriation of the word *shadow*," a code that cannot be correctly interpreted until the reader adjusts his or her perspective to the implied world of the text. Engelberg notes also that, after the subtitle, "shadow" does not appear in the text until chapter 5, "Release of Iola Leroy," after which it appears frequently and strategically. See also Sundquist's consideration of the narrative voice of "Benito Cereno" as "a kind of 'shadow,' at once merged with but partially suspended above or outside his conscious point of view" (*To Wake the Nations* 150).

15. Harper here echoes a scene from Haviland's *A Woman's Life-Work*. In this episode of Haviland's narrative of her Underground Railroad work, two fugitive slaves in a skiff on the Licking River are hailed by two men and asked where they are going. They answer, " 'To market, sir' "; and when asked what they have for the market, they respond, " 'Butter and eggs, sir,' " (116).

16. This usage of the term *mystery* has persisted, as in James J. Kilpatrick's assertion that the black South is "mysterious and incomprehensible to most white men" (qtd. in Zinn, 89).

17. On Harper's poetry, see J. Sherman; and Foster, *Written by Herself*, 131–53.

18. This concern with effectual transformation from white to black—that is, the revision of one's identity according to the demands of law and culture—is, of course, one of the many connections between *Iola Leroy* and William Wells Brown's *Clotel*. Harper, though, emphasizes the terms of this self-discovery (including the reenvisionment of attitudes about race and culture) and thus heightens the extent to which cultural tragedy engenders individual revelation and power.

19. In *Trial and Triumph*, a nameless merchant serves Mr. Cloten's function, though the reader is not offered his reflections; see *MST*, 283. In that novel, also, we encounter many white employers who lack Mr. Cloten's conviction.

20. Harper presents a similar lesson in *Minnie's Sacrifice*; see *MST*, 72.

21. See also Sanchez-Eppler.

22. One thinks particularly of the 1845 edition of Frederick Douglass's *Narrative*, and especially of the extent to which the Appendix to that work serves as the hermeneutical key to the narrative; one thinks also of William Wells Brown's sequential chapters in *Clotel*: "A True Democrat," followed by "The Christian's Death."

23. On the changing relationships between nineteenth-century African Americans and the Protestant church, see Reimers; Rabinowitz; Touchstone; and Dvorak.

24. Addressing the tragic limitations of Eugene Leroy's own enlighten-

ment, Harper uses a similar image: "Even while Leroy dreamed of safety the earthquake was cradling its fire; the ground was growing hollow beneath his tread; but his ear was too dull to catch the sound; his vision too blurred to read the signs of the times" (*IL* 78).

25. Interestingly, one of the notable changes from one account to the next concerns the number of bullets that hit Black Tom/Big Bob/Tom Anderson: seven bullets in the Yankee soldier's version, five in Brown's, "seven or eight" in Harper's.

26. These letters were widely distributed in African-American publications. See Wells, chs. 3 and 4. Tate also speculates that Harper, in naming her protagonist Iola, is referring to Wells (145). See also duCille's speculation that Harper "may have been paying tribute to the antilynching activist" (35–36).

27. In 1840, John Brown Russwurm, the governor of the colony of Maryland in Liberia, purchased for the colony (for business ventures) a ship he named the *Latrobe*, though immediately it had to be repaired, and was soon sold. Ironically, Russwurm lived in the colonial town called "Harper." For the history of this colony and of Latrobe's involvement in it, see P. Campbell. Martin Delany mentions John Hazlehurst Boneval Latrobe—in Latrobe's role as the biographer of Benjamin Bannaker—in *The Condition*, 91. See also Griffith, 109.

28. For an example of the African-American response to the American Colonization Society, see that of the Colored Citizens of Pittsburgh in Ullman, 11–16.

29. Among Latrobe's other notable projects are a penitentiary at Richmond, Virginia, and various educational buildings in Pennsylvania, completing this symbolic framework of the cultural system. I mention in the text only those prominent landmarks with which one can assume that Harper was familiar.

30. The possible connection between Dr. Gresham and Gresham's law was first pointed out to me by Ms. Joan Duhamel, an undergraduate at the University of New Hampshire. In her paper on *Iola Leroy*, Duhamel argues that Iola's father, Eugene Leroy, "falsely inflated the worth of his family by denying their association with the Black race" instead of challenging the standards of value; and "When Eugene dies, the bottom falls out of his investment as Eugene is no longer able to support the illusion of their Whiteness." Similarly, Duhamel argues, Mr. Gresham bases his initial estimate of Iola on her "face value." Ultimately, Duhamel concludes, Harper cautions her readers that "the cycle of Gresham's law must be broken for our country to achieve all it is capable of achieving. Otherwise, the acquisitions of selfish, personal fortunes will override any benefits to society as a whole."

31. On the significance of Iola's choice, see duCille, 44–46; on Harper's

commentary on color and character in her handling of the novel's characters and their choices, see Tate, 144–49.

32. An interesting coincidence beyond the historical presences I've suggested is a novel that Harper might not have read or heard of, *Uncle Daniel's Story of "Tom" Anderson and Twenty Great Battles*, published anonymously in 1886 after appearing serially in the *National Tribune* in 1885. This novel of the Civil War and Reconstruction is as fiercely critical of Reconstruction politics—and the North's abandonment of its cause—as anything found in novels by Tourgée. The story is narrated by "Uncle Daniel," who is white, and concerns in part his nephew, Tom Anderson; Uncle Daniel is so filled with grief over the events and conditions he describes that he dies in his chair after narrating this story. Tom Anderson serves prominently in and survives the Civil War (rising to the rank of general) only to be attacked and killed, with his family, by a southern mob after the war.

33. The episode on which this scene is based occurred in the Freedmen School in Louisville, Kentucky, in 1866, as reported by Henry Lee Swint in *The Northern Teacher in the South, 1862–1870* (1941), quoted in Litwack, *Been in the Storm So Long*, 386:

> "Now children, you don't think white people are any better than you because they have straight hair and white faces?"
>
> "No, sir."
>
> "No, they are no better, but they are different, they possess great power, they formed this great government, they control this vast country. . . . Now what makes them different from you?"
>
> "MONEY." (Unanimous shout)
>
> "Yes, but what enabled them to obtain it? *How* did they get money?"
>
> "Got it off us, stole it off we all!"

34. For an excellent examination of the "narrative architecture" in *Iola Leroy*, see Holloway.

## Epilogue

1. I say influential in part because from *The Clansman* sprang *The Birth of a Nation*, in part because of the novel's ongoing importance to the members of the Ku Klux Klan, and in part because of its indirect influence on subsequent writers—for example, Margaret Mitchell, who admired Dixon's fiction long before she wrote *Gone with the Wind*. As Thomas D. Clark notes in his 1970 introduction to the novel, "No scholarly historian of Reconstruction was

ever able to reach so wide or impressionable an audience as did Thomas Dixon" (xvii).

2. On the intersections of "eugenics, motherhood, and racial patriarchy," see Doyle, ch. 1.

# Works Cited

Abbott, Richard H. *Cotton & Capital: Boston Businessmen and Antislavery Reform, 1854–1868*. Amherst: University of Massachusetts Press, 1991.

Adams, Henry. *The Education of Henry Adams*. Ed. Ernest Samuels. Boston: Houghton Mifflin, 1973.

———. *The Letters of Henry Adams*. Vol. 2. Ed. J. C. Levenson, Ernest Samuels, Charles Vandersee, and Viola Hopkins Winner. Cambridge: Harvard University Press, 1982.

Ammons, Elizabeth. *Conflicting Stories: American Women Writers at the Turn into the Twentieth Century*. New York: Oxford University Press, 1992.

———. "*Legacy* Profile: Frances Ellen Watkins Harper (1825–1911)." *Legacy* 2.2 (1985): 61–66.

Anbinder, Tyler. *Nativism and Slavery: The Northern Know Nothings and the Politics of the 1850s*. New York: Oxford University Press, 1992.

Andrews, William L. "The Changing Moral Discourse of Nineteenth-Century African American Women's Autobiography: Harriet Jacobs and Elizabeth Keckley." In *De/Colonizing the Subject: The Politics of Gender in Women's Autobiography*. Minneapolis: University of Minnesota Press, 1992. 225–41.

———. Introduction. In *From Fugitive Slave to Free Man: The Autobiographies of William Wells Brown*. Ed. William L. Andrews. New York: Mentor, 1993. 1–12.

———. Introduction. In *Two Biographies by African American Women*. New York: Oxford University Press, 1991. xxxiii–xliii.

———. "Mark Twain, William Wells Brown, and the Problem of Authority in New South Writing." In *Southern Literature and Literary Theory*. Ed. Jefferson Humphries. Athens: University of Georgia Press, 1990. 1–21.

———. *To Tell a Free Story: The First Century of Afro-American Autobiography, 1760–1865*. Urbana: University of Illinois Press, 1986.

*Anglo-African Magazine, Volume 1—1859*. New York: Arno Press and The New York Times, 1968.

*The Anti-Slavery Record, Volumes 1–3, 1835–1837*. Westport, Conn.: Negro Universities Press, 1970.

Ashmore, Harry. *The Negro and the Schools*. Chapel Hill: University of North Carolina Press, 1954.

Austin, Allan D. "The Significance of Martin Robison Delany's *Blake, or the Huts of America*." Ph.D. diss., University of Massachusetts, 1975.

Awkward, Michael. "Negotiations of Power: White Critics, Black Texts, and the Self-Referential Impulse." *American Literary History* 2 (Winter 1990): 581–606.

———. "The Politics of Positionality: A Reply to Kenneth Warren." *American Literary History* 4 (Spring 1992): 104–9.

———. "Race, Gender, and the Politics of Reading." *Black American Literature Forum* 22 (1988): 5–27.

Baker, Houston A., Jr. *Blues, Ideology, and Afro-American Literature: A Vernacular Theory*. Chicago: University of Chicago Press, 1984.

———. "In Dubious Battle." *New Literary History* 18 (1987): 363–69.

———. *Long Black Song: Essays in Black American Literature and Culture*. Charlottesville: University Press of Virginia, 1972.

———. *Workings of the Spirit: The Poetics of Afro-American Women's Writing*. Chicago: University of Chicago Press, 1991.

Bakhtin, Mikhail. *The Dialogic Imagination*. Trans. Caryl Emerson and Michael Holquist. Ed. Michael Holquist. Austin: University of Texas Press, 1981.

Bancroft, George. *History of the United States from the Discovery of the American Continent*. 10 vols. Boston: Little, Brown, 1872–74.

Baym, Nina. "At Home with History: History Books and Women's Sphere Before the Civil War." *Proceedings of the American Antiquarian Society* 101.2 (1991): 275–95.

———. *Woman's Fiction: A Guide to Novels by and about Women in America, 1820–70*. Urbana: University of Illinois Press, 1993.

Beard, John R. *The Life of Toussaint L'Ouverture, the Negro Patriot of Hayti*. London, 1853.

Becker, Elizabeth C. "Harriet Jacobs's Search for Home." *CLA Journal* 35 (June 1992): 411–21.

Bell, Bernard W. *The Afro-American Novel and Its Tradition*. Amherst: University of Massachusetts Press, 1987.

Bender, Thomas, ed. *The Antislavery Debate: Capitalism and Abolitionism as a Problem in Historical Interpretation*. Berkeley: University of California Press, 1992.

Bennett, David H. "Women and the Nativist Movement." In *"Remember the Ladies": New Perspectives on Women in American History. Essays in Honor of Nelson Manfred Blake*. Ed. Carol V. R. George. Syracuse, N.Y.: Syracuse University Press, 1975. 71–89.

Bentley, Nancy. "White Slaves: The Mulatto Hero in Antebellum Fiction." *American Literature* 65 (1993): 501–22.

Bercovitch, Sacvan. *The American Jeremiad*. Madison: University of Wisconsin Press, 1978.

———. *The Office of the Scarlet Letter*. Baltimore: Johns Hopkins University Press, 1991.

Berlant, Lauren. *The Anatomy of National Fantasy: Hawthorne, Utopia, and Everyday Life*. Chicago: University of Chicago Press, 1991.

Bloch, Ruth H. "The Gendered Meanings of Virtue in Revolutionary America." *Signs: Journal of Women in Culture and Society* 13.1 (1987): 37–58.

Bone, Robert. *The Negro Novel in America*. 1958. Reprint. New Haven, Conn.: Yale University Press, 1965.

Boyd, Melba Joyce. *Discarded Legacy: Politics and Poetics in the Life of Frances E. W. Harper, 1825–1911*. Detroit: Wayne State University Press, 1994.

Braxton, Joanne M. *Black Women Writing Autobiography: A Tradition within a Tradition*. Philadelphia: Temple University Press, 1989.

Brown, Gillian. *Domestic Individualism: Imagining Self in Nineteenth-Century America*. Berkeley: University of California Press, 1990.

Brown, Sterling A., Arthur P. Davis, and Ulysses Lee. *The Negro Caravan: Writings by American Negroes*. New York: The Dryden Press, 1941.

Brown, William Wells. *The American Fugitive in Europe. Sketches of Places and People Abroad*. 1855. Reprint. Freeport, N.Y.: Books for Libraries Press, 1970.

———. *The Black Man, His Antecedents, His Genius, and His Achievements*. 4th ed. 1865. Reprint. Salem, N.H.: Ayer, 1992.

———. *Clotel; or, The President's Daughter: A Narrative of Slave Life in the United States*. Ed. William Edward Farrison. New York: Carol Publishing Group, 1969.

———. *My Southern Home: or, The South and Its People*. In *From Fugitive Slave to Free Man: The Autobiographies of William Wells Brown*. Ed. William L. Andrews. New York: Mentor, 1993.

———. *Narrative of William W. Brown, a Fugitive Slave*. In *From Fugitive Slave to Free Man: The Autobiographies of William Wells Brown*. Ed. William L. Andrews. New York: Mentor, 1993.

———. *The Negro in the American Rebellion: His Heroism and His Fidelity*. 1867. Reprint. New York: Kraus Reprint, 1969.

———. *The Rising Son; or, The Antecedents and Advancement of the Colored Race*. 1874. Reprint. New York: Negro Universities Press, 1970.

———. *St. Domingo: Its Revolutions and its Patriots. A Lecture, Delivered Before the Metropolitan Athenaeum, London, May 16, and at St. Thomas' Church, Philadelphia, December 20, 1854*. 1855. Afro-American History Series. Philadelphia: Rhistoric Publications, n.d.

Bruce, Dickson D., Jr. *Black American Writing from the Nadir: The Evolution of a Literary Tradition, 1877–1915*. Baton Rouge: Louisiana State University Press, 1989.

Buell, Lawrence. *New England Literary Culture: From Revolution through Renaissance*. Cambridge: Cambridge University Press, 1986.

Bullock, Henry Allan. *A History of Negro Education in the South from 1619 to the Present*. Cambridge: Harvard University Press, 1967.

Butterfield, Stephen. *Black Autobiography in America*. Amherst: University of Massachusetts Press, 1974.

Callcott, George H. *History in the United States, 1800–1860: Its Practice and Purpose*. Baltimore: Johns Hopkins University Press, 1970.

Campbell, Jane. *Mythic Black Fiction: The Transformation of History*. Knoxville: University of Tennessee Press, 1986.

Campbell, Penelope. *Maryland in Africa: The Maryland State Colonization Society, 1831–1857*. Urbana: University of Illinois Press, 1971.

Carby, Hazel V. Introduction. In *Iola Leroy; or, Shadows Uplifted*, by Frances E. W. Harper. Boston: Beacon Press, 1987. ix–xxvi.

———. *Reconstructing Womanhood: The Emergence of the Afro-American Novelist*. New York: Oxford University Press, 1987.

Cartwright, Samuel A. *Essays, being inductions drawn from the Baconian philosophy proving the truth of the Bible and the justice and benevolence of the decree dooming Canaan to be a servant of servants. . . .* Natchez, 1843.

Castronovo, Russ. "Radical Configurations of History in the Era of American Slavery." *American Literature* 65 (1993): 523–47.

Chase, Warren. *The American Crisis; or, Trial and Triumph of Democracy*. Boston: Bela Marsh, 1865.

Chase-Riboud, Barbara. *The President's Daughter*. New York: Crown, 1994.

Chesnutt, Charles W. *The Journals of Charles W. Chesnutt*. Ed. Richard Brodhead. Durham: Duke University Press, 1993.

———. *The Marrow of Tradition*. Ann Arbor: University of Michigan Press, 1969.

Child, L. Maria. *The American Frugal Housewife. Dedicated to Those Who Are Not Ashamed of Economy*. Boston, 1832.

———. *An Appeal in Favor of That Class Americans Called Africans*. 1836. Reprint. New York: Arno Press and The New York Times, 1968.

———. *The Mother's Book*. 2d ed. Boston, 1831.

———. "The Quadroons." *Fact and Fiction: A Collection of Stories*. New York, Boston, 1846.

Christian, Barbara. *Black Women Novelists: The Development of a Tradition, 1892–1976*. Westport, Conn.: Greenwood Press, 1980.

———. "The Highs and the Lows of Black Feminist Criticism." In *Reading*

*Black, Reading Feminist: A Critical Anthology.* Ed. Henry Louis Gates, Jr. New York: Meridian, 1990. 44–51.

Christy, David. *Cotton is King: or the Culture of Cotton, and Its Relation to Agriculture, Manufactures and Commerce; and also to the Free Colored People of the United States, and to those who hold that Slavery is in itself sinful.* 2d ed. New York, 1856.

Clark, Thomas D. Introduction. In *The Clansman: An Historical Romance of the Ku Klux Klan,* by Thomas Dixon, Jr. Lexington: University Press of Kentucky, 1970. v–xviii.

Clarke, James Freeman. "Condition of the Free Colored People of the United States." In *The Free People of Color.* Ed. Benjamin Quarles. New York: Arno Press and The New York Times, 1969.

Cmeil, Kenneth. *Democratic Eloquence: The Fight over Popular Speech in Nineteenth-Century America.* New York: William Morrow, 1990.

Code, Lorraine. *What Can She Know? Feminist Theory and the Construction of Knowledge.* Ithaca: Cornell University Press, 1991.

Cooper, Anna Julia. *A Voice from the South by a Black Woman of the South.* New York: Oxford University Press, 1988.

Croly, David Goodman. *Miscegenation: The Theory of the Blending of the Races, Applied to the American White Man and Negro.* 1864. Reprint. Upper Saddle River, N.J.: Literature House, 1970.

Davis, Arthur. Introduction. In *Clotel; or, The President's Daughter: A Narrative of Slave Life in the United States,* by William Wells Brown. New York: Collier Books, 1970. vii–xvi.

Davis, Cynthia J. "Speaking the Body's Pain: Harriet Wilson's *Our Nig.*" *African American Review* 27 (Fall 1993): 391–404.

Davis, David Brion. *The Slave Power Conspiracy and the Paranoid Style.* Baton Rouge: Louisiana State University Press, 1969.

Dearborn, Mary V. *Pocahontas's Daughters: Gender and Ethnicity in American Culture.* New York: Oxford University Press, 1986.

Delaney, Lucy A. *From the Darkness Cometh the Light or Struggles for Freedom.* In *Six Women's Slave Narratives.* Ed. William L. Andrews. New York: Oxford University Press, 1988.

Delany, Martin Robison. "The Attractions of Planets." *Anglo-African Magazine, Volume 1—1859.* New York: Arno Press and The New York Times, 1968. 17–20.

———. *Blake, or The Huts of America; A Tale of the Mississippi Valley, the Southern United States, and Cuba.* Ed. Floyd J. Miller. Boston: Beacon Press, 1970.

———. "Comets." *Anglo-African Magazine, Volume 1—1859.* New York: Arno Press and The New York Times, 1968. 59–60.

————. *The Condition, Elevation, Emigration, and Destiny of the Colored People of the United States.* 1852. Reprint. New York: Arno Press and The New York Times, 1968.

————. *Official Report of the Niger Valley Exploring Party.* In *Search For A Place: Black Separatism and Africa, 1860.* Ed. Howard H. Bell. Ann Arbor: University of Michigan Press, 1971.

————. *The Origin and Objects of Ancient Freemasonry; its Introduction into the United States, and Legitimacy Among Colored Men.* Pittsburgh, 1853.

————. *The Origin of Races and Color.* 1879. Reprint. Baltimore: Black Classic Press, 1991.

————. "Political Destiny of the Colored Race on the American Continent." In *The Ideological Origins of Black Nationalism.* Ed. Sterling Stuckley. Boston: Beacon Press, 1972. 195–236.

Denslow, Van Buren. *Principles of the Economic Philosophy of Society, Government and Industry.* 1888. Reprint. New York: Garland, 1974.

Dixon, Thomas, Jr. *The Clansman: An Historical Romance of the Ku Klux Klan.* Lexington: University Press of Kentucky, 1970.

Doriani, Beth Maclay. "Black Womanhood in Nineteenth-Century America: Subversion and Self-Construction in Two Women's Autobiographies." *American Quarterly* 43.2 (1991): 199–222.

Douglas, Ann. *The Feminization of American Culture.* 1977. Reprint. New York: Doubleday, 1988.

Douglass, Frederick. "Did John Brown Fail?: An Address Delivered in Harpers Ferry, West Virginia, on 30 May 1881." *The Frederick Douglass Papers, Series One: Speeches, Debates, and Interviews.* Vol. 5: *1881–95.* Ed. John W. Blassingame, and John R. McKivigan. New Haven, Conn.: Yale University Press, 1992. 7–35.

————. "The Douglass Institute: An Address Delivered in Baltimore, Maryland, on 29 September 1865." *The Frederick Douglass Papers, Series One: Speeches, Debates, and Interviews.* Vol. 4: *1864–80.* Ed. John W. Blassingame, and John R. McKivigan. New Haven, Conn.: Yale University Press, 1991. 86–96.

————. "The Heroic Slave." In *Violence in the Black Imagination: Essays & Documents.* Expanded edition. Ed. Ronald T. Takaki. New York: Oxford University Press, 1993.

————. *Life and Times of Frederick Douglass.* In *Frederick Douglass: Autobiographies.* Ed. Henry Louis Gates, Jr. New York: Literary Classics of the United States, 1994.

————. *My Bondage and My Freedom.* In *Frederick Douglass: Autobiographies.* Ed. Henry Louis Gates, Jr. New York: Literary Classics of the United States, 1994.

———. *Narrative of the Life of Frederick Douglass, an American Slave*. In *Frederick Douglass: Autobiographies*. Ed. Henry Louis Gates, Jr. New York: Literary Classics of the United States, 1994.

Doyle, Laura. *Bordering the Body: The Racial Matrix of Modern Fiction and Culture*. New York: Oxford University Press, 1994.

duCille, Ann. *The Coupling Convention: Sex, Text, and Tradition in Black Women's Fiction*. New York: Oxford University Press, 1993.

Dvorak, Katharine L. "After Apocalypse, Moses." *Masters & Slaves in the House of the Lord: Race and Religion in the American South, 1740–1870*. Ed. John B. Boles. Lexington: University Press of Kentucky, 1988. 173–91.

Elaw, Zilpha. *Memoirs of the Life, Religious Experience, Ministerial Travels and Labours of Mrs. Zilpha Elaw, an American Female of Colour; Together with Some Account of the Great Religious Revivals in America*. In *Sisters of the Spirit: Three Black Women's Autobiographies of the Nineteenth Century*. Ed. William L. Andrews. Bloomington: Indiana University Press, 1986. 49–160.

Elkins, Marilyn. "Reading Beyond the Conventions: A Look at Frances E. W. Harper's *Iola Leroy, or Shadows Uplifted*." *American Literary Realism, 1870–1910* 22 (1990): 44–53.

Fabi, M. Giulia. "The 'Unguarded Expressions of the Feelings of the Negroes': Gender, Slave Resistance, and William Wells Brown's Revisions of *Clotel*." *African American Review* 27 (1993): 639–54.

Farrison, William Edward. *William Wells Brown: Author & Reformer*. Chicago: University of Chicago Press, 1969.

Faust, Drew Gilpin. *Southern Stories: Slaveholders in Peace and War*. Columbia: University of Missouri Press, 1992.

Field, Henry M. *Bright Skies and Dark Shadows*. New York, 1890.

Fishkin, Shelley Fisher, and Carla Peterson. " 'We Hold These Truths to Be Self-Evident': The Rhetoric of Frederic Douglass's Journalism." In *Frederick Douglass: New Literary and Historical Essays*. Ed. Eric J. Sundquist. Cambridge: Cambridge University Press, 1990. 189–204.

Fitzhugh, George. *Cannibals All! or, Slaves Without Masters*. Cambridge: Belknap Press of Harvard University Press, 1960.

———. *Sociology for the South: Or the Failure of Free Society*. Richmond, 1854.

Foner, Eric. *Reconstruction: America's Unfinished Revolution, 1863–1877*. New York: Harper & Row, 1988.

Foner, Philip S. *Women and the American Labor Movement: From Colonial Times to the Eve of World War I*. New York: The Free Press, 1979.

Foster, Frances Smith. Introduction. In *Iola Leroy, or Shadows Uplifted*, by Frances E. W. Harper. New York: Oxford University Press, 1988. xxvii–xxxix.

———. Introduction. In *"Minnie's Sacrifice," "Sowing and Reaping," "Trial*

*and Triumph": Three Rediscovered Novels by Frances E. W. Harper.* Ed.
Frances Smith Foster. Boston: Beacon, 1994. xi–xxxvii.

———. *Witnessing Slavery: The Development of Ante-Bellum Slave Narratives.*
2d ed. Madison: University of Wisconsin Press, 1979.

———. *Written by Herself: Literary Production by African American Women,
1746–1892.* Bloomington: Indiana University Press, 1993.

Foucault, Michel. *The Archaeology of Knowledge.* Trans. A. M. Sheridan Smith.
New York: Pantheon, 1972.

———. "Truth and Power." In *The Foucault Reader.* Ed. Paul Rabinow. New
York: Pantheon, 1984. 51–75.

Fox-Genovese, Elizabeth. "My Statue, My Self: Autobiographical Writings of
Afro-American Women." In *Reading Black, Reading Feminist: A Critical
Anthology.* Ed. Henry Louis Gates, Jr. New York: Meridian, 1990. 176–203.

Franchot, Jenny. "The Punishment of Esther: Frederick Douglass and the
Construction of the Feminine." In *Frederick Douglass: New Literary and
Historical Essays.* Ed. Eric J. Sundquist. Cambridge: Cambridge University
Press, 1990. 141–65.

Fredrickson, George M. *The Black Image in the White Mind: The Debate on
Afro-American Character and Destiny, 1817–1914.* New York: Harper, 1971.

Gara, Larry. Introduction. *Narrative of William W. Brown, A Fugitive Slave,
Written by Himself.* In *Four Fugitive Slave Narratives.* Ed. Robin W. Winks
et al. Reading, Mass.: Addison-Wesley, 1969. ix–xvii.

———. *The Liberty Line: The Legend of the Underground Railroad.* Lexington:
University of Kentucky Press, 1961.

———. "William Still and the Underground Railroad." In *Blacks in the
Abolitionist Movement.* Ed. John H. Bracey, Jr., August Meier, and Elliott
Rudwick. Belmont, Calif.: Wadsworth Publishing Co., 1971. 44–52.

Gardner, Eric. " 'This Attempt of Their Sister': Harriet Wilson's *Our Nig*
from Printer to Readers." *The New England Quarterly* 66.2 (1993): 226–46.

Gates, Henry Louis, Jr. "Canon-Formation, Literary History, and the Afro-
American Tradition: From the Seen to the Told." In *Afro-American Literary
Study in the 1990s.* Ed. Houston A. Baker, Jr., and Patricia Redmond.
Chicago: University of Chicago Press, 1989. 14–39.

———. *Figures in Black: Words, Signs, and the "Racial" Self.* New York:
Oxford University Press, 1987.

———. "From Wheatley to Douglass: The Politics of Displacement." In
*Frederick Douglass: New Literary and Critical Essays.* Ed. Eric J. Sundquist.
Cambridge: Cambridge University Press, 1990. 47–65.

———. Introduction. In *Our Nig; or, Sketches from the Life of a Free Black,* by
Harriet E. Wilson. New York: Vintage, 1983. xi–lv.

———. *The Signifying Monkey: A Theory of African-American Literary Criticism.* New York: Oxford University Press, 1988.

———. " 'What's Love Got To Do with It?': Critical Theory, Integrity, and the Black Idiom." *New Literary History* 18 (1987): 345–62.

Geertz, Clifford. *The Interpretation of Cultures: Selected Essays.* New York: Basic Books, 1973.

Genovese, Eugene D. *The World the Slaveholders Made: Two Essays in Interpretation.* New York: Random House, 1969.

Gerteis, Louis S. *Morality & Utility in American Antislavery Reform.* Chapel Hill: University of North Carolina Press, 1987.

Gibson, Donald B. "Faith, Doubt, and Apostasy: Evidence of Things Unseen in Frederick Douglass's *Narrative.*" In *Frederick Douglass: New Literary and Historical Essays.* Ed. Eric J. Sundquist. Cambridge: Cambridge University Press, 1990. 84–98.

———. "Reconciling Public and Private in Frederick Douglass' *Narrative.*" *American Literature* 57 (1985): 549–69.

———. "Response." In *Afro-American Literary Study in the 1990s.* Ed. Houston A. Baker, Jr., and Patricia Redmond. Chicago: University of Chicago Press, 1989. 44–50.

Ginzberg, Lori D. *Women and the Work of Benevolence: Morality, Politics, and Class in the 19th–Century United States.* New Haven, Conn.: Yale University Press, 1990.

Gossett, Thomas F. *Race: The History of an Idea in America.* 1963. New York: Schocken Books, 1965.

———. *Uncle Tom's Cabin and American Culture.* Dallas: Southern Methodist University Press, 1985.

Graham, Maryemma. "Frances Ellen Watkins Harper." In *Afro-American Writers Before the Harlem Renaissance.* Ed. Trudier Harris and Thadious M. Davis. Detroit: Gale, 1986.

Grammer, John. "What Shall This Land Produce? Pastoral and Politics in the Old South." Ph.D. diss., University of Virginia, 1991.

Griffith, Cyril E. *The African Dream: Martin R. Delany and the Emergence of Pan-African Thought.* University Park: Pennsylvania State University Press, 1975.

Grimké, A[ngelina] E. "Appeal to the Christian Women of the South." *The Anti-Slavery Examiner: Nos. 7–14, 1838–1845.* Westport, Conn.: Negro Universities Press, 1970. 1–36.

Grimshaw, William H. *Official History of Freemasonry Among the Colored People in North America.* 1903. Reprint. New York: Negro Universities Press, 1969.

Hall, Peter Dobkin. *The Organization of American Culture, 1700–1900: Private Institutions, Elites, and the Origins of American Nationality.* New York: New York University Press, 1984.

Halttunen, Karen. *Confidence Men and Painted Women: A Study of Middle-*

*class Culture in America, 1830–1870*. New Haven, Conn.: Yale University Press, 1982.

Harding, Sandra. "Rethinking Standpoint Epistemology: What is 'Strong Objectivity'?" In *Feminist Epistemologies*. Ed. Linda Alcoff, and Elizabeth Potter. New York: Routledge, 1993. 49–82.

Harper, Frances E. W. "Christianity." In *A Brighter Coming Day: A Frances Ellen Watkins Harper Reader*. Ed. Frances Smith Foster. New York: Feminist Press, 1990. 96–99.

———. "Enlightened Motherhood." In *A Brighter Coming Day: A Frances Ellen Watkins Harper Reader*. Ed. Frances Smith Foster. New York: Feminist Press, 1990. 285–92.

———. "A Factor in Human Progress." In *A Brighter Coming Day: A Frances Ellen Watkins Harper Reader*. Ed. Frances Smith Foster. New York: The Feminist Press, 1990. 275–80.

———. *Iola Leroy, or Shadows Uplifted*. New York: Oxford University Press, 1988.

———. *"Minnie's Sacrifice," "Sowing and Reaping," "Trial and Triumph": Three Rediscovered Novels by Frances E. W. Harper*. Ed. Frances Smith Foster. Boston: Beacon, 1994.

———. "Miss Watkins and the Constitution." In *A Brighter Coming Day: A Frances Ellen Watkins Harper Reader*. Ed. Frances Smith Foster. New York: Feminist Press, 1990. 47–48.

———. "The Two Offers." In *A Brighter Coming Day: A Frances Ellen Watkins Harper Reader*. Ed. Frances Smith Foster. New York: Feminist Press, 1990. 105–14.

Hatch, Nathan. *The Sacred Cause of Liberty: Republican Thought and the Millennium in Revolutionary New England*. New Haven, Conn.: Yale University Press, 1977.

Haviland, Laura S. *A Woman's Life-Work: Labors and Experiences of Laura S. Haviland*. 1881. Reprint. Salem, N.H.: Ayer, 1984.

Hedin, Raymond. "Probable Readers, Possible Stories: The Limits of Nineteenth-Century Black Narrative." In *Readers in History: Nineteenth-Century American Literature and the Contexts of Response*. Ed. James L. Machor. Baltimore: Johns Hopkins University Press, 1993. 180–205.

Heermance, J. Noel. *William Wells Brown and Clotelle: A Portrait of the Artist in the First Negro Novel*. Hamden, Conn.: Archon Books, 1969.

Henderson, Mae Gwendolyn. "Speaking in Tongues: Dialogics, Dialectics, and the Black Woman Writer's Literary Tradition." In *Changing Our Own Words: Essays on Criticism, Theory, and Writing By Black Women*. Ed. Cheryl A. Wall. New Brunswick, N.J.: Rutgers University Press, 1989. 16–37.

Herzog, Kristin. *Women, Ethnics, and Exotics: Images of Power in Mid-Nine-*

*teenth-Century American Fiction*. Knoxville: University of Tennessee Press, 1983.

Hite, Molly. "Romance, Marginality, and Matrilineage: *The Color Purple* and *Their Eyes Were Watching God*." In *Reading Black, Reading Feminist: A Critical Anthology*. Ed. Henry Louis Gates, Jr. New York: Meridian, 1990. 431–53.

Holloway, Karla F. C. "Economies of Space: Markets and Marketability in *Our Nig* and *Iola Leroy*." In *The (Other) American Traditions: Nineteenth-Century Women Writers*. New Brunswick, N.J.: Rutgers University Press, 1993. 126–40.

"The Homes of America The Hope of the Republic." *The United States Democratic Review* 7 (November 1856): 292–97.

Hopkins, Pauline E. *Contending Forces: A Romance Illustrative of Negro Life North and South*. New York: Oxford University Press, 1988.

Hord, Fred Lee. *Reconstructing Memory: Black Literary Criticism*. Chicago: Third World Press, 1991.

Horton, James Oliver. *Free People of Color: Inside the African American Community*. Washington: Smithsonian Institution Press, 1993.

Hughes, Henry. "A Treatise on Sociology." In *Slavery Defended: The Views of the Old South*. Ed. Eric L. McKitrick. Englewood Cliffs, N.J.: Prentice-Hall, 1963. 51–56.

Hurston, Zora Neale. *Their Eyes Were Watching God*. 1937. Reprint. New York: Harper & Row, 1990.

"Intellectual Culture of Woman." *Southern Literary Messenger: A Magazine Devoted to Literature, Science and Art* 28 (May 1859): 321–32.

Jackson, Blyden. *A History of Afro-American Literature*. Vol. I: *The Long Beginning, 1746–1895*. Baton Rouge: Louisiana State University Press, 1989.

Jacobs, Harriet A. *Incidents in the Life of a Slave Girl, Written by Herself*. Ed. Jean Fagan Yellin. Cambridge: Harvard University Press, 1987.

James, Henry Field. *Abolitionism Unveiled; or, Its Origin, Progress, and Pernicious Tendency Fully Developed*. Cincinnati, 1856.

Jay, William. *Condition of the Free People of Color*. In *The Free People of Color*. Ed. Benjamin Quarles. New York: Arno Press and The New York Times, 1969.

Jefferson, Paul. Introduction. In *The Travels of William Wells Brown, including "Narrative of William Wells Brown, A Fugitive Slave" and "The American Fugitive in Europe. Sketches of Places and People Abroad."* Ed. Paul Jefferson. New York: Markus Wiener, 1991. 1–20.

Jenkins, William Sumner. *Pro-Slavery Thought in the Old South*. 1935. Reprint. Gloucester, Mass.: Peter Smith, 1960.

Johnson, H. U. *From Dixie to Canada: Romances and Realities of the Under-*

*ground Railroad*. Vol. 1. 2d ed. 1896. Reprint. Westport, Conn.: Negro Universities Press, 1970.

Jordan, Winthrop D. *White Over Black: American Attitudes Toward the Negro, 1550–1812*. New York: Norton, 1977.

Joyce, Joyce A. "The Black Canon: Reconstructing Black American Literary Criticism." *New Literary History* 18 (1987): 335–44.

———. "Black Woman Scholar, Critic, and Teacher: The Inextricable Relationship between Race, Sex, and Class. *New Literary History* 22 (1991): 543–65.

———. " 'Who the Cap Fit': Unconsciousness and Unconscionableness in the Criticism of Houston A. Baker, Jr., and Henry Louis Gates, Jr." *New Literary History* 18 (1987): 371–84.

Kerber, Linda K. *Women of the Republic: Intellect and Ideology in Revolutionary America*. Chapel Hill: University of North Carolina Press, 1980.

Kibbey, Ann. "Language in Slavery: Frederick Douglass's *Narrative*." *Prospects* 8 (1983): 163–82.

Kaufman, Allen. *Capitalism, Slavery, and Republican Values: Antebellum Political Economists, 1819–1848*. Austin: University of Texas Press, 1982.

Larsen, Nella. *Quicksand. Quicksand and Passing*. Ed. Deborah E. McDowell. New Brunswick, N.J.: Rutgers University Press, 1986.

Latrobe, Benjamin Henry. *The Journals of Benjamin Henry Latrobe*. Vol. 3: *1799–1820: From Philadelphia to New Orleans*. Ed. Edward C. Carter II, John C. Van Horne, and Lee W. Formwalt. New Haven, Conn.: Yale University Press, 1980.

Lauter, Paul. "Is Frances Ellen Watkins Harper Good Enough to Teach?" *Legacy* 5.1 (1988): 27–32.

Lepenies, Wolf. *Between Literature and Science: The Rise of Sociology*. Trans. R. J. Hollingdale. Cambridge: Cambridge University Press, 1992.

Lerner, Gerda. *The Majority Finds Its Past: Placing Women in History*. Oxford: Oxford University Press, 1979.

Levenson, J. C. *The Mind and Art of Henry Adams*. Boston: Houghton Mifflin, 1957.

Leverenz, David. *Manhood and the American Renaissance*. Ithaca, N.Y.: Cornell University Press, 1989.

Levin, David. *History as Romantic Art: Bancroft, Prescott, Motley, and Parkman*. Stanford, Calif.: Stanford University Press, 1959.

Levine, Lawrence W. *Highbrow/Lowbrow: The Emergence of Cultural Hierarchy in America*. Cambridge: Harvard University Press, 1988.

Lewis, Richard O. "Literary Conventions in the Novels of William Wells Brown." *CLA Journal* 29 (December 1985): 129–56.

Lindberg, Gary. *The Confidence Man in American Literature*. New York: Oxford University Press, 1982.

Litwack, Leon F. *Been in the Storm So Long: The Aftermath of Slavery.* New York: Knopf, 1980.

———. *North of Slavery: The Negro in the Free States, 1790–1860.* Chicago: University of Chicago Press, 1961.

Lively, Robert A. *Fiction Fights the Civil War: An Unfinished Chapter in the Literary History of the American People.* Westport, Conn.: Greenwood Press, 1957.

Loggins, Vernon. *The Negro Author: His Development in America.* New York: Columbia University Press, 1931.

Lott, Eric. *Love & Theft: Blackface Minstrelsy and the American Working Class.* New York: Oxford University Press, 1993.

Lown, Judy. *Women and Industrialization: Gender and Work in the Nineteenth Century.* Minneapolis: University of Minnesota Press, 1990.

McDowell, Deborah E. " 'The Changing Same': Generational Connections and Black Women Novelists." *New Literary History* 18 (1987): 281–302.

McFeely, William S. *Frederick Douglass.* New York: Touchstone, Simon & Schuster, 1991.

Margolis, Maxine L. *Mothers and Such: Views of American Women and Why They Changed.* Berkeley: University of California Press, 1984.

Marsh-Lockett, Carol P. "Martin Robinson [*sic*] Delany." In *Afro-American Writers Before the Harlem Renaissance.* Ed. Trudier Harris and Thadious M. Davis. Detroit: Gale, 1986. 74–80.

Martin, Waldo E., Jr. *The Mind of Frederick Douglass.* Chapel Hill: University of North Carolina Press, 1984.

Meier, August. *Negro Thought in America, 1880–1915: Racial Ideologies in the Age of Booker T. Washington.* Ann Arbor: University of Michigan Press, 1969.

Mills, Bruce. "Lydia Maria Child and the Endings to Harriet Jacobs's *Incidents in the Life of a Slave Girl.*" *American Literature* 64 (1992): 255–72.

Mitchell, Angelyn. "Her Side of His Story: A Feminist Analysis of Two Nineteenth-Century Antebellum Novels—William Wells Brown's *Clotel* and Harriet E. Wilson's *Our Nig.*" *American Literary Realism* 24.3 (Spring 1992): 7–21.

Mixon, Wayne. "The Shadow of Slavery: Frederick Douglass, the Savage South, and the Next Generation." In *Frederick Douglass: New Literary and Historical Essays.* Ed. Eric J. Sundquist. Cambridge: Cambridge University Press, 1990. 233–52.

Morrison, Toni. *Playing in the Dark: Whiteness in the Literary Imagination.* New York: Vintage, 1992.

Moses, Wilson J. "Writing Freely? Frederick Douglass and the Constraints of Racialized Writing." In *Frederick Douglass: New Literary and Historical Essays.* Ed. Eric J. Sundquist. Cambridge: Cambridge University Press, 1990. 66–83.

Moss, Elizabeth. *Domestic Novelists in the Old South: Defenders of Southern Culture*. Baton Rouge: Louisiana State University Press, 1992.

Munford, Howard M. "Henry Adams: The Limitations of Science." *Southern Review* 4 (Winter 1968): 59–71.

Nelson, Dana D. *The Word in Black and White: Reading "Race" in American Literature, 1638–1867*. New York: Oxford University Press, 1992.

Newcomb, Simon. *Principles of Political Economy*. 1886. Reprint. New York: Augustus M. Kelley, 1966.

Norton, Anne. *Alternative Americas: A Reading of Antebellum Political Culture*. Chicago: University of Chicago Press, 1986.

Nott, Josiah Clark, and George R. Gliddon. *Types of Mankind: Or, Ethnological Researches, Based upon the Ancient Monuments, Paintings, Sculptures, and Crania of Races, and upon Their Natural, Geographical, Philological, and Biblical history*. . . . Philadelphia, 1854.

Nudelman, Franny. "Harriet Jacobs and the Sentimental Politics of Female Suffering." *ELH* 59 (1992): 939–64.

Oakes, James. *Slavery and Freedom: An Interpretation of the Old South*. New York: Knopf, 1990.

Olcott, Charles. *Two Lectures on the Subjects of Slavery and Abolition*. 1838. Reprint. Freeport, N.Y.: Books for Libraries Press, 1971.

Olney, James. "The Founding Fathers—Frederick Douglass and Booker T. Washington." In *Slavery and the Literary Imagination: Selected Papers from the English Institute, 1987*. Ed. Deborah E. McDowell and Arnold Rampersad. Baltimore: Johns Hopkins University Press, 1989. 1–24.

———. " 'I Was Born': Slave Narratives, Their Status as Autobiography and as Literature." In *The Slave's Narrative*. Ed. Charles T. Davis and Henry Louis Gates, Jr. Oxford: Oxford University Press, 1985. 148–74.

O'Meally, Robert G. "Frederick Douglass' 1845 *Narrative*: The Text Was Meant to Be Preached." In *Afro-American Literature: The Reconstruction of Instruction*. Ed. Dexter Fisher and Robert B. Stepto. New York: Modern Language Association of America, 1979. 192–211.

"On the Moral and Political Effect of the Relation between the Caucasian Master and the African Slave." *Southern Literary Messenger* 10 (June 1844): 329–39.

Painter, Nell Irvin. "Martin R. Delany: Elitism and Black Nationalism." In *Black Leaders of the Nineteenth Century*. Ed. Leon Litwack and August Meier. Urbana: University of Illinois Press, 1988. 149–71.

Parker, Theodore. *The Trial of Theodore Parker, for the "Misdemeanor" of A Speech in Faneuil Hall against Kidnapping, Before the Circuit Court of the United States, at Boston, April 3, 1855. With the Defense, by Theodore Parker*. 1855. New York: Negro Universities Press, 1970.

Pease, Donald E. Introduction. In *The American Renaissance Reconsidered*. Ed. Walter Benn Michaels, and Donald E. Pease. Baltimore: Johns Hopkins University Press, 1985.

Peterson, Carla L. "Capitalism, Black (Under)development, and the Production of the African-American Novel in the 1850s." *American Literary History* 4 (1992): 559–83.

Pettit, Eber M. *Sketches in the History of the Underground Railroad, Comprising Many Thrilling Incidents of the Escape of Fugitives from Slavery, and the Perils of Those Who Aided Them*. 1879. Reprint. Freeport, N.Y.: Books for Libraries Press, 1971.

"Pocahontas." *Cousin Franck's Household, Scenes in the Old Dominion*. Boston, 1853.

Rabinowitz, Howard N. *Race Relations in the Urban South, 1865–1890*. New York: Oxford University Press, 1978.

Reed, Ishmael. *Flight to Canada*. New York: Atheneum, 1989.

Reilly, John M. "History-Making Literature." In *Studies in Black American Literature*. Volume II: *Belief vs. Theory in Black American Literary Criticism*. Greenwood, Fla.: Penkevill, 1986. 85–120.

Reimers, David M. *White Protestantism and the Negro*. New York: Oxford University Press, 1965.

Reynolds, David S. *Beneath the American Renaissance: The Subversive Imagination in the Age of Emerson and Melville*. Cambridge: Harvard University Press, 1989.

Ricoeur, Paul. "Christianity and the Meaning of History." *History and Truth*. Trans. Charles A. Kelbley. Evanston, Ill.: Northwestern University Press, 1965. 81–97.

Ripley, C. Peter, ed. *The Black Abolitionist Papers*. Volume IV: *The United States, 1847–1858*. Chapel Hill: University of North Carolina Press, 1991.

Roediger, David R. *The Wages of Whiteness: Race and the Making of the American Working Class*. London: Verso, 1991.

Rollin, Frank [Frances] A. *Life and Public Services of Martin R. Delany, Sub-Assistant Commissioner Bureau Relief of Refugees, Freedmen, and of Abandoned Lands, and Late Major 104th U.S. Colored Troops*. 1883. In *Two Biographies by African-American Women*. Ed. William L. Andrews. New York: Oxford University Press, 1991.

Ruffin, Edmund. "The Political Economy of Slavery." In *Slavery Defended: The Views of The Old South*. Ed. Eric L. McKitrick. Englewood Cliffs, N.J.: Prentice-Hall, 1963.

Sanchez-Eppler, Karen. "Bodily Bonds: The Intersecting Rhetorics of Feminism and Abolition." *Representations* 24 (1988): 28–59.

Saxton, Alexander. *The Rise and Fall of the White Republic: Class Politics and Mass Culture in Nineteenth-Century America*. London: Verso, 1990.

Sherman, Joan R. *Invisible Poets: Afro-Americans of the Nineteenth Century.* 2d ed. Urbana: University of Illinois Press, 1989.

Sherman, Sarah Way. "Moral Experience in Harriet Jacobs's *Incidents in the Life of a Slave Girl.*" *NWSA Journal* 2 (1990): 178–82.

Shore, Laurence. *Southern Capitalists: The Ideological Leadership of an Elite, 1832–1885.* Chapel Hill: University of North Carolina Press, 1986.

"Slavery." *The North American Review* 41 (July 1835): 170–93.

*Slavery in America: with Notices of the Present State of Slavery and the Slave Trade Throughout the World. Conducted by The Rev. Thomas Price, D.D.* London: G. Whightman, 1837.

Smith, Sidonie. "Resisting the Gaze of Embodiment: Women's Autobiography in the Nineteenth Century." In *American Women's Autobiography: Fea(s)ts of Memory.* Ed. Margo Culley. Madison: University of Wisconsin Press, 1992. 75–110.

Smith, Stephanie A. "Heart Attacks: Frederick Douglass's Strategic Sentimentality." *Criticism* 34 (Spring 1992): 193–216.

Smith, Valerie. Introduction. In *Incidents in the Life of a Slave Girl.* New York: Oxford University Press, 1988. xxvii–xl.

Smith, W. L. G. *Life at the South: or "Uncle Tom's Cabin" As It Is. Being Narratives, Scenes, and Incidents in the Real "Life of the Lowly."* Buffalo, 1852.

Sollors, Werner, Caldwell Titcomb, and Thomas A. Underwood, eds. *Blacks at Harvard: A Documentary History of African-American Experience at Harvard and Radcliffe.* New York: New York University Press, 1993.

Southern, Eileen. *The Music of Black Americans: A History.* New York: Norton, 1971.

Spurlin, William J. "Theorizing Signifyin(g) and the Role of the Reader: Possible Directions for African-American Literary Criticism." *College English* 52 (1990): 732–42.

Stanton, William. *The Leopard's Spots: Scientific Attitudes toward Race in America, 1815–59.* 1960. Reprint. Chicago: University of Chicago Press, 1982.

Staudenraus, P. J. *The African Colonization Movement, 1816–1865.* New York: Columbia University Press, 1961.

Stebbins, G. B. *Facts and Opinions Touching the Real Origin, Character, and Influence of the American Colonization Society: Views of Wilberforce, Clarkson, and Others, and Opinions of the Free People of Color of the United States.* 1853. New York: Negro Universities Press, 1969.

Stepto, Robert B. "Distrust of the Reader in Afro-American Narratives." In *Reconstructing American Literary History.* Ed. Sacvan Bercovitch. Cambridge: Harvard University Press, 1986. 300–322.

———. *From Behind the Veil: A Study of Afro-American Narrative.* 2d ed. Urbana: University of Illinois Press, 1991.

Sterling, Dorothy. *The Making of an Afro-American: Martin Robison Delany, 1812–1885*. Garden City, N.Y.: Doubleday, 1971.

——. *Turning the World Upside Down: The Anti-Slavery Convention of American Women*. New York: Feminist Press, 1987.

Stewart, Maria W. *Productions of Mrs. Maria W. Stewart*. In *Spiritual Narratives*. New York: Oxford University Press, 1988.

Still, William. *The Underground Rail Road: A Record of Facts, Authentic Narratives, Letters, &c., Narrating the Hardships Hair-breadth Escapes and Death Struggles of the Slaves in their efforts for Freedom, as related by Themselves and Others, or Witnessed by the Author; Together with Sketches of Some of the Largest Stockholders, and Most Liberal Aiders and Advisers, of the Road*. 1871. Reprint. Chicago: Johnson Publishing Co., 1970.

Stowe, Harriet Beecher. *Uncle Tom's Cabin; or, Life among the Lowly*. New York: Vintage Books/Library of America, 1991.

Stuckey, Sterling. " 'Ironic Tenacity': Frederick Douglass's Seizure of the Dialectic." In *Frederick Douglass: New Literary and Historical Essays*. Ed. Eric J. Sundquist. Cambridge: Cambridge University Press, 1990. 23–46.

Sundquist, Eric J. *To Wake the Nations: Race in the Making of American Literature*. Cambridge: The Belknap Press of Harvard University Press, 1993.

Takaki, Ronald. *Iron Cages: Race and Culture in 19th-Century America*. New York: Oxford University Press, 1990.

Tate, Claudia. *Domestic Allegories of Political Desire: The Black Heroine's Text at the Turn of the Century*. New York: Oxford University Press, 1992.

Temperly, Howard. "Capitalism, Slavery and Ideology." *Past and Present* 75 (May 1977): 94–118.

Thoreau, Henry D. *Walden and "Resistance to Civil Government."* 2d ed. New York: Norton, 1992.

Tise, Larry E. *Proslavery: A History of the Defense of Slavery in America, 1701–1840*. Athens: University of Georgia Press, 1987.

Tompkins, Jane. *Sensational Designs: The Cultural Work of American Fiction, 1790–1860*. New York: Oxford University Press, 1985.

Touchstone, Blake. "Planters and Slave Religion in the Deep South." In *Masters & Slaves in the House of the Lord: Race and Religion in the American South, 1740–1870*. Ed. John B. Boles. Lexington: University Press of Kentucky, 1988. 99–126.

Turbin, Carole. "Beyond Dichotomies: Interdependence in Mid-Nineteenth Century Working Class Families in the United States." *Gender & History* 1.3 (Autumn 1989): 293–308.

Tuveson, Ernest Lee. *Redeemer Nation: The Idea of America's Millennial Role*. Chicago: University of Chicago Press, 1968.

Ullman, Victor. *Martin R. Delany: The Beginnings of Black Nationalism*. Boston: Beacon Press, 1971.

*Uncle Daniel's Story of "Tom" Anderson and Twenty Great Battles*. New York, 1886.

Van Leer, David. "Reading Slavery: The Anxiety of Ethnicity in Douglass's *Narrative*." In *Frederick Douglass: New Literary and Critical Essays*. Ed. Eric J. Sundquist. Cambridge: Cambridge University Press, 1990. 118–40.

Vermillion, Mary. "Reembodying the Self: Representations of Rape in *Incidents in the Life of a Slave Girl* and *I Know Why the Caged Bird Sings*." *Biography* 15 (Summer 1992): 243–60.

"Vidi." *Mr. Frank, the Underground Mail-Agent*. Philadelphia, 1853.

Vitzthum, Richard C. *The American Compromise: Theme and Method in the Histories of Bancroft, Parkman, and Adams*. Norman: University of Oklahoma Press, 1974.

Walker, Clarence E. *Deromanticizing Black History: Critical Essays and Reappraisals*. Knoxville: University of Tennessee Press, 1991.

Warren, Kenneth W. "Frederick Douglass's *Life and Times*: Progressive Rhetoric and the Problem of Constituency." In *Frederick Douglass: New Literary and Critical Essays*. Ed. Eric J. Sundquist. Cambridge: Cambridge University Press, 1990. 253–70.

———. "From the Superscript: A Response to Michael Awkward." *American Literary History* 4 (Spring 1992): 97–103.

Washington, Mary Helen. " 'The Darkened Eye Restored': Notes Toward a Literary History of Black Women." In *Reading Black, Reading Feminist: A Critical Anthology*. Ed. Henry Louis Gates, Jr. New York: Meridian, 1990. 30–43.

Weld, Theodore Dwight. *American Slavery As It Is: Testimony of a Thousand Witnesses*. 1839. Reprint. New York: Arno Press and The New York Times, 1968.

Wells, Ida B. *Crusade for Justice: The Autobiography of Ida B. Wells*. Ed. Alfreda M. Duster. Chicago: University of Chicago Press, 1970.

Welter, Barbara. "The Cult of True Womanhood: 1820–1860." *American Quarterly* 18.2 (1966): 151–74.

Wesling, Donald. "Writing as Power in the Slave Narrative of the Early Republic." *Michigan Quarterly Review* 26 (1987): 459–72.

Whelpley, Samuel. *A Compend of History, from the Earliest Times; Comprehending a General View of the Present State of the World, with respect to Civilization, Religion, and Government; and A Brief Dissertation on the Importance of Historical Knowledge*. Boston, 1823.

White, Barbara A. " 'Our Nig' and the She-Devil: New Information about Harriet Wilson and the 'Bellmont' Family." *American Literature* 65.1 (March 1993): 19–52.

White, Hayden. *Tropics of Discourse: Essays in Cultural Criticism*. Baltimore: Johns Hopkins University Press, 1978.

Williams, Loretta J. *Black Freemasonry and Middle-Class Realities*. Columbia: University of Missouri Press, 1980.

Williams, Sherley Anne. "Some Implications of Womanist Theory." In *Reading Black, Reading Feminist: A Critical Anthology*. Ed. Henry Louis Gates, Jr. New York: Meridian, 1990. 68–75.

Willis, Susan. *Specifying: Black Women Writing the American Experience*. Madison: University of Wisconsin Press, 1987.

Wilson, Harriet E. *Our Nig; or, Sketches from the Life of a Free Black, in a Two-Story White House, North. Showing that Slavery's Shadows Fall Even There. By "Our Nig."* New York: Vintage, 1983.

"Woman and the 'Woman's Movement.'" *Putnam's Monthly* 1 (March 1853): 279–88.

Wood, Gordon S. *The Creation of the American Republic, 1776–1787*. New York: Norton, 1972.

Yarborough, Richard. "Race, Violence, and Manhood: The Masculine Ideal in Frederick Douglass's 'The Heroic Slave.'" *Frederick Douglass: New Literary and Historical Essays*. Ed. Eric J. Sundquist. Cambridge: Cambridge University Press, 1990. 166–88.

Yee, Shirley J. *Black Women Abolitionists: A Study in Activism, 1828–1860*. Knoxville: University Press of Knoxville, 1992.

Yellin, Jean Fagan. *The Intricate Knot: Black Figures in American Literature, 1776–1863*. New York: New York University Press, 1972.

———. Introduction. In *Incidents in the Life of a Slave Girl*. By Harriet A. Jacobs. Ed. Jean Fagan Yellin. Cambridge: Harvard University Press, 1987. xiii–xxxiv.

———. "Texts and Contexts of Harriet Jacobs' *Incidents in the Life of a Slave Girl: Written by Herself*." In *The Slave's Narrative*. Ed. Charles T. Davis and Henry Louis Gates, Jr. Oxford: Oxford University Press, 1985. 262–82.

———. *Women & Sisters: The Antislavery Feminists in American Culture*. New Haven, Conn.: Yale University Press, 1989.

Young, Elizabeth. "Warring Fictions: *Iola Leroy* and the Color of Gender." *American Literature* 64.2 (1992): 273–97.

Zafar, Rafia. "Franklinian Douglass: The Afro-American as Representative Man." In *Frederick Douglass: New Literary and Critical Essays*. Ed. Eric J. Sundquist. Cambridge: Cambridge University Press, 1990. 99–117.

Zinn, Howard. *The Southern Mystique*. 1959. Reprint. New York: Simon and Schuster, 1972.

# Index

86–89, 101–02, 117; and relation to
politics and the state, 34, 42, 49, 89–
92; and violation of, 34, 37, 38–41, 60
Wood, Gordon S., 218 *n*19

Yarborough, Richard, 217 *n*14, 231 *n*2
Yee, Shirley J., 223 *n*9

Yellin, Jean Fagan, 81, 84, 215 *n*2,
216 *n*10, 222 *n*3, 223 *n*17, 224 *n*22,
229 *n*26
Young, Elizabeth, 238 *n*7

Zafar, Rafia, 231 *n*6, 233 *n*15